Other Selves

SUNY Series in Ethical Theory
Robert B. Louden, editor

Other Selves

Aristotle on Personal and Political Friendship

Paul Schollmeier

State University of New York Press

Published by
State University of New York Press, Albany

© 1994 State University of New York

For information, address State University of New York
Press, State University Plaza, Albany, N.Y., 12246

Production by Dana Foote
Marketing by Bernadette LaManna

Library of Congress Cataloging-in-Publication Data

Schollmeier, Paul.
    Other selves : Aristotle on personal and political friendship /
Paul Schollmeier.
        p.   cm.   (SUNY series in ethical theory)
        Includes bibliographical references and index.
        ISBN 0–7914–1683–6 (alk. paper) — ISBN 0–7914–1684–4 (pbk. :
alk. paper)
        1. Aristotle.   2. Friendship.   I. Title.   II. Series.
B491.F7S36   1993
177'.6—dc20
                                                              93–18102
                                                              CIP

10 9 8 7 6 5 4 3 2 1

To the Memory
of
S.H.J.

CONTENTS

Acknowledgments   ix

Abbreviations   xi

   I. Introduction   1

  II. Happiness and Virtue   17

 III. A Definition of Friendship   35

  IV. A Motivation for Friendship   53

   V. Political Friendship   75

  VI. Political Justice   97

 VII. Conclusion   113

Appendix A. Lawrence Blum   123

Appendix B. John Rawls   139

Notes   155

Select Bibliography   209

Subject Index   213

Author Index   219

ACKNOWLEDGMENTS

The author wishes to express his gratitude to the University Research Council at the University of Nevada, Las Vegas. With a generous grant the Council provisioned me with scholarly resources necessary to bring my research on this study to completion. A debt of gratitude is due the Center for Values and Social Policy at the University of Colorado, Boulder. A visiting fellowship from the center ensconced me in an academic arcadia most conducive to completing my manuscript. And I must surely not forget to acknowledge my debt to my dissertation committee at the University of Chicago for their many encouragements and cautions during the early stages of my research on this topic. I also gratefully acknowledge permission to reprint "An Aristotelian Motivation for Good Friendship," which appeared in *Revue de Métaphysique et de Morale*, vol. 91 (1986), pp. 379–88, and "An Aristotelian Origin for Good Friendship," which appeared in *Revue de Philosophie Ancienne*, vol. 8 (1990), pp. 173–90. Finally, I wish especially to thank the Ministry of Culture in Athens for granting permission to use the photograph of the kouros who graces the cover of this book and the National Gallery of Art in Washington for furnishing the photograph.

ABBREVIATIONS

Eth. = *Nicomachean Ethics*

Eud. Eth. = *Eudemian Ethics*

His. Ani. = *History of Animals*

Mor. = *Magna Moralia*

Pol. = *Politics*

Pr. Ana. = *Prior Analytics*

Psy. = *Psychology*

INTRODUCTION

Moral philosophers for the most part tend to regard the Aristotelian theory of friendship much as they might a kinsman of distant and perhaps dubious descent. They treat the theory more with perfunctory courtesy than with perfect cordiality when they do not utterly ignore it.[1]

These philosophers allow themselves to cultivate an unfortunate attitude toward Aristotle's theory, for they prevent themselves from comprehending his theory fully. Failing to see its integrity, they are blind to both its theoretical subtilty and its practical versatility. They indeed leave central problems in the theory without generally accepted resolutions. One rather important problem left unresolved is the very problem of what Aristotelian friendship is: Is friendship an altruistic relationship or an egoistic one? That is to say, when we enter a friendship, do we perform acts of friendship for the sake of our friend or for the sake of ourselves? Classical philosophers resolve this problem in ways diametrically opposed to one another. One philosopher argues, for example, that all friendship is altruistic. When we do something for them, we intend to act not for our own benefit but for the benefit of our friends.[2] But another philosopher argues that all friendship is egoistic. When we act for them, we do so with the intention of benefiting ourselves through our friends.[3]

Another important problem left without a generally accepted resolution is the problem of why Aristotelian friendship is: Does friendship have a motivation that is altruistic or egoistic? Again we find diametrically opposed interpretations. One commentator argues that friendship has a motivation which is altruistic. We act out of sympathy. As we relate to the thoughts and emotions of our own, so too we relate to the thoughts and emotions of our friends.[4] Another commentator argues that friendship has an egoistic motivation. We act out of self-love. When we benefit our friends, we really achieve our own good, for we do what is noble for us.[5]

Other related, yet unresolved, problems concerning Aristotelian friendship include the problems of what political friendship is[6] and why it is.[7] There also remains the problem of what affinity, if any, might exist between political friendship and justice. Is friendship of this sort a condition of justice? Or is justice a condition of it? One classical scholar argues that justice is a condition of friendship in any community. That is, we must render advantages and honors to one another if we are to have friendship.[8] Another scholar argues that without friendship there can be no justice. Only in a community with mutual confidence do we effect private and public advantage through contract and division of labor. Unless we are friends, we secure advantage only by murder and plunder.[9]

And these philosophers are negligent not only about problems of theory but also about problems of application. They especially leave a crucial problem concerning political friendship unresolved. And so I also wish to ask: What is the likelihood of establishing political friendship in a society?[10]

The fact that they fail to resolve these problems, I take to be a sign that moral philosophers fail to have recourse to a principle to guide them in their consideration of Aristotle's theory. In this study I do intend to use a principle to resolve the ethical and political problems awaiting us and to show that the theory has unity as well as theoretical and practical merit. I shall not introduce any novel principle of analysis but merely make use of Aristotle's own principle, that of happiness.

My intention is both exegetic and heuristic. Aristotle's principle permits us to see that his theory of friendship is an integral part of his ethical and political theories; but it also permits us to see that his theory has a unique conception of a human good—a conception of another self. This conception of another self in turn shows us that his theory of friendship is more sophisticated and more feasible than usually supposed. His theory appears to be at once altruistic and pluralistic.[11]

I shall accordingly apply Aristotle's conception of happiness in an analysis of his conceptions of personal friendship, political friendship, and justice. I shall begin by addressing the problem of what personal friendship is. With Aristotle's conception of happiness, we shall be able to see in the third chapter that personal friendship is essentially good will and good wishes, reciprocated and recognized, for the sake of the happiness of another person. Friendship of this kind is only accidentally good will and good wishes, reciprocated and recognized, for the sake of profit or pleasure for ourselves. Friendship is thus essentially altruistic and accidentally egoistic.

The problem of the motivation for personal friendship I shall take up in the fourth chapter. This chapter is an analysis of Aristotle's explanation of why personal friendship is. The problem is especially acute with regard to altruistic friendship, in which we act for the sake of the happiness of another person. The problem is why we do so. In friendship of the egoistic sort, we act for the sake of our own happiness or what we conceive it to be. The problem thus has an obvious solution.

Aristotle argues that the motive for friendship is an object of mental pleasure. We act for the sake of the happiness of another person because we find that the happiness of another is an object of pleasant apperception. He also argues that the happiness of another in either its primary or its secondary sense is an object of mental pleasure. Thus friendship is also pluralistic.

Aristotle's resolution for the problem of motivation appears at first to be a paradox. Aristotle argues that we find the happiness of another to be an object of pleasant apperception because the happiness of another is a good belonging to us. But how can the happiness of another be our own good? To say that it is might seem to reduce altruistic friendship to egoistic friendship, for we might seem to act for the sake of our own profit or pleasure.

We shall see that Aristotle's conception of another self overcomes this paradox. Another self is an actualization of Aristotle's moral principle in the character and activity of another person. That is to say, it is an actualization of happiness and virtue in another person. Another self is therefore a good, for someone who is happy has human goodness; and another self belongs to us, for we make other selves ours by helping them attain or retain their happiness. They become our work, so to speak.

In the fifth chapter we shall see that political friendship is unanimity and that friendship of this type has a definition and a motivation quite similar to those of personal friendship. Political friends are fellow citizens, and fellow citizens exhibit good will and good wishes, most probably with reciprocity and recognition, for the sake of other citizens. At least citizens act for the sake of others when their constitution is healthy; but when their constitution is corrupt, they have no political friendship. Political friendship is thus altruistic.

We shall also see that fellow citizens appear to act for the sake of the happiness of others because they find the happiness of others to be an object of pleasant apperception. And they find either primary or secondary happiness to be an object of mental pleasure. Thus political friendship, too, is pluralistic.

Those people who are political friends would accordingly appear to act for the sake of other selves as do personal friends. Indeed, we shall see that they do. But political friends have a conception of another self more general than do personal friends. Fellow citizens define their conception of happiness politically rather than personally, for they define happiness for themselves through a constitution and its laws.

The final chapter of analysis compares political friendship with justice of the political kind. We shall see that political justice is only a mark of political friendship, though its end and motive are similar. People who are just act for the sake of the happiness of other people, and they appear to find the happiness of another to be an object of mental pleasure. However, political justice differs from political friendship because just people do not act on the same emotion that political friends do. Justice is only a condition of friendship, for we exhibit marks of friendship to others before we become friends with them.

Aristotle's theory of friendship is thus an integral part of his ethical and political theories, for his theory of friendship relies on his principle of happiness. The feasibility of Aristotle's theory of political friendship is apparent if we remember that Aristotle distinguishes healthy constitutions of three kinds. If friendship underlies these constitutions, political friendship would also have three kinds. Friendship of the political variety may in fact spring up and flourish among people pursuing either primary or secondary happiness; or a statesman may attempt to introduce and cultivate friendship among people pursuing these ends.

Why other philosophers do not attempt the obvious maneuver of using Aristotle's conception of happiness to analyze his theory of friendship, I cannot say for certain. But one cause of their failure appears to be that philosophers discussing Aristotle's theory have purposes that are either very broad or very narrow. Most philosophers who discuss friendship intend to comment on the whole of Aristotle's *Ethics* or *Politics*. They thus give their attention to the theory merely in passing.[12] More recently, some philosophers consider only one or two problems in his theory and thus examine the theory piecemeal.[13]

But a more profound cause may lie in our linguistic habits. These habits appear to explain why philosophers often fail to take an appropriate perspective on the theory. We usually use "friendship" to designate a rather narrow range of phenomena, but the Greeks use "friendship" to designate a rather broad range of phenomena. We would therefore very likely benefit from an effort to free ourselves from these prejudicious habits. To do this, I suggest that we make a preliminary survey of our subject.[14]

If we turn to the opening chapter of his discussion, we can see at once that Aristotle's arguments reflect a very wide range of human relationships. Aristotle sets out the two central problems concerning friendship in his first sentence:

> After these things a discussion of friendship would follow, for friendship is a virtue or follows from a virtue, and it is most necessary for life. (*Eth.* 8.1.1155a3–5)

In this sentence he raises the problem of the nature of friendship when he states that it is a virtue or follows from a virtue. When he states that friendship is necessary for life, he raises the problem of the motivation for friendship, for a problem of necessity is a problem of causation.[15]

But what is of interest to us is that Aristotle takes special care to indicate that there is a problem about the necessity of friendship. He offers several arguments to show that friendship is indeed necessary, and his arguments cover relationships of several different kinds. The first argument concerns friendship and external goods and pertains to our usual conception of friendship—personal friendship:

> No one would choose to live without friends though he had all other goods. For both rich men and those possessed of office and dynasty seem to need friends the most. What is the use of such property without beneficence, which is best and most praiseworthy when exercised toward friends? Or how can such prosperity be guarded and preserved without friends? For the greater it is, the more precarious it is. And in poverty and other misfortunes, men think that friends are the only refuge. (*Eth.* 8.1.1155a5–12)

Another argument concerned with goods of the soul and the body also applies to personal friendship:

> The young friendship rescues from mistakes. The old it helps in their needs and supplements their actions that are failing because of their weakness. And those in the prime of life it stimulates to noble actions. For "two heads are better than one" and they are more able to intuit and to act. (*Eth.* 8.1.1155a12–16)

He thus indicates that personal friendship is necessary for rich and poor, for young and old, and even for those in the prime of life.

But Aristotle continues with an argument about parenthood among human beings and other animals and about less-intimate relationships among different races and groups traveling together:

> Friendship seems to be inherent by nature in the relationship of parent to offspring and of offspring to parent not only among men but also among birds and most animals. And friendship also seems to be present among those of a similar race in their relationship with one another, especially among men. Hence, we praise lovers of fellow men. One may also see in his travels how every man belongs to each man and is friendly. (*Eth.* 8.1.1155a16–22)

And he suggests that friendship occurs among fellow citizens:

> Friendship also seems to hold cities together, and statesmen seem to be more zealous about it than about justice. For unanimity seems to be something like friendship, and this they aim at most of all and expel faction as their worst enemy. (*Eth.* 8.1.1155a22–26)

He does not quite say that political friendship is unanimity, but he does imply that unanimity is friendly relationship of some sort among fellow citizens. It apparently holds cities together because it is the opposite of faction.

We may glean an even more striking conception of the range of Aristotle's theory of friendship if we bring together several seemingly disparate statements that Aristotle makes about friendships and other relationships. These diverse statements suggest that Aristotle uses "friendship" as a homonymic genus. He appears to use the word sometimes as a specific term to signify only personal friendship and sometimes as a generic term to signify both personal friendship and other relationships. These other relationships include both kinships and political relationships. By bringing these statements together, we shall also obtain an initial glimpse of what the cause of friendship is—and of what another self is.

In the *Ethics* Aristotle divides friendship into two major genera. He distinguishes kinship and comradeship from political friendship and other friendships:

> All friendship exists in a community, as we have said. One might, however, mark off from the rest kinships and comradeships. Political friendship and the friendship of fellow tribesmen and that of fellow travelers and all friendships of such sort seem to be more in communities. For they appear to be in accordance with some convention. Among these someone might also place hospitality. (*Eth.* 8.12.1161b11–16)

He apparently divides friendship into natural relationships and conventional relationships. At least, he asserts that friendships other than kinship and comradeship are in accordance with some convention.[16]

If we consider kinship first, we can begin to see why Aristotle might call kinship and comradeship natural relationships. Friendships of both kinds have the same natural object—another self. When he discusses parenthood, Aristotle in fact introduces his conception of another self. He asserts that parenthood is the source of kinship of all other species and explains that parents and children love one another because parents reproduce themselves in their children:

> Kinship seems to be of many species, and all species appear to depend on parenthood. For parents feel fondness for their children as being something of themselves, and children feel fondness for their parents as being something from them. (*Eth.* 8.12.1161b16–19)

Apparently, because of reproduction parents and children are what he calls "other selves" or "different selves":

> Parents therefore love their children as themselves, for their issue are like different selves in being separate. And children love their parents as being from them by nature. (*Eth.* 8.12.1161b27–30)

He unfortunately does not pause to define his conception of another self explicitly. But he does indicate that other selves are different from one another in one sense and yet identical to one another in another sense. We can see that other selves are obviously different from one another, for parents and children are different individuals. Yet other selves are also identical with or very similar to one another, for parents and children have the same or very similar natural qualities. He also indicates that another self is the cause of friendship, for he implies that someone who is another self is a lovable object of some kind.

Parents and children thus love one another because they have similar natural qualities. And so parents and children are what one might call natural other selves to one another.

Though they are primarily natural other selves, Aristotle suggests that parents and children are also what one might call cultural other selves to one another. He implies that parents perpetuate their cultural characteristics in their children. Parents are the cause not only of the existence of their children but also of their upbringing and their education:

> The friendship of children to parents, and of men to gods, is a relationship to them as to something good and superior. For parents have rightly done the most things, being the cause of the existence and the upbringing and also the education of their children. (*Eth.* 8.12.1162a4–7)

He argues that children love their parents not only as the source of their natural existence but also as the source of their moral and intellectual development. And he implies that parents act for the sake of the moral and intellectual virtues and activities of their children. He thus takes into account the biological life of children as well as their moral and intellectual life.

Parents and children are thus cultural other selves, too. Parents and children again are in one sense different from one another, for they are different individuals; but they are again in another sense the same as one another, for they have the same or very similar moral and intellectual qualities.

Aristotle confirms our inferences about his conception of another self when he discusses brotherhood. He argues that brothers, too, are natural other selves. Brothers love each other because they have the same parents:

> Brothers love each other as being born of the same parents, for their identity with them makes them identical with each other. That is why people speak of the same blood and the same stock and so on. They are somehow the same thing in different individuals. (*Eth.* 8.12.1161b30–33)

He does not literally say that brothers are other selves, but he does say that they are "the same thing in different individuals." And he argues that brothers are identical with each other because they are identical with their parents. That is, they have the same natural qualities because they have natural qualities from the same parents.

He appears to imply that brothers are cultural other selves, too, when he argues that they are similar to comrades. Though he does not mention education, he explains that brothers are similar to comrades with respect to age and moral character:

> Great contributors to friendship are a common upbringing and similarity of age. For "two of an age take to each other," and people of similar habits tend to be comrades. That is why brothers are similar to comrades. (*Eth.* 8.12.1161b33–1162a1; see also 1162a9–14)

He argues that comrades have a friendship with one another because of their similar age and upbringing. He would thus imply that they have some natural identity with each other, for they have natural similarities because of their similar age. But he also implies that they have some cultural identity with each other. Because of their common upbringing, they have similar habits.

We conclude then that in more natural friendships the friends appear to be both natural and cultural other selves to one another. Parents and children are primarily natural other selves to one another because the parents are the cause of the existence of their children; but parents and children are also cultural other selves to one another because parents are the cause of the moral and mental development of the children. Siblings are both natural and cultural other selves, too, because they have the same parents and the same upbringing.[17]

We can also see that the friends in more conventional friendships appear to be other selves to one another. Though initially they have more of a natural identity, these friends eventually acquire an identity that is more cultural. Aristotle's conception of their development shows that not only the family but also the village and the city rest on his conception of another self. As he argues in the *Ethics* that parents and children love each other because they are other selves, so, too, Aristotle implies in the *Politics* that fellow villagers and fellow citizens love each other because they are other selves.

Aristotle argues, of course, that the family naturally develops into the village, and the village into the city. He appears to assume that family members are primarily natural other selves, for marriage arises from a natural desire to create other selves:

> Those who are not capable of being without one another must
> first of all be united. For example, male must be united with fe-
> male for the sake of reproduction. And this they do not do from
> choice. But as with other animals and plants, they naturally long
> to leave behind another of the same sort as themselves. (*Pol.*
> 1.2.1252a26–30)

He does not literally assert that parents and children are other selves, but he
does say that parents reproduce "another of the same sort as themselves."
He thus implies that they are different individuals with a natural identity.
He also argues that the family comes to be for the sake of daily needs (*Pol.*
1.2.1252b12–15). If they come to be for these needs, parents and children
again appear to be primarily biological other selves.

Aristotle implies that parents have some cultural identity, too, for he
argues that marriage extends beyond reproduction:

> But human beings dwell together not only for the sake of re-
> production but also for the sake of the things important for life.
> For their functions are clearly divided, and the functions of men
> and women are different. They therefore toil for one another
> by contributing their own good to the common good. (*Eth.*
> 8.12.1162a20–24)

He even asserts that marriage may promote virtue:

> But their friendship may also exist for the sake of virtue if they
> are good. For there is a virtue for each, and they may delight in
> virtue of such sort. (*Eth.* 8.12.1162a25–27)

If it promotes virtue, marriage promotes cultural other selves, for humans
cultivate virtuous activity.

Aristotle argues that the village is an expansion of the family. At least,
the village that is "most in accordance with nature" is:

> The village most in accordance with nature appears to be an
> expansion of the family, composed of children and grand-
> children, whom some say to be suckled with the same milk.
> (*Pol.* 1.2.1252b16–18)

By stating that it is "composed of children and grandchildren," he clearly
implies that this village has villagers who are natural other selves.

He also argues that cousins are friends because of their ultimate common parents:

> Cousins and other kinsmen have ties by derivation from the ties of brothers, for they have ties as being from the same parents. And they belong more to each other or more to others in accordance with the nearness or distance of their ancestor. (*Eth.* 8.12.1162a1–4)

Cousins, too, thus appear to be natural other selves.

But he implies that fellow villagers are at least in part cultural other selves as well, for he argues that these villages satisfy "not only everyday needs" (*Pol.* 1.2.1252b15–16). These villages accordingly appear to satisfy some cultural needs, too.

By referring to the village of this type as most natural, Aristotle leaves open the possibility that villages may also be of other types. These other villages more clearly advance an identity that is cultural. He appears to refer to these villages when he argues that tribes and clans, sailors and soldiers, religious congregations and social clubs are friendships. Though they do not develop from a family, relationships of these kinds are villagelike relationships because they develop into cities:

> Cities cannot be established among those who do not live in one and the same place and do not intermarry. That is why families arise in cities, and kinships and sacrifices and festivals. Relationships of such sort are the function of friendship, for friendship is the choice to live together. And the end of a city is to live well, and these relationships also exist for the sake of this end. (*Pol.* 3.9.1280b35–40)

He implies that not only families and other kinships but also religious groups and social gatherings are the means toward a city, for he argues that these relationships have the ends of living together and living well, and he explicitly asserts that a city has the end of living well and implies that a city has the end of living together.[18]

Aristotle explains that relationships of these sorts are parts of a city. They are parts because they only partially advance the interest of a political community:

> All communities seem to be parts of a political community. For men journey together to attain some interest and to provide something that pertains to life. (*Eth.* 8.9.1160a8–11)

He explicitly asserts that religious congregations and social clubs, sailors and soldiers, tribesmen and clansmen, all advance the interest of a city only in part:

> These other communities seek their interest in part. For example, sailors seek their interest at sea, either monetary profit or some such thing, and soldiers seek their interest at war, whether they desire money or victory or a city. Similarly tribesmen and clansmen. Some of these communities also seem to arise for the sake of pleasure—religious congregations and social clubs. For they exist for the sake of sacrifices and social events. (*Eth.* 8.9.1160a14–20)

He promptly states again not only that these relationships are parts of a city but also that all these relationships are friendships:

> All these communities appear to be parts of the political community. And friendship of these kinds attend communities of these kinds. (*Eth.* 8.9.1160a28–30)

He asserts at least that friendships attend them.

Aristotle does not explicitly say how people in these friendships are other selves to one another, nor does he even say that they are other selves. We might, however, conjecture that these people are primarily cultural other selves. People clearly do not have to have natural identities with one another to join religious congregations or social clubs or to serve in armies or navies. Neither are all tribesmen nor all clansmen kin. But people in these relationships do have cultural identities with one another. Individuals in congregations and clubs, in navies and armies, and in tribes and clans have moral and intellectual identities of some kind. Though they provide some biological benefits, members of these groups primarily provide moral or intellectual benefits for one another, for they do have—in part at least—the end of living well.

Finally, Aristotle argues that several villages may combine into a city, and that a city satisfies all needs of its citizens:

> The complete community formed from several villages is the city, a community having, in a word, the goal of full self-sufficiency, coming to be for the sake of life, and being for the sake of good life. (*Pol.* 1.2.1252b27–30)

He asserts explicitly that a city exists for the sake of happiness:

> A city is a community of families and villages in a complete and self-sufficient life. And, as we say, this life is to live happily and nobly. Therefore, that the political community is for the sake of noble actions and not merely for living together, must be laid down. (*Pol.* 3.9.1280b40–1281a4)

Fellow citizens appear to be primarily cultural other selves and to have some moral and intellectual identity with one another. If it exists for the sake of happiness, their city exists for the sake of a moral and intellectual life, for happiness consists in a life of such sort.

Fellow citizens also appear to have moral and intellectual identities because a political community advances the interest of an entire life and other communities only the interest of part of life:

> But all other communities seem to fall under the political community. For the political community seeks not present interest but an interest for an entire life, even making sacrifices and arranging assemblies for them and assigning honors to the gods and providing pleasant relaxations for themselves. For early sacrifices and assemblies appear to have arisen after the grain harvest as first fruits. (*Eth.* 8.9.1160a21–28)

The interest of an entire life would surely include both moral and intellectual interests. But citizens most clearly have a moral identity, for they have a common interest, which is justice:

> And a political community seems to come together in the beginning and to endure for the sake of an interest. For this statesmen aim at, and they say that justice is the common interest. (*Eth.* 8.9.1160a11–14)

We see then that Aristotle's theory of friendship includes not only what we call personal friendships but also families, villages, and cities and that these natural and conventional relationships all rest on his conception of another self (Figure 1.1). We see, too, that Aristotle's conception of another self is a conception of people who are different individuals but who have natural or cultural identities. And, we begin to grasp the unity and diversity of Aristotle's conception of friendship, not to mention its sublimity.[19]

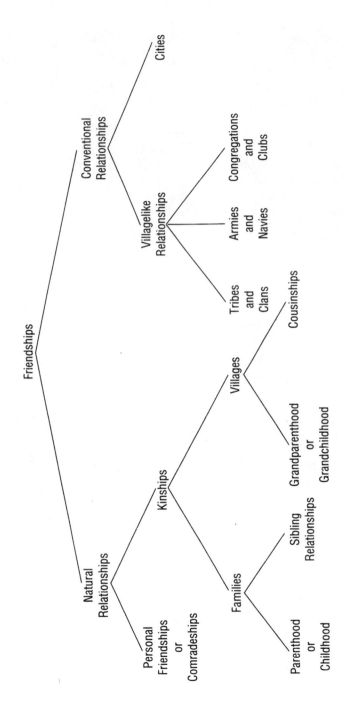

Figure 1.1

In the chapters that follow we shall use Aristotle's principle to examine the extremes in this spectrum of human friendship. I shall analyze personal friendship and political friendship. I wish to analyze personal friendship in order to determine what friendship is and why it is. Aristotle discusses friendship of this kind to define friendship and to explain its cause. I wish to analyze political friendship and also justice in order to compare Aristotle's definition of personal friendship and his explanation of it with his definition and explanation of political friendship and justice. I also intend to see what insight, if any, this comparison might yield for political philosophy. I would suggest that Aristotle's political philosophy might turn out to be both altruistic and pluralistic and that these properties would make his theory more sophisticated and more feasible than usually supposed.

HAPPINESS AND VIRTUE

Before beginning my analysis, I would like to define explicitly the principle that I intend to use for analyzing Aristotle's theory of friendship. The principle in question is that of happiness. But I shall examine both Aristotle's definition of happiness and his definition of virtue, for the two are closely connected. I shall also discuss his conception of the object of friendship—another self. For he does not explicitly define this conception for us. And we shall consider other conceptions that are not Aristotle's but are useful for our present purpose.

When he defines happiness, Aristotle first shows that there is a human good. He argues that there is an end for all our actions and that this end is the best good:

> We have an end for all actions that we wish for its own sake, and all other actions are for the sake of it. And we do not choose every action for the sake of another action, for this would go on to infinity, and our desire would be vain and empty. This end then is clearly the good and the best good. (*Eth.* 1.2.1094a18–22)

His argument is simply that an end for our actions is a good that is best because we direct our other actions toward it and that we would fall into an infinite regress if we did not direct our actions toward an end.[1]

After examining other alternatives, he ultimately concludes that the good that is best is happiness:

We call what is pursued for itself more complete than what is pursued for the sake of something else. And what is never choiceworthy for the sake of something else more complete than what is choiceworthy for itself and for the sake of something else. What is absolutely complete is choiceworthy ever for itself and never for the sake of something else. And a thing of such sort happiness seems to be most of all, for this we always choose for the sake of itself and noway for the sake of something else. (*Eth.* 1.7.1097a30–1097b1)

He appears to argue that happiness is the best good because happiness is the most complete good. He assumes that an end choiceworthy for the sake of itself and not for the sake of something else is the most complete good, and he asserts that happiness we always choose for the sake of itself and not for the sake of something else.

But what is happiness? Aristotle argues that happiness is activity in accordance with virtue:

The human good is an activity of soul in accordance with virtue. (*Eth.* 1.7.1098a16–17)

He establishes this definition by using the conception of a function. An analogy suggests to him that the goodness of something that has a function resides in its function:

Just as for a flute player, a sculptor, and all craftsmen, and generally, for things that have some function and action, the good and the well seem to be in the function, so it would seem to be for a human being if indeed he has some function. (*Eth.* 1.7.1097b25–28)

As flute players and sculptors have a good residing in their function, so, too, human beings have a good residing in the human function.

To determine what the human function is, he eliminates functions common to other live beings:

What then is this function? For life appears to be common even to plants, and we are seeking the function peculiar to man. We must therefore exclude the life of nutrition and growth. A certain life of perception would follow next. But this life appears to be common to a horse, an ox, and all animals. There remains then a certain practical life of the element having a principle. (*Eth*. 1.7.1097b33–1098a4)

As such, human beings have only the function of a life of intellection. That is, we have the function of the principled element of our soul. As organisms, we do have the functions of intellection, perception, and nutrition; but perception and nutrition we share with other living beings.

To fulfill it well, humans must fulfill their function in accordance with virtue. Aristotle again relies on an analogy:

> The human function is an activity of soul in accordance with a principle or not without a principle. And we say that the function of a this and of a good this is the same in kind, as is the function of a lyre player and a good lyre player. And as is this absolutely in all cases, the superiority in accordance with virtue being added to the function, for a lyre player plays the lyre, but a good lyre player does so well. And it is also thus, we assert that the function of a man is a certain life, that this life is the same as an activity or action of soul with a principle, that the function of a good man is to fulfill this function well and nobly, and that each function is fulfilled well when fulfilled in accordance with its own virtue. (*Eth*. 1.7.1098a7–15)

Put more simply, the analogy states that as a good lyre player plays the lyre in accordance with virtue, so a good man fulfills the human function in accordance with virtue.

Notice one significant difference between Aristotle's conception of happiness and our common conception. Derived from "hap," meaning luck, the very word "happiness" suggests that we tend to think of being happy as having good fortune, especially as possessing external goods. In fact, we often do think of happiness as the possession of wealth of one kind or another, such as real estate or machines, if not simply as the possession of money, preferably in a large quantity.

Our tendency to identify happiness with good fortune seems to find confirmation in the fact that someone who is happy requires wealth to act virtuously. We must have the means necessary to perform actions and to perform them well. Aristotle himself observes that happiness requires external goods. He argues that to do noble deeds without provisions is difficult or impossible: "Yet happiness appears to need external goods, as we said. For to do noble deeds without provisions is either impossible or not easy. We do many deeds through friends and wealth and political power as through instruments" (*Eth.* 1.8.1099a31–1099b2). He even notes that because happiness requires these goods, some people in the ancient world also identified happiness with good fortune (*Eth.* 1.8.1099b6–8).

Yet Aristotle implies that to be happy, a person need only have external goods sufficient to engage in virtuous actions: "What prevents us from saying that a happy man is active in accordance with complete virtue and sufficiently equipped with external goods, not for some fortunate period but for a complete life" (*Eth.* 1.10.1101a14–16; also see *Eth.* 10.8.1179a1–16)? He does argue that good fortune can indeed make people extremely happy and that bad fortune prevents us from having extreme happiness: "The small strokes of good fortune and similarly those of opposite fortune clearly do not weigh much on the scales of life. Many great strokes of fortune, if they turn out well, will make life most extremely happy. For they themselves naturally provide adornments and their use may be noble and good. But if they turn out ill, they crush and cripple extreme happiness. For they bring pains and hinder many activities" *(Eth.* 1.10.1100b24–30). But he also adds that a good man has the ability to make the best of his circumstances even though he may be hindered by poverty: "If activities are the chief things in life, as we said, no one who is extremely happy could become miserable. For he never does hateful and petty deeds. The truly good and practically wise man, we think, bears all fortune with dignity and always makes the best of circumstances, just as a good general makes the best campaign with the army at his command, and the best cobbler makes the best shoes out of the hides given him" (*Eth.* 1.10.1100b33–1101a5). That is, a person who has a good character but finds himself in bad circumstances will not be able to do great deeds but will not do evil deeds, either. He will do what he can with what he has.

We thus see that to be happy is to act in accordance with virtue and that action in accordance with virtue requires wealth, but the possession of wealth is not virtuous action. What then is virtue? Aristotle divides virtue into two kinds—intellectual and moral. Unfortunately he does not offer a general definition of intellectual virtue. Instead, he defines the intellectual virtues one by one. He distinguishes two important kinds. Theoretical wisdom appears to be the virtue of the intellect concerned with invariable things; practical wisdom is apparently the virtue concerned with variable things:

> Let us assert that there are two parts of the soul which have a principle. The one part is that by which we see the sort of things of which the first principles cannot be otherwise, the other is that by which we see things which can be otherwise. For with

respect to objects different in kind, the parts of the soul answering to each of the two objects naturally differ in kind, since the knowledge belongs to these parts in accordance with some similarity and kinship. Of these parts let us call the one scientific and the other calculative, for to deliberate and to calculate are the same, and no one deliberates about that which cannot be otherwise. (*Eth.* 6.1.1139a6–14)

Theoretical wisdom would, of course, be the virtue of the scientific part, and practical wisdom the virtue of the calculative part.

Wisdom of the theoretical kind appears only to grasp truth; wisdom of the practical kind apparently grasps truth and controls desire:

Of the theoretical intellect, which is neither practical nor productive, the good and bad activity is truth and falsity, for this is the function of all thought. Of the practical intellect, the good activity is truth in agreement with desire—right desire. (*Eth.* 6.2.1139a27–31)

The practical intellect, however, is not only in agreement with desire but also makes desire right:

The appetitive part in a strong-willed man obeys a principle. And in the temperate and courageous man it is even more obedient. For on all matters it speaks with the same voice as principle. (*Eth.* 1.13.1102b26–28)

The practical intellect would thus command desire, for desire obeys its principle.

Theoretical wisdom Aristotle defines as knowledge of first principles and of what follows from them:

The theoretically wise man must know not only what follows from first principles but also know the truth about first principles. Theoretical wisdom would thus be intuition and science— science of the highest objects, being their fruition. (*Eth.* 6.7.1141a17–20)

He implies that wisdom of this kind is a unity of two other intellectual virtues—intuition and science. By "science of the highest objects," he appears to mean that science concerns invariable objects rather than variable ones (*Eth.* 6.7.1141a20–1141b8).

But what is intuition? What is science? Aristotle implies that intuition is knowledge of first principles, for he argues by elimination that intuition is a habit that grasps first principles:

> If science and practical wisdom and theoretical wisdom and in-
> tuition are the habits by which we know the truth and are never
> deceived about things that are invariable and things that are
> variable, then not being these three—practical wisdom, science,
> and theoretical wisdom—intuition grasps first principles. (*Eth.*
> 6.6.1141a3–8)

Obviously, theoretical wisdom cannot be intuition for it includes science (*Eth.* 6.6.1141a1–3). But science cannot be intuition, for it assumes first principles (1140b33–35). And practical wisdom concerns variable things (1140b35–1141a1).

He implies that science is knowledge of what follows from first prin-ciples. For he argues that science is a habit productive of demonstration:

> Science is therefore a habit that is productive of demonstration
> and has the other qualities that we additionally defined in the
> *Analytics,* for when a man is persuaded in a certain way, and the
> first principles are known to him, he has science. (*Eth.*
> 6.3.1139b31–34)

First principles, of course, are premises of science:

> And there are first principles of demonstration and of all science,
> for science follows from a principle. (*Eth.* 6.6.1140b32–35)

In other words, intuition grasps indemonstrable propositions, and science grasps those propositions that are demonstrable.

Aristotle argues that practical wisdom is an intellectual habit that is practical:

> The alternative remaining is that practical wisdom is a true habit
> that follows from a principle and that is practical and concerns
> human goods and evils. (*Eth.* 6.5.1140b4–6)

He argues that practical wisdom is not science, for science con-cerns that which is necessary and not that which can be otherwise (*Eth.* 6.5.1140a33–1140b4). We may add that wisdom of this kind is not theoretical intuition, which does not concern that which can be otherwise, either.

Why does practical wisdom follow from a principle? As does theoretical wisdom, practical wisdom appears to require intuition of some sort to supply its premises. Aristotle implies that intuition is of two kinds. Intuition of the theoretical kind grasps invariable premises for demonstration; intuition of the practical kind grasps variable premises for deliberation:

> Intuition concerns the ultimate facts in two ways. For intuition concerns both the first definitions and the ultimate facts, and argument does not. The intuition in accordance with which there are demonstrations grasps the definitions that are immovable and first. The intuition that is in practical arguments grasps the fact that is ultimate and variable and yields a proposition of a different kind. (*Eth.* 6.11.1143a35–1143b3)

These variable premises appear to include a grasp of the ends for the sake of which we act, for they include a grasp of universals:

> The first principles of that for the sake of which are these ultimate facts, for from the particulars arise the universals. Of these, we must therefore have apperception, and this apperception is intuition. (*Eth.* 6.11.1143b4–5)

He asserts, in effect, that practical intuition grasps the ends of our actions, for it grasps the ultimate facts, and these facts include the first principles for the sake of which we act. The first principles are universals arising from particulars.[2]

To be practical, practical wisdom must also include deliberation, which allows us to choose proper means to our ends:

> To the man of practical wisdom seems to belong the capacity to deliberate well about the things good for himself and the things in his interest. But not about things good in part. For example, not things of the sort conducive to health or to strength. But things of the sort conducive to living well generally. (*Eth.* 6.5.1140a25–28)

When he defines deliberation, Aristotle argues more explicitly that deliberation is not about ends but about means:

Deliberation seems to concern actions to be done by oneself, and these actions are for the sake of other actions. For the object of deliberation is not the end but the things that lead to the end. (*Eth.* 3.3.1112b32–34)

He uses examples drawn from the professions of medicine, rhetoric, and politics to show that we assume our end and consider through what means we may attain it (*Eth.* 3.3.1112b11–16).

We thus see that intellectual virtue includes theoretical wisdom and practical wisdom. And theoretical wisdom includes theoretical intuition and demonstration; practical wisdom is practical intuition and deliberation.

Aristotle explicitly defines moral virtue. Virtue of this kind is a habit that concerns choice and lies on a mean:

Virtue therefore is a habit concerned with choice, lying on a mean relative to us—a mean defined by the principle by which a man of practical wisdom would define it. (*Eth.* 2.6.1106b36–1107a2)

He argues by elimination that virtue has the genus of habit. The soul contains only capacities, emotions, and habits (*Eth.* 2.5.1105a19–21). But virtue cannot be a capacity or an emotion, so it must be a habit (1105b28–1106a10, 1106a10–12).

He shows that virtue concerns choice in two ways. Choice for actions of a certain kind produces virtue, for we acquire habits by repetition of actions:

By doing what we do in transactions with human beings, we become just or unjust. And by doing what we do among fearful objects, and by being habituated to feel fear or confidence, we become courageous or cowardly. And similarly for the rest, what we do concerning the appetites and the passions of anger. Some become temperate and good-tempered, some intemperate and bad-tempered. In the same circumstances, some turn this way, some that way. In a word, habits thus arise out of similar activities. (*Eth.* 2.1.1103b14–22)

Virtue also produces choice for actions of the same kind, for our habits incline us toward certain actions:

By abstaining from pleasures, we become temperate, and having become temperate, we also are most able to abstain from
them. Similarly, with courage. By being habituated to feel con-
tempt for fearful objects and to stand our ground against them,
we become courageous. And having become courageous, we
are most able to stand our ground against fearful objects. (*Eth.*
2.2.1104a34–1104b3)

Our actions thus produce habits originally, but eventually our habits in
turn produce actions.

The mean of virtue is an intermediate between two extremes: excess,
which is to overdo something, and defect, which is to underdo something:

He who fears and flies from everything and does not stand
his ground against anything becomes a coward, and he who
generally fears nothing but marches out to meet everything
becomes rash. And similarly he who indulges in every pleasure and abstains from none becomes self-indulgent, and
he who shuns every pleasure as rustics do becomes an insensi
ble sort. Temperance and courage are then destroyed by excess
and deficiency, and they are preserved by the mean. (*Eth.*
2.2.1104a20–27)

But the mean may be relative to an object or relative to us (*Eth.*
2.6.1106a26–32). A mean relative to an object is an arithmetic mean:

If ten is many and two is few, then six may be taken to be an
intermediate in accordance with the thing. For six exceeds and
is exceeded by an equal amount. This is a mean in accordance
with an arithmetic proportion. (*Eth.* 2.6.1106a32–36)

Without saying so explicitly, Aristotle indicates that a geometric mean is a
mean relative to us:

If ten pounds is too much for some to eat and two too little,
then the trainer will not order us six pounds. This is perhaps too
much for the man who takes it or too little. Too little for Milo,
too much for the beginner in athletics. (*Eth.* 2.6.1106a36–
1106b4)

He thus implies that virtue lies on a geometric mean, which is relative to us (*Eth*. 2.6.1106b5–7).

Finally, virtue is an intermediate that concerns our actions and emotions, either of which may be excessive or defective:

> Moral virtue is concerned with passions and actions, and in these, there is an excess and a defect and an intermediate. For example, fear and confidence and appetite and anger and generally pleasure and pain may be felt too much or too little. In both cases, they are not felt well. But they must be felt at this time or place, with respect to this object, for the sake of this object, and in this way to be an intermediate and best—the very thing required of virtue. Similarly concerning actions, there is an excess and a defect and an intermediate. (*Eth*. 2.6.1106b16–24)

We also see that what action or passion is intermediate depends on the situation in which we find ourselves.

Assuming that practical wisdom determines the mean, Aristotle thus defines moral virtue as a habit concerned with choice and lying on a mean. Aristotle's conception of moral virtue differs from our usual conception in an important respect. This difference concerns his conception of habit. We usually think of habits not as good qualities but rather as bad qualities, perhaps because we most often think of a habit as an addiction of some kind. For example, a drug addiction.

Aristotle would have to agree that habits in our usual sense are bad qualities, but he would distinguish these habits from virtues. These habits are vices, which concern extremes rather than means: "Virtue is a mean between two vices—one vice in accordance with an excess and another in accordance with a defect" (*Eth*. 2.6.1107a2–3). We have to admit that even a drug taken in accordance with a mean relative to us can be beneficial.

Aristotle also explains why these vices arise. both virtues and vices concern pleasures and pains. We acquire virtues by standing up to pains as we ought and by abstaining from pleasures as we ought; but we acquire vices by fleeing from pains and by indulging in pleasures. Pleasure persuades us to perform bad actions; pain dissuades us from performing good actions: "Moral virtue concerns pleasures and pains. Because of pleasures we do base things, and because of pains we fail to do noble things" (*Eth*. 2.3.1104b8–11). That is why Plato was right to say that we must be brought up from our youth to feel pleasure and pain in the proper things (*Eth*. 2.3.1104b11–13).

Another difference between Aristotle's conception of habit and our usual one is that we often think that habits —especially bad habits—arise and persist almost without our knowledge. We seem to slip into them and to act out of them almost unawares. Consider smoking or drinking, for example.

Aristotle discusses habits of this sort, too, but he discusses good habits rather than bad. Habits that arise unawares appear to him to result from natural dispositions: "All men seem to think that each of the habits belongs to us somehow by nature. For we are just or temperate or courageous or the rest at once from birth" (*Eth.* 6.13.1144b4–6). But he clearly distinguishes habits acquired through our natural dispositions from virtue. Habits resulting merely from dispositions can be harmful: "Yet we seek to believe that something else is the chief good and that these qualities belong to us in some other way. For children and beasts naturally have these habits, but without intuition they appear to be harmful" (*Eth.* 6.13.1144b6–9). Habits arising from our dispositions are harmful, precisely because they cause us to act without knowledge, for intuition is knowledge of practical principles. That is, practical intuition grasps these principles.

With the addition of knowledge, habits resulting from natural dispositions can become virtues: "We seem to see this far—that as a strong body that moves without sight might stumble with its strength because of not having sight, so in these things. If he has intuition, a man acts differently. And his habit, though similar to what it was, will be virtue strictly speaking" (*Eth.* 6.13.1144b10–14). But to be a moral virtue, Aristotle adds, a habit must be not only in accordance with a principle but also from a principle (*Eth.* 6.13.1144b21–28).

Aristotle thus argues that happiness is an activity in accordance with virtue and that virtue is a habit that lies on a mean. His definitions of happiness and virtue are not entirely satisfactory, however. He does not specify what virtue happiness actualizes. He states only that this virtue is the best and the most complete: "And if the virtues are many, the human good is an activity of soul in accordance with the best and most complete virtue" (*Eth.* 1.7.1098a 17–18). But if we wish to be happy, which virtue would we find to be best and most complete? We discussed six intellectual virtues: theoretical wisdom, theoretical intuition, science, practical wisdom, practical intuition, and deliberation. Though we did not define them, we mentioned four moral virtues: justice, courage, temperance, and good-temperedness. And there are many more virtues, both intellectual and moral.

What Aristotle does is indicate merely that we are happy in a primary way when we act in accordance with theoretical wisdom. Wisdom of this kind, he argues, is the best virtue: "If happiness is an activity in accordance with virtue, happiness would be well said to be in accordance with the best virtue. And the best virtue would be that of the best part of us. Whether this part is intuition or some other part that in accordance with nature appears to rule and to lead us and to have thought of things noble and divine, or whether it is divine itself or the most divine part in us, complete happiness would be the activity of this part in accordance with its own virtue. That this activity is theoretical wisdom has been said" (*Eth.* 10.7.1177a11–18). He also indicates that we may be happy in a secondary way when we act in accordance with moral virtue: "But life in accordance with another virtue is happiness secondarily. For actions in accordance with another virtue are human. We perform for one another just actions and courageous actions and other actions in accordance with the virtues in regard to contracts and transactions and actions of all sorts. And with regard to the passions, we observe what is proper for each. All these activities appear to be human" (*Eth.* 10.8.1178a9–14). So we are happy in a primary sense when we exercise theoretical wisdom, and we are happy in a secondary sense when we exercise practical wisdom and moral virtue. For we have seen that practical wisdom is necessary for moral virtue.

Aristotle still leaves us with the problem of how we ought to integrate the activities of primary happiness and secondary happiness: Ought we to let the pursuit of primary happiness dominate our lives? Or ought we to include the pursuit of both primary and secondary happiness in our lives? This philosophical problem has generated a controversy of some magnitude, but fortunately we need not participate in it. The fact that we may be happy in either a primary or a secondary sense is sufficient for our purposes. Indeed, the fact that we may be happy in either sense will prove to be an advantage for us.[3]

We are now in a position to appreciate the importance of using a principle in our analysis of Aristotle's theory of friendship. Aristotle's principle has primarily a theoretical significance for us. We now know that when he speaks of human goodness, Aristotle speaks of an activity in accordance with virtue. And when he speaks of good character, he speaks of virtuous character, for good character is made up of virtues. I shall soon show more specifically that friendship itself is an activity in accordance with virtue and that it is also a virtue. I shall show, too, that friendship takes as its end the activity and virtue of a friend.

Aristotle's principle of happiness is also useful for defining his conception of a different self or another self more clearly. We have seen that Aristotle uses the term "another self" or "different self" to designate the object of friendship of the best kind but also that he does not define what another self or a different self is. Why he neglects to define this conception, I do not know. But by applying his conception of happiness to his discussion of the object of friendship, I believe that we may define it for ourselves.

Aristotle's conception of happiness allows us to define what identity other selves have with one another. We have already seen that other selves are numerically different than one another, for they are different individuals. We have also seen that other selves are naturally or culturally identical to one another, for they have the same or very similar natural or cultural qualities. For example, though they are different individuals, parents and children usually have very similar natural qualities as well as very similar moral and intellectual qualities.

We can now see how Aristotle's principle of happiness defines the qualities that constitute the cultural identity of other selves. Happiness defines what moral and intellectual activities constitute good activities, and these good activities in turn indicate what moral and intellectual virtues constitute good character. These moral and intellectual virtues, which give us our character, are the cultural identity of other selves. Happiness is, after all, what human beings cultivate.

The conception of happiness does not appear to define the natural identity of other selves, however. Moral and intellectual virtues arise in us in accordance with nature but not by nature (*Eth.* 2.1.1103a18–1103b2). Yet cultural identity, of course, does find its material in our nature, for culture supplants nature, as virtue supplants emotion.

Using his principle of happiness, I can indeed show how we might explain the unity and diversity of Aristotle's conception of friendship. We have seen that Aristotelian friendship encompasses relationships of many species, for friendship of the Aristotelian sort includes personal friendships as well as the relationships of families, villages, and cities. We have seen that the friends in these different relationships are other selves to one another. Though different individuals, family members share identical qualities, and so do fellow villagers and fellow citizens.

Aristotle's definition of happiness appears to explain the generic unity within the specific diversity of these relationships. The conception of happiness shows how other selves are of one genus and yet of several species. Happiness itself includes virtuous activities of different sorts, for happiness includes activities of intellectual and moral virtues as well as activities of different intellectual and moral virtues. What would prevent one from using different conceptions of happiness to define the ends of different friendships and to define the qualities of different friends? For example, we might use one conception of happiness and virtue in a personal relationship and another conception of happiness and virtue in a political relationship. Indeed, we might use different conceptions for different personal relationships and different conceptions for different political relationships.[4]

We thus see that other selves appear to be different individuals who share identical conceptions of happiness. I assume that Aristotle would most likely use his principle of happiness to define the cultural identity of other selves. We shall, in fact, discover that he does strongly imply that happiness defines the identity of other selves, when he discusses friendship.

We ought to be careful not to confuse Aristotle's conception of another self with the conception of another human being, however. The two are not the same. We differ from another self and another human being in the same way. Both other selves and other humans are numerically different. But we are not the same as another self and another human being in the same way. Other selves have the same natural or cultural identity, for they have very similar natural or cultural qualities. But other human beings need not share these specific qualities. We share only the most general natural qualities with other humans, who may be of different natural stock and may have different natural abilities. And other humans need not cultivate any activity of happiness. They may have no culture at all; they may indulge in the acquisition of wealth, for example, or wantonly pursue pleasure.

We also ought to define two terms that will prove useful in our analysis of Aristotle's theory of friendship. Aristotle does not use these terms, but we do today. They are "altruistic" and "egoistic." These terms are convenient for characterizing the difference between two subgenera of Aristotelian friendship. The difference between these subgenera is primarily a difference in the intentions of the friends. In an altruistic friendship, both friends act for the sake of each other. That is, the one friend acts for the sake of the other, and the other acts for the sake of the one. Each one intends to benefit the other one. In an egoistic friendship, both friends act for the sake of themselves. That is, the one friend acts for the sake of the other but only so that the other will act for the sake of the one. The other friend does the same. Each intends to benefit himself.

Please note that the difference between an altruistic friendship and an egoistic friendship is not necessarily a difference between a self-sacrificing relationship and a non-self-sacrificing relationship. In an altruistic friendship, the one friend does not have to sacrifice himself for the sake of the other. If he wishes, he may of course do so. But he need not. The difference between an altruistic and an egoistic friendship is only one of intention.[5]

Other non-Aristotelian terms worth defining are "monistic" and "pluralistic." I use both terms to indicate how many goods a moral theory recognizes. A monistic theory recognizes only one good; a pluralistic theory recognizes several goods. One could argue that Aristotle advances a monistic theory because he argues that the human good is happiness, which is activity in accordance with virtue. But one would better argue that his theory is pluralistic because he recognizes happinesses of more than one kind. He himself explicitly distinguishes virtuous intellectual activity, which he calls primary happiness, and virtuous moral activity, which he calls secondary happiness. He also discusses many different intellectual activities, such as those of theoretical and practical wisdom, and many different moral activities, such as just, courageous, and temperate actions, to name only a few.

So when I oppose monism with pluralism, I do not have in mind a moral eclecticism of any sort. I wish merely to draw attention to the fact that in his moral theory Aristotle recognizes many human activities that we may perform for their own sakes and that we may perform in accordance with good habits.

My methodological assumptions I shall keep to a minimum. I shall assume what Aristotle himself espouses in the *Logic*. These assumptions include the principles of contradiction and excluded middle, of course, as well as the schemata of the syllogism and other derivative schemata, among them induction, enthymeme, and example.

I have found one technique in the *Prior Analytics* especially helpful for research of this kind. Aristotle calls this technique a way, and he implies that it helps us make syllogisms:

> We must discuss how we shall always be well supplied with syllogisms relevant to a proposed problem and by what way we shall grasp the first causes of each subject. For perhaps we ought not only to theorize about the origin of syllogisms but also to have the capacity to make them. (*Pr. Ana.* 1.27.43a20–24)

Asserting that this way is the same in all fields, he gives a brief description of it in one passage:

> This way is the same in all subjects—both in philosophy and in art and learning of whatever kind. One must consider the predicates and the subjects of each term and supply oneself with as many of these as possible. And one must examine these terms in threes, disproving propositions in one way and proving them in another. (*Pr. Ana.* 1.30.46a3–7)

In other words, this technique is a way of collecting terms and of using them to examine one another.

Aristotle explains that these terms are set out in two sets of lists, each set containing four lists. The first list contains one of the terms of a problem, the second list contains the consequents of this term, the third contains the antecedents of this term, and the final list the terms that are not consequents. The final list also includes terms that are not antecedents of the term in the first list because universal negative propositions convert simply (*Pr. Ana.* 1.27.43b1–6).

The sets of lists for both terms of a problem can be represented in a schema:

$$C \quad A \quad B \qquad D$$
$$G \quad E \quad F \qquad H$$

A and *E* stand for the terms of a problem, *B* and *F* stand for their consequents, *C* and *G* stand for their antecedents, and *D* and *H* for the terms that are neither consequents nor antecedents (*Pr. Ana.* 1.28.44a11–17).

This schema produces syllogisms relating the terms of a problem by isolating middle terms. For example, an identical term among the *C*'s and *F*'s will serve as a middle term for a syllogism proving that all *E* is *A*:

> All *C* is *A*
> All *E* is *C*
> Therefore, all *E* is *A* (*Pr. Ana.* 1.28.44a17–19).

Or an identical term among the *D*'s and the *F*'s will produce a syllogism proving that no *E* is *A*:

> No *A* is *D*
> All *E* is *D*
> Therefore, no *E* is *A* (*Pr. Ana.* 1.28.44a21–24).

The major premise converts simply, for it is a universal negative premise.

The schema thus uses the figures of the syllogism as criteria for the production of syllogisms out of the terms of the two sets of lists. The modes of the figures show which terms can be used to produce different types of propositions. A mode of the first figure shows how to select terms to produce universal affirmative propositions; a mode of the second figure shows how to produce universal negative propositions; and modes of the third figure show how to produce particular affirmative and negative propositions (*Pr. Ana.* 1.28.44b6–19).

The difficulty with this schema, of course, is how to determine what terms fall into its lists. I use two rules to determine what terms to put into what lists. The first rule is to follow Aristotle's explicit connection of one term with another; the second is to follow his implicit connection between terms. The second rule we may apply by induction. Examples may allow us to generalize an implicit relationship between terms. We may also apply the second rule by deduction. Enthymemes may leave implicit an obvious relationship between terms.

The first rule is, of course, the better for placing terms in the lists of our schema. It allows us to be about as certain as we can be about Aristotle's conception of the relations between terms. The second rule only allows us to conjecture about his conception. Applications of the second rule yield an inference with a strength dependent upon the amount of inductive or deductive evidence that we can muster. That is, upon how many instances or how many properties we can take into account.[6]

A DEFINITION OF FRIENDSHIP

I shall begin my analysis of Aristotle's theory of friendship by examining his definition of friendship. My examination will show that his conception of friendship is altruistic. We shall see that friendship is essentially good friendship and that friendship of this sort is altruistic. For those who are good friends act with the intention of advancing the happiness of one another.

Actually, Aristotle defines friendship twice: explicitly as an activity and implicitly as a virtue. These two definitions complement one another quite nicely, and their complementarity yields an insight into how his conception of friendship fits into his theory of ethics. This insight will, in turn, facilitate our examination of the motivation for friendship.

When he defines it as an activity, Aristotle states his definition of friendship more as he might a definition of a friend:

> Friends must bear good will and good wishes for one another,
> not without recognition, for the sake of one of the objects dis-
> cussed. (*Eth.* 8.2.1156a3–5)

This definition states what friends must do, how they must do it, and why they must. Friends must bear good will and good wishes, they must reciprocate and recognize their good will and good wishes, and they must do so for the sake of their goodness, their usefulness, or their pleasantness, for these three qualities distinguish the lovable objects under discussion (*Eth.* 8.2.1155b18–19).

Aristotle establishes each element of his definition with a succinct argument. These arguments present us with an initial impression of what each element is. He begins with the object of love:

> Not everything seems to be loved but only the lovable, and this seems to be either good or pleasant or useful. But the useful would seem to be that by means of which some good or pleasure comes to be so that the good and the pleasant would be lovable as ends. (*Eth.* 8.2.1155b18–21)

He states simply that love is for the sake of the lovable and that the lovable is divisible into the good, the useful, and the pleasant. He adds that the useful is a means and the good and the pleasant are ends. With this addition he implies that his division of lovable objects is exhaustive, for the lovable is what is immediately or mediately good or pleasant.

He next considers the elements of good wishes and their reciprocity. He uses a counterexample to show that friendship requires good wishes and that these wishes must be reciprocated. His counterexample contrasts friendship with love for wine:

> . . . love for a lifeless object we do not call friendship. For there is no reciprocal love nor is there a good wish for the other. To bear a good wish for wine would be ridiculous. If anything, we wish that it may keep so that we may drink it. But we say that is it necessary to wish the good for a friend for his sake. (*Eth.* 8.2.1155b27–31)

He uses the contrast between love for a friend and love for wine to show what a good wish in friendship is. A good wish is one for the sake of the object of our wish. We apparently wish a friend well for his sake, but we do not usually wish wine well for its sake.[1]

Aristotle's contrast between our love for a friend and our love for wine also shows that a good wish in friendship is reciprocated. For a friend would return a good wish, but wine would not. Aristotle gives another explanation for the element of reciprocity by distinguishing between good will and friendship:

> To those who wish what is good we ascribe only good will, if the same wishes do not arise from another. For friendship lies in reciprocal good will. (*Eth.* 8.2.1155b32–34)

He asserts that even if we feel good will for him, we cannot yet say that we are friends with another person unless he reciprocates our good will.

Aristotle argues finally that friends must recognize their good wishes for one another:

> Or must we add that they do so not without recognition? For many people bear good wishes for those whom they have not seen but suppose to be good or useful. And someone among these may feel the same toward them. These people therefore seem to bear good will for one another. But how could someone call them friends when they do not recognize how they feel about themselves? (*Eth.* 8.2.1155b34–1156a3)

Obviously friends are aware of the good wishes borne toward one another; but other people who bear good wishes for each other need not be aware that they do.

In establishing each element of this definition, Aristotle thus appears to follow the usual sequence of events in the development of a friendship. We first feel affection for another person because of his goodness, usefulness, or pleasantness. We allow ourselves to express our affection with good will and good wishes for that person. We do him a favor, in other words. We may then find that he reciprocates our good wishes and good actions. And eventually we may both recognize a continued exchange of good wishes and actions. We are then friends.

Having defined friendship, Aristotle qualifies one element of his definition—the element of bearing good will and good wishes for another. This qualification allows him to distinguish what he calls essential friendship from what he calls accidental friendship. An examination of this distinction will permit us to understand more clearly what friendship itself is and what its species are. We shall see that friendship of one species is altruistic and that friendship of two species is egoistic.

Aristotle first divides friendship into its species by distinguishing the loves exhibited in them. He distinguishes these loves by distinguishing their objects:

> The lovable objects differ as species from one another, and therefore so do their loves and their friendships. There are therefore three species of friendship, equal in number to the lovable objects. For in accordance with each object there is reciprocal love and it is recognized. Those loving one another

wish what is good to one another in the respect in which they
love each other. (*Eth.* 8.3.1156a6–10)

He argues that friendship has three species. One person may bear good
wishes with reciprocation and recognition for another person as for someone good, someone useful, or someone pleasant. For one may love another
as someone good, useful, or pleasant.

Aristotle now makes his qualification. He implies that because of
these differences in lovable objects, some friends bear good wishes for others altruistically, and some friends bear good wishes for others egoistically.
He argues that those whom he calls good friends act for the sake of another essentially, advancing the good of another as an end. Those who are
useful and pleasant friends act for the sake of another accidentally, advancing the good of another only as a means to some other end of their own.

In his argument Aristotle uses a distinction that he explains more fully
in other passages. The distinction is that between acting essentially and acting accidentally. When he discusses justice, he assumes that someone who
does what is just for its own sake does what is essentially just. At least he
clearly asserts that someone who does what is just for the sake of something
else does what is accidentally just (*Eth.* 5.8.1135b2–8). But he explains
more explicitly in his discussion of weakness of will that when we choose or
pursue one thing for the sake of another, we choose or pursue our end essentially and our means accidentally (*Eth.* 7.9.1151a35–1151b2). In other
words, Aristotle assumes that we act essentially for the sake of an end and
accidentally for the sake of a means.[2]

Aristotle takes up useful and pleasant friendships first. He implies
that useful and pleasant friends bear good wishes for one another egoistically, for, he argues, useful and pleasant friends love one another only as
a means to an ulterior end of their own. Instead of loving each other as
who they are, friends of these kinds love each other as having useful or
pleasant qualities:

These people feel affection for another not as someone loved
but as someone useful or pleasant. (*Eth.* 8.3.1156a15–16)

They thus love one another not essentially but for the sake of something
received from the other:

Those loving for the sake of utility do not love one another essentially but rather as some good comes to be for themselves
from each other. Similarly those loving for the sake of pleasure,

for men do not feel affection for witty people for having certain qualities but because they give themselves pleasure. (*Eth.* 8.3.1156a10–14)

These friends therefore love one another accidentally, for they love each other only to procure some good for themselves:

> These friendships are therefore accidentally friendships, for the person loved is not loved as the very man he is but as he furnishes them some good or pleasure. (*Eth.* 8.3.1156a16–19)

A useful friend thus loves for the sake of his own good, a pleasant friend for the sake of his own pleasure (*Eth.* 8.3.1156a14–15).[3]

When he argues that good friends love each other as an end, Aristotle implies that good friends love one another altruistically. Good friends love one another for the sake of the goodness of the other because they are good men and wish what is good to each other as being good:

> Perfect friendship is the friendship of good men and of men who are similar according to their virtue. For they wish things that are good similarly to each other as good men and they are essentially good. (*Eth.* 8.3.1156b7–9)

These friends thus love one another for the sake of the other and not accidentally:

> Those who wish the good to their friends for the sake of them are the most friends, for they do this for their sake and not accidentally. (*Eth.* 8.3.1156b9–11)

The one friend thus loves the other friend for the sake of the other.[4]

Thus friendship is essentially altruistic, for it is essentially good will and good wishes, reciprocated and recognized, for the sake of the goodness of another. Friendship is only accidentally good will and good wishes, reciprocated and recognized, for the sake of the usefulness or pleasantness of another.[5]

When he discusses good will itself, Aristotle also maintains that we may feel good will for the sake of another or for the sake of ourself. That is, he distinguishes altruistic from egoistic good will, though he does not distinguish essential from accidental good will. With an analogy to erotic love, he reminds us that good will is the beginning of friendship: "Good will seems to be the beginning of friendship, as the pleasure of sight is the beginning of erotic love. For no one loves erotically unless he has been carried away by the form of his lover" (*Eth.* 9.5.1167a3–5). Continuing with his analogy, he asserts that without good will no one can be friends, but to be friends, good will by itself is not enough: "He who delights in the form of another does not yet feel erotic love, but he does so only when he also longs for him when absent and desires his presence. And thus it is not possible for people to be friends unless they come to have good will, but those who feel good will are not yet friends. For they wish only what is good for those for whom they have good will, but they would do nothing with them and nor would they trouble themselves for them" (*Eth.* 9.5.1167a5–10). But with time and familiarity, good will can become friendship: "Therefore, someone might say metaphorically that good will is idle friendship and that when it is prolonged and has arrived at familiarity, good will becomes friendship. But it does not become friendship for the sake of utility nor friendship for the sake of pleasure. For good will does not come to be for these things" (*Eth.* 9.5.1167a10–14). The implication is that good will can become good friendship, for it does not become useful or pleasant friendship.

Aristotle also explains that we feel good will for the sake of the good qualities of another: "Generally good will comes to be for the sake of virtue and goodness when a man appears to someone to be noble or courageous or to have a quality of such sort ..." (*Eth.* 9.5.1167a18–20). But we do not feel good will for the sake of the useful qualities of another: "But he who wishes someone to do well in the hopes of enriching himself through him does not seem to feel good will for him but rather for himself, just as no one is a friend of another if he treasures him for the sake of some utility" (*Eth.* 9.5.1167a15–18). We obviously feel good will toward ourself when we act for the sake of our own benefit. Presumably we also feel good will for ourself when we act for the sake of the pleasant qualities of another, for we would act for the sake of our own pleasure.[6]

We might note that friends who are essentially friends need not appear to differ in their actions from those who are accidentally friends. A good friend performs good actions for another, and his friend returns the good actions. Similarly, a useful or pleasant friend might also perform good actions for another, and his friend might return his good actions. But essential friends differ greatly from accidental friends in their intentions. Good friends intend to advance the good of another; useful and pleasant friends intend to advance their own good.

Aristotle does, in fact, argue that only because they resemble good friendships, do useful and pleasant friendships appear to be friendship at all. Because of their similarities to good friends, people call friends those who love one another for the sake of utility or pleasure:

> People call friends even those who feel affection for the sake of utility, just as cities may be called friends. For alliances among cities seem to come to be for the sake of their own interests. People also call friends those who feel affection for each other for the sake of pleasure, just as children do. So perhaps we must also say that such people are friends and that the species of friendship are many—primarily and chiefly the friendship of good men as good men and, in the accordance with similarities, the other species. For as having some good and some similarity, in that respect they are friends. (*Eth*. 8.4.1157a25–32)

Useful friends resemble good friends because good men are useful to one another; pleasant friends resemble good friends because good men are pleasant to one another: "Friendship for the sake of pleasure is similar to good friendship, for good men are pleasant to one another. Similarly friendship for the sake of utility is, too, for good men are also useful to one another" (*Eth*. 8.4.1156b35 1157a3). But good friendship remains distinct from useful and pleasant friendship. Good friends are useful and pleasant to one another for the sake of each other; but useful and pleasant friends are so for their own sake.[7]

The fact that they differ as essential and accidental friendship also explains another noteworthy difference. Good friendship is more stable than either useful or pleasant friendship. Because they continue to be like each other, good friends have a lasting relationship: "Friendship of good men lasts as long as they are good, and virtue endures" (*Eth*. 8.3.1156b11–12). Only a transitory relationship exists between useful and pleasant friends: "Useful and pleasant friendships are easily dissolved if the friends do not remain like one another, for if they are no longer pleasant or useful, they cease to love each other" (*Eth*. 8.3.1156a19–21). After they attain their own ends, useful and pleasant friends often find each other to be no longer useful or pleasant (see also *Eth*. 8.3.1156a21–24, 1156a34–1156b1).

Aristotle does admit that pleasant friendship can become stable, but his admission only reinforces his distinction between essential and accidental friendships: "However, many pleasant friends are constant if, from familiarity, they feel fondness for their characters, these being similar" (*Eth*. 8.4.1157a10–12). Pleasant friendships become stable if the friends become aware of their characters and their characters are similar. In a word, pleasant friends may become good friends.

Aristotle thus argues that good friendship is good will and good wishes, reciprocated and recognized, for the sake of another. And that good friendship is altruistic, but useful and pleasant friendships are egoistic.

Unfortunately Aristotle does not establish his definition of friendship as a virtue with either an explicit argument or a single argument. He presents separate arguments to prove that the elements in the definition of virtue belong to friendship, not troubling himself to collect these elements together into an explicit definition. He shows that friendship is a habit, that it is in accordance with a mean, and that it concerns an emotion. But assuming that practical wisdom determines the mean, a habit that is productive of choice in accordance with a mean and that concerns an emotion is obviously a virtue (see again *Eth.* 2.6.1106b36–1107a2; see also *Eth.* 2.5.1105b25–28).

To prove that friendship is a habit, Aristotle first asserts not only that friendship is a habit but also that love is a passion:

> It seems that love is a passion and that friendship is a habit. (*Eth.* 8.5.1157b28–29).

With this assertion he implies that love is a homonymic genus and that this genus divides into two species—a passion and a habit. At least, he cannot deny that love is both a passion and a habit, for he states that love is a passion and that friendship is not only a habit but also love. Recall that friends love what is lovable in each other (see again *Eth.* 8.2.1155b17–19, 1156a3–5).

He, in fact, proves that love—the species—is a passion by using love for a lifeless object as an example. He could hardly be more terse:

> For love is felt no less for lifeless objects. (*Eth.* 8.5.1157b29–30)

His argument leaves much room for conjecture, having only one premise. But this lone premise might call to mind another argument about love for a lifeless object—the argument about love for wine. This argument furnishes middle terms for additional premises:

> . . . love for a lifeless object we do not call friendship. For there
> is no reciprocal love nor is there a good wish for the other. (*Eth.*
> 8.2.1155b27–29)

In this argument we find two differences between love for a lifeless object and friendship: Love for a lifeless object is neither reciprocal nor for the sake of another. Our terse argument thus appears to have two implicit premises. Completed it would be: Love neither reciprocal nor for the sake of another is a passion; love for a lifeless object is neither reciprocal nor for the sake of another; love is felt for a lifeless object; therefore love is a passion.

Though stated in full, our argument still leaves us with a question: Why is love that is neither reciprocal nor for the sake of another a passion? In other words, why is reciprocal love for the sake of another a habit? Aristotle appears to take up this question next. He proves that friendship is a habit by using both its quality of being reciprocal and its quality of being for the sake of another. The quality of being for the sake of another is the crucial quality. This proof is more generous than the other one—it has two parts. The first part is:

> Friends love each other reciprocally from choice and their choice springs from a habit. (*Eth.* 8.5.1157b30–31)

The argument has two premises and its conclusion is obvious—that friends love reciprocally from habit. Its major premise is easy enough to grasp. That choice springs from habit merely implies that friendly activity may produce a habit and that this habit may, in turn, cause someone to choose the activity (see again *Eth.* 2.2.1104a34–1104b3).

The minor premise of this argument is more difficult: Why do friends who love reciprocally love from choice? The second part of the argument appears to show why they do. This part restricts friendship to reciprocal love of one kind:

> And friends wish the good to those whom they love for their sake not in accordance with passion but in accordance with habit. (*Eth.* 8.5.1157b31–32)

This argument appears to leave its premises implicit and to state only its conclusion. Fully stated, the argument would be: Love for the sake of another is in accordance with habit; friends love for the sake of another; therefore friends love in accordance with habit. The argument clearly restricts reciprocal love to that found in good friendship, for only good friends love one another for the sake of the other.

Now we can see that the reciprocal love in good friendship is likely to become a habit. If we wish him well essentially, we wish another good for the sake of his character and his activity, for a good friend loves the character and activity of another. In fact, Aristotle reminds us at the beginning of this discussion that one good man finds another good man lovable:

> The absolutely good or pleasant would seem to be lovable and
> choiceworthy, and for each man the good or pleasant for him.
> And the good man is lovable and choiceworthy for a good man
> for the sake of both qualities. (*Eth*. 8.5.1157b26–28)

He might better say that a good man is choiceworthy for the sake of all
four qualities. But his meaning is clear: One good man finds the character
and activity of another good and pleasant absolutely and relatively to him.

But we must know someone if we are to wish him good for the sake
of his character and activity. Without knowing him we cannot determine
if his character is good or bad, and we cannot determine if he is lovable or
not. That is why good friendship takes time to develop:

> Good friendship requires time and familiarity, for we say ac-
> cording to the proverb that men do not know one another
> until they have eaten salt together. Neither do they accept
> one another nor are they friends until each calls the other lov-
> able and trusts him. Those exhibiting the marks of friendship
> to one another wish to be friends but are not unless they are
> lovable and know it. The wish for friendship arises quickly, but
> friendship does not. (*Eth*. 8.3.1156b25–32)

We are therefore likely to make a knowledgeable wish when we wish another what is good for his sake. And to realize a wish of this sort, we would
most probably act from choice, for we would be likely to deliberate before
acting. In good friendship, reciprocal love therefore most likely follows
from choice.

We can also see that the object of our choice is a good character and
its activities. But a good character and its activities are stable. Again, good
friendship lasts a long time:

> A good friendship is well said to be permanent. For in it come
> together all the qualities that must belong to friends. All friend-
> ship is either for the sake of the good or the pleasant, either ab-
> solutely or for him who loves, and all friendship is in accordance
> with some similarity. All these qualities mentioned belong to
> good friendship in accordance with the friends themselves.
> (*Eth*. 8.3.1156b17–21)

In good friendship we would therefore most likely form a habit out of our
love, for we love a stable character.[8]

We thus see that good friendship is a habit. But friendship of this kind also lies on a mean because it entails equality. Aristotle proves that it does with another argument not quite so terse. He argues that good friends love qualities that are good for themselves:

> In loving a friend, men love what is good for themselves, for in becoming a friend, a good man becomes a good for his friend. (*Eth.* 8.5.1157b33–34)

The main clause of this sentence states the conclusion of this argument. The major premise being implicit, the subordinate clause of the sentence contains the minor premise. The full argument is: A man becoming a good for a friend loves what is good for himself; a good man loving a friend becomes a good for his friend; therefore, a good man loving a friend loves what is good for himself.

The implicit major premise might present a difficulty: How does a person who becomes a good for his friend love what is good for himself? Someone who is good appears to love what is good for himself because he loves a good that is good absolutely and relatively to him as well as to his friend. Good friends are absolutely good and good relatively to each other, and friends of this sort are also absolutely pleasant and pleasant relatively to each other:

> Each friend is absolutely good and good to his friend, for good men are absolutely good and advantageous to one another. Similarly they are pleasant, for good men are absolutely pleasant and pleasant to one another. (*Eth.* 8.3.1156b12–15)

Aristotle explains why each friend is pleasant absolutely and to one another by reminding us that what is pleasant absolutely and relatively to good men is human action:

> For each man, his own actions and other such actions are in accordance with pleasure, and the actions of good men are the same or similar. (*Eth.* 8.3.1156b15–17)

Because they enjoy happiness, good men enjoy the same or similar actions. He does not explain why each friend is advantageous absolutely and relatively to his friend, but he could make a similar argument to show why they are. Again, they are happy.

Aristotle concludes that a good man and his friend love one another equally:

Each therefore both loves what is good for himself and gives in turn an equal share in wishes and pleasures. For equality is said to be friendship, and this belongs most to the friendship of good men. (*Eth.* 8.5.1157b34–1158a1)

He implies that good men tend to love one another equally and asserts that they tend to reciprocate actions for one another equally. Obviously good men would have similar feelings for the character and activity of one another because their virtues and activities are similar. And because they have similar feelings, they would be inclined to perform similar actions for one another.

We might note that friendship has a mean in a different way than do the other virtues. Friendship has a mean with respect to the reciprocity of its activity, not a mean with respect to its activity simply. Though Aristotle himself does not state so, we can, however, see that this mean concerned with reciprocated action arises out of a mean concerned with unreciprocated action. Good friends attain a mean in the reciprocity of their action by aiming at a mean in their own action. Good friends love one another neither too much nor too little, for they find good qualities and activities lovable in each other, and these qualities and activities are in accordance with a mean. Good friends consequently attain a mean in their own actions by aiming at a mean in the actions of each other.

Aristotle also says very little about what extremes friendship might have, but he does indicate why sour and elderly people are defective and have fewer friends. They are less good-tempered and enjoy companionship less: "Among ill-tempered people and older people friendship comes to be less frequently to the extent that they are ill-content and delight in company less. For these qualities seem to be marks of friendship and to be productive of friendship most of all. That is why young people make friends quickly and old people do not. For friendships arise among those who take delight in one another. Similarly, ill-tempered people do not make friends quickly either" (*Eth.* 8.6.1158a1–7). He might also argue that young and good-tempered people tend to be excessive because they are more content and enjoy company more.

In addition to being a habit that lies on a mean, friendship concerns an emotion. Aristotle limits his discussion of the emotion of friendship to two possibilities: the emotion of loving and that of being loved. One might love for the sake of being loved in return, as useful and pleasant friends do, for example. And he admits that people do delight in being loved:

> People delight in being loved for itself. That is why it seems to be better than being honored, and why friendship seems to be desirable for itself. (*Eth*. 8.8.1159a25–27)

However, he produces a counterexample in favor of the emotion of loving. Mothers sometimes love without any thought of being loved.

> But friendship seems to lie in loving rather than in being loved. A sign of this is that mothers delight in loving. For some mothers hand over their children to be brought up, and they love them so long as they know their fate. They do not seek to be loved reciprocally if they cannot have both. But they seem to be satisfied if they see them doing well. And they also love their children, even if they, through ignorance, do not assign them what is due to a mother. (*Eth*. 8.8.1159a27–33)

One might not find this example entirely satisfactory, for it is a rhetorical argument, proceeding from a sign. But Aristotle does make his position clear, and he will argue with causes when he explains the motivation for good friendship.

Assuming that practical wisdom determines its mean, we thus see that good friendship is a virtue: it is a habit, it lies on a mean, and it concerns an emotion.[9]

We can also see, however, that useful and pleasant friendships are not likely to become virtues. Friendships of these types are unlikely to develop into habits, for they concern objects less stable than good character. What is useful changes, so useful friendship changes. Such friendships occur mostly among older people: "The useful does not remain constant, but it changes from one thing to another. When that for the sake of which they were friends goes away, the friendship too dissolves, since it existed for that. This sort of friendship seems to arise most among old people, for those of such age do not pursue pleasure but utility. And among young people or people in their prime, those who pursue their own interest form such friendships" (*Eth*. 8.3.1156a21–27). Pleasant friendship changes because the friends change. As their fancy changes, pleasant friends seek different pleasures. These friendships are found among the young: "The friendship of young people seems to be for the sake of pleasure. For they live according to passion, and they pursue most what is pleasant to them and what is before them. But as their fancy changes, their pleasures become different. That is why they make friends and change them quickly, for their friendship changes with their pleasures and the changes in their pleasures are quick" (*Eth*. 8.3.1156a31–1156b1). But friendships of utility and pleasure do involve equality: "Friendships of utility and pleasure do involve equality. For the same thing comes from both people. They wish the same things to one another, or they exchange one thing for another, such as pleasure or utility" (*Eth.* 8.6.1158a1–3). Friends of these types are obviously concerned more with being loved than with loving, for they love what they receive from each other.

The three species of friendship thus appear to have genera in different categories. Good friendship falls under the category of quality, for it is a virtue, and its genus is habit. Useful friendship belongs in the category of action. A useful friend would act because he calculates that his friend is a means to an end. Pleasant friendship may well fall under the genus of passion. No calculation need be involved, for a pleasant friend may even be weak-willed.

Why does Aristotle argue that friendship has three species if these species are in different categories? He appears to use the term "species" in a non-scientific sense. As do Plato and other Greek philosophers, he notoriously uses philosophical terms in accordance with loose philosophical usage as well as in accordance with everyday usage. However, his non-scientific usage of this term is not without precedent even in the *Ethics*. He divides courage into six species, for example. Only one species is a species in the strict sense—the virtue courage; the other species appear to fall under the categories of action and passion (*Eth.* 3.6–8).

We can now see how Aristotle's conception of friendship is an integral part of his theory of ethics. Aristotle's principle of happiness allows us to see how it is. This principle integrates his conception of friendship into his ethics in two ways. First of all, happiness is the end of friendship—at least of good friendship, which is the essential species. A good friend acts for the sake of the goodness of another, and the goodness of another can only be happiness. That is why Aristotle argues not only that good friends are absolutely good and good to each other but also that these friends are absolutely pleasant and pleasant to each other (see again *Eth.* 8.3.1156b12–17).

To apply Aristotle's conception of happiness in this way to his conception of friendship is important for our analysis. We have already seen that the conception of happiness considered as the end of friendship allows us to distinguish altruistic friendship from egoistic friendship. An altruistic friend loves another for the sake of the goodness of the other. That is, he acts for the sake of the happiness of the other. We shall soon see that the conception of happiness allows us to explain the motivation for altruistic friendship. This conception will also explain the pluralism of altruistic friendship.

Aristotle's conception of happiness integrates his conception of friendship into his ethics in a second way, too. Obviously happiness includes friendship, for happiness is an activity in accordance with virtue, and one activity in accordance with virtue is friendship itself. To wish and to do what is good for the sake of another is an activity that follows from a habit lying on a mean. That is, good friends engage in an activity that follows from the moral virtue of friendship.

This application of the conception of friendship may be troublesome, however. The fact that happiness includes friendship might tempt one to conclude that even good friendship is egoistic. One might argue that a person in a good friendship acts for the sake of the happiness of himself rather than for the sake of the happiness of his friend, for friendship with another is itself an activity in accordance with a virtue.

Aristotle even presents arguments that seem to support this objection. When discussing self-love, he argues that we might act for a friend out of self-love. To show that we might, he first distinguishes between praiseworthy and blameworthy self-love. He explains that some people who love themselves are reproachable. They concern themselves with goods of the body and external goods: "Those using the term as one of reproach ascribe self-love to those assigning to themselves the greater share of wealth, honor, and bodily pleasure. For most people desire these things and busy themselves about them as though they were the best things. That is why they become competitive goods" (*Eth.* 9.8.1168b15–19). Men who love themselves in this way satisfy the irrational part of their souls. Aristotle refers to them as greedy: "Those who are greedy with regard to these things gratify their appetites and generally their passions and the irrational part of their soul" (*Eth.* 9.8.1168b19–21). Because most men are greedy, the term "self-love" usually has a reproachful sense (*Eth.*9.8.1168b21–23).

We do not usually apply the term "self-love" to other people who love themselves. But because they are good, these people most deserve the epithet in a laudatory sense. They clearly act for the sake of themselves in a good way: "If someone were always anxious that he himself should most of all do what is just or temperate or in accordance with any other virtue, and in general if he were always to try to secure for himself what is noble, no one would call such a man a lover of self or blame him. But such a man would seem more a lover of self than the other" (*Eth.* 9.8.1168b25–29). Aristotle amplifies this argument by adding that a man of this sort strives to act for the sake of his rationality. He tries to please the chief element in himself (*Eth.* 9.8.1168b29–31). But the chief element in him is his intuition: "A man is said to be strong-willed or weak-willed depending on whether his intuition controls him or not as if this were each man. And those things done most from principle men themselves seem to have done and to have done voluntarily. That each man is this element or most so, is no longer unclear, and that the good man is fond of this element most of all" (*Eth.* 9.8.1168b34–1169a3). He explains that a man who acts in this way acts out of self-love in a laudable way because he acts for the sake of a principle: "Therefore he is most a lover of self but according to a different species than that which is reproached. And he differs as much as living according to principle differs from living according to passion and as much as desiring what is noble differs from desiring what seems to be in his interest" (*Eth.* 9.8.1169a3–6). Aristotle probably refers to practical intuition and its principle because this virtue of our practical intellect grasps the universal for the sake of which we act (see again *Eth.* 6.11.1143a35–1143b5). Of course, we use our practical intellect and its principle to control our emotions (again see *Eth.* 6.2.1139a27–31 and *Eth.* 1.13.1102b26–28).

But Aristotle argues that someone who loves himself in a good way gives up many things for his friends and, by doing so, he gains happiness for himself: "Truly it concerns a good man to do many acts for the sake of his friends and his country, and if necessary, to die for them. He will give up both wealth and honor and in general the goods of competition, gaining for himself nobility, for he would prefer a short period of intense pleasure to a long one of mild enjoyment, a year of noble life to many years of humdrum life, one great and noble deed to many trivial ones" (*Eth.* 9.8.1169a18–25). He may even forgo action so that his friend may act: "It is possible that he might give up actions to a friend, and that it might be nobler for him to become the cause of action for his friend than to act himself" (*Eth.* 9.8.1169a33–34). But again he assigns more of what is noble to himself (*Eth.* 9.8.1169a34–1169b1).

Now I must admit that this objection does hold sometimes, but I also have to argue that sometimes it does not. In this argument Aristotle discusses only a good man who loves himself. This man does act out of self-love when he performs these acts of friendship. But we need not always perform an act of friendship out of self-love. We may also act out of love for another. A good friend does, in fact, so act.

What intention a person has is what tells us if his friendship is for the sake of himself or for the sake of another. We act essentially for another when we intend to act for the sake of the activity and virtue of another— when we intend to advance the happiness of another. We may even act in this way for the sake of the activity of friendship and its virtue; we do so when we help another cultivate happiness and virtue of this sort. We especially need to help children in this way. But when we intend to help another, we only accidentally advance our own happiness. We do engage in the activity of friendship in accordance with its virtue, but we do not intend to advance our own happiness.

A person acts essentially for himself when he intends to act for the sake of his own activity and virtue. We may enter what appears to be a good friendship with the intention of advancing our own happiness. But we do not in fact enter a good friendship, for we advance the happiness of another only accidentally. We essentially advance our own happiness, for we act for the happiness of another only as a means to our happiness. Indeed, we also act for ourselves when we intend to act for the sake of our activity of friendship and its virtue. This we most often do, of course, when we attempt to cultivate this activity and virtue in ourselves.[10]

We may conclude then that friendship includes three species, that good friendship is the essential species, and that good friendship is altruistic. We may also conclude that the principle of happiness defines the end of good friendship and that happiness includes the activity of good friendship in accordance with its virtue.

A MOTIVATION FOR FRIENDSHIP

In my analysis I have so far been concerned with the problem of what Aristotelian friendship is. We have seen that friendship is essentially good friendship and that good friendship is altruistic. Good friends act with the intention of advancing the happiness of their friends. I shall now consider the problem of why Aristotelian friendship is: Why does someone enter into a good friendship and acquire its virtue? What is the motivation for a relationship of this kind? We shall find that the resolution of this problem will take us to the conception lying at the heart of Aristotle's theory—the conception of another self. The resolution will also allow us to see that good friendship is pluralistic.

Aristotle appears to present a two-part solution to the problem of why one person would act for the sake of the happiness of another. Assuming that we may be a friend with ourself, he shows first that friendships with ourselves are similar to friendships with others and then that friendships of both kinds have the same motive. In the first part, he sets up an analogy between our friendships with ourselves and those with others; in the second part, he proves that we act for the sake of an object of the same kind in both friendships.

Aristotle begins the first part of his proof when he argues that the marks of a friendship with ourself are the same as the marks of a friendship with another. Though he does not do so, he claims that he will prove that the marks of a relationship with another come from the marks of a relationship with oneself:

> The marks of friendship in a relationship with our neighbor
> and the marks by which friendship is defined seem to have come
> from the marks of a relationship of a man with himself. (*Eth.*
> 9.4.1166a1–2)

He only implies that the marks of a relationship of a man with himself are
the same as those of a relationship with a friend. But we shall see that this
proposition his proof establishes. He asserts that the marks of our relationship with ourself are the source of the marks of our relationship with another.
This proposition he does not establish. But when we analyze the motive of
these relationships, we shall see without undue difficulty how he could show
that a friendship with ourself is the origin of a friendship with another.

   To understand his proof, we would probably do well to follow Aristotle's own lead. He proves that the marks of a friendship with another belong to a friendship with ourself. He thus appears to establish a more strict
analogy than usually thought between a friendship with another and a
friendship with ourself, for he suggests that a friendship with ourself exists
between ourself somehow acting as a friend acts and ourself somehow acting as someone befriended acts.[1]

   We would also do well to bear in mind two restrictions that Aristotle places on his proof and their implications. Aristotle proves that the
marks of friendship with another belong to a friendship of a good man with
himself (*Eth.* 9.4.1166a10–11). He bases his proof on this relationship because a good man and his virtue are the measure of human activity
(1166a12–13). He does concede that a man who believes that he is good,
when he is not, may have these same marks in his relationship with himself, too (1166a11). But he argues that these marks depend not solely on
the good opinion that a man may have of himself but also on the fact that
his opinion has some truth. For he uses the relationships of a vicious man
and a weak-willed man with themselves to prove that those who are not
good do not have these marks (1166b2–25).

   He also appears to prove that the marks of friendship belong to a
good friendship with oneself. For we shall soon see that he characterizes
the first mark of friendship as wishing and doing what is good for the sake
of another. But we have already seen that he defines good friendship as
good wishes and good actions for the sake of another—when these wishes
and actions are reciprocated and recognized.

   We shall find these restrictions and their implications helpful in our
analysis of Aristotle's proof. Aristotle begins to prove that the marks of a
friendship with another belong to a friendship with ourself by presenting
us with a list of five marks of friendship:

(1) That a friend wishes and does what is good, or what appears to be good, for the sake of his friend, and
(2) that he wishes his friend to exist and to live for his sake, the very thing that mothers do for their children and friends who are at odds, is laid down by us.
(3) That a friend lives with his friend, and
(4) that he chooses the same things as his friend, and
(5) that he grieves and rejoices with his friend, which happens most of all with mothers, is added by others. (*Eth.* 9.4.1166a2–9)

Though he attributes some marks to others when he lists them, he clearly endorses all five marks in the succeeding arguments.

He takes up the fourth mark first—choosing the same things as a friend. To prove that this mark belongs to the friendship of a good man with himself, he merely asserts two propositions:

A good man agrees with himself, and he desires the same thing with all his soul. (*Eth.* 9.4.1166a13–14)

Consider the first proposition. We can see how a good man would agree with himself if we ask how the fourth mark exists in a good friendship with another. In a good friendship, one person chooses actions that lead to happiness for another person. For the one chooses actions that lead to what is good for the sake of the other, and what is good for the other is happiness. The one friend consequently chooses the same actions that the other would choose, for the one chooses actions that lead to happiness for the other, and the other would choose actions that lead to happiness for himself. Someone befriending another would therefore agree with someone who is befriended that these actions ought to be chosen and that these actions lead to happiness for whoever is befriended.

How then does the fourth mark exist in a friendship with ourself? In a good friendship with ourself, we would appear to choose actions that lead to happiness for ourself. As someone befriending ourself we choose the same actions that we would choose as someone befriended by ourself. We would therefore agree with ourself that we ought to choose these actions and that these actions lead to our happiness.

Aristotle's second proposition explains his first. Someone who wishes to be happy and chooses actions leading to happiness would desire the same things with his whole soul, for not only someone who is virtuous but also someone who is strong-willed desires the same thing with the rational and irrational elements of the soul. Individuals of these types use their rational element to train their irrational element so that both elements desire the same thing. For the theoretical and practical parts of the rational element have functions that differ. The theoretical part only grasps the truth, but the practical part grasps truth and coerces desire: "Of the theoretical intellect, which is neither practical nor productive, the good and bad activity is truth and falsity, for this is the function of all thought. Of the practical intellect, the good activity is truth in agreement with desire—right desire" (*Eth.* 6.2.1139a27–31). The proof that the practical intellect coerces desire lies in the source of action. Pursuit and avoidance originate in virtue, virtue in choice, and choice—good choice—in true principle and right desire: "That very thing that affirmation and denial are in thought, pursuit and avoidance are in desire. And since moral virtue is a habit productive of choice, and since choice is deliberate desire, for the sake of these things, the principle must be true and the desire right if choice is to be good. And the former must assert and the latter pursue the same things" (*Eth.* 6.2.1139a22–26). But true principle persuades or coerces desire: "This unprincipled element of the soul appears to share in a principle, as we said. This element in a strong-willed man is obedient to principle. And it is more eager to listen in a temperate man and brave man. For it speaks with a voice similar to principle on all matters" (*Eth.* 1.13.1102b25–28). The practical intellect controls desire because desire obeys its principle.

Aristotle's statements, though terse, thus show that a good man chooses the same things as himself. As someone who is a friend to ourself we choose the same actions that we would choose as someone who is befriended by ourself. We choose those actions that lead to happiness for ourself, for we desire the same things with both our practical wisdom and our moral virtue. We also see that Aristotle draws a rather strict analogy between our friendship with another and our friendship with ourself.[2]

Aristotle takes up the first three marks of friendship in succession— wishing and doing what is good for a friend, wishing a friend to live, and wishing to live with a friend. He again implies that we have these marks in a friendship with ourself because we exist both as someone who is a friend and as someone who is befriended.

Aristotle offers an explicit proof that the first mark belongs to a friendship of a good man with himself:

> A good man wishes what is good for himself and what appears to be good, and he does these things, for being good he works out the good. And he also does these things for his own sake, for he does them for the sake of his intellect, the very thing that each man seems to be. (*Eth.* 9.4.1166a14–17)

Aristotle's argument is quite clear. At least formally. We may paraphrase it without difficulty: A good man wishes and does what is good for his own sake because he wishes and does what is good for the sake of his intellect, his intellect being the man himself. The conclusion is first; the minor premise is second; and, finally, the major premise is implicit in the last subordinate clause.

We can see that Aristotle takes his formulation of the first mark almost word for word from his definition of a good friendship, for when we befriend another, we bear good wishes and do what is good for the sake of whoever we befriend. We thus exhibit good friendship for the sake of ourself when we bear good wishes and do what is good for ourself. As someone befriending ourself we consequently wish and do what is good for the sake of ourself as someone befriended by ourself.

But for us to see how we exhibit practical wisdom and virtue is also important. Aristotle's assertions that the intellect of a man is the man himself and that a good man wishes and does what is good for the sake of his intellect, these assertions might appear almost absurd when stated so baldly.

That the intellect of a man is the man appears to be an assertion about our intellectual and moral character. Though he mentions the theoretical intellect later, Aristotle now speaks primarily of the practical intellect (see *Eth.* 9.4.1166a18–23). But the practical intellect is a combination of practical wisdom and moral virtue. A good man does not dispense with practical wisdom even though he completely conditions his desires into virtues. Action originates in choice and choice in argument and desire: "Therefore, the first cause of action is choice—that from which the motion arises, not that for the sake of which. And the first cause of choice is desire and principle—that for the sake of which" (*Eth.* 6.2.1139a31–33). That is why actions originate in truth and habit: "That is why choice is not without intuition and thought nor without ethical habit, for good action and its opposite are not without thought and habit" (*Eth.* 6.2.1139a33–35). Choice itself appears to be a combination of practical wisdom and moral virtue: "Therefore, choice is either desireful intuition or thoughtful desire, and a first cause of such sort is a human being" (*Eth.* 6.2.1139b4–5). The principled element of the soul, indeed, includes the appetitive element, when the appetitive element is obedient to a principle: "If this principled element must be said to have a principle, the element having a principle is twofold. The one element has a principle chiefly and in itself. The other element has a principle as does someone who listens to his father" (*Eth.* 1.13.1103a1–3). If it is obedient to a principle, the unprincipled element of the soul becomes principled.

To say that we are our practical intellect would therefore mean that we are our practical wisdom taken together with our moral virtue. To say that he acts for the sake of his intellect would thus mean that a good man acts for the sake of a combination of practical wisdom and moral virtue. When he wishes and does what is good for his practical intellect, a man thus wishes and does what is good for the sake of his intellectual and moral character.[3]

Aristotle's proof of the second mark—wishing a friend to live and to exist for his sake—is quite similar to his proof of the first:

> A good man wishes himself to live and to be secure, most of all that part through which he exercises practical wisdom. . . . And the part that intuits would seem to be the individual man, or to be so more than any other part of him. (*Eth.* 9.4.1166a18–23)

The first sentence of this argument contains the conclusion and the minor premise, and the second sentence proves the major premise: A good man wishes himself to live and to be secure because he wishes that part through which he is practically wise to live and to be secure, and that part would seem to be the individual man.

This argument is plainly of the same form as the argument proving the first mark of friendship. If we wished, we might analyze it in similar fashion. However, our analysis of this mark would turn not on living well but on living; our principle would be not good life but simply life. Aristotle does assert that we are more our intuition and our practical wisdom than our practical intellect. But in doing so, he presents no real problem. Practical intuition is the primary part of practical wisdom, for through intuition we see what is good; and practical wisdom is the primary virtue of the practical intellect, for through it we see truth and coerce desire.

What is interesting about this proof is that the conclusion, that a good man wishes to live and to be secure, is proved with additional interjected arguments:

> For existence is good for the virtuous man, and each man wishes for himself what is good. No one chooses to possess the whole world if he has first to become someone else, for even now God possesses the good by always being only what he is. (*Eth.* 9.4.1166a19–22)

This passage presents two arguments. The first sentence, which offers the first argument, contains two premises, its conclusion being implicit. Explicitly the argument would run: Existence is good for the virtuous man; each man desires what is good; therefore, each man desires existence. The argument might seem to be invalid. The major premise does not appear to convert to a universal premise, for it is affirmative. But a subject and its essential properties do convert universally. Recall that the subject of the argument is a virtuous man, that a virtuous man is essentially his practical intellect, and that the practical intellect and its activity is essentially what is good for a good man.

The second sentence contains the second argument. The argument consists of two contrary-to-fact premises and their conclusion. One may paraphrase it in this way: To possess the world would be to become someone else; no one would wish to possess the world; therefore, no one would wish to become someone else. To understand this conclusion, we might bear in mind again that the subject of this argument is a good man. A good man would not wish to be someone else if to be someone else would be for him to be bad, for no one who knows what happiness is and has a good character would want to do or would do something else. Indeed, he would destroy his practical intellect by doing so.

Aristotle's subordinate clause suggests that he has a good man in mind, for it is an example supporting this argument. Because he is what he is, God does what he does. If he were to change his thought, God would no longer possess the world. For he would change only for the worse if he could change at all. The good man is like God, for our practical wisdom regulates our conduct much as the divine intellect regulates the world.[4]

Aristotle proves the third mark of friendship—wishing to live with a friend—with an argument similar to that used to prove the first and second mark:

> A man such as a good man wishes himself to live with himself, for he does so with pleasure. For the memories of his past actions are delightful, and the hopes for his future actions are good, and thoughts of such sort are pleasant. And he has stocked his intellect with objects of theoretical wisdom. (*Eth.* 9.4.1166a23–27)

This argument presents no serious difficulties. It is amenable to the same interpretation as the arguments concerned with the first and second marks. It takes the same form: The intellect of a man is that man himself; a good man wishes to live with his memories of past actions and hopes for future actions; therefore, a good man wishes to live with himself.

Aristotle here makes more explicit his assumption that a friendship with ourself exists between ourself acting as a friend and ourself acting as someone befriended. At least, he clearly distinguishes a self existing at one time from a self existing at another time. He also assumes that we may take pleasure in the recollection or anticipation of our virtuous actions. One might surmise that we may take pleasure in intuiting our present actions, too (but see *Eth.* 9.9).

For the first time, he mentions theoretical wisdom. By so doing, he explicitly widens the scope of happiness. He now reminds us that his arguments also apply to theoretical wisdom; until now they have centered on practical wisdom and moral virtue. Though he need not do so, a good man may wish another or himself to be happy in the primary sense, too.

The remaining mark of friendship to be proved is the fifth—rejoicing and grieving with a friend. Aristotle presents another explicit argument to show that a good man rejoices and grieves with himself:

A good man both grieves and rejoices most of all with himself, for always the same action is painful and the same action pleasant and not one action at one time and another at another time. He has, so to speak, no need to repent. (*Eth.* 9.4.1166a27–29)

When we examined the fourth mark, we saw that a virtuous man agrees with himself because he chooses actions that lead to what is good. But what is good is always the same—happiness. A good man accordingly at all times chooses actions that lead to happiness for himself, he always takes pleasure in his actions when they are successful attempts to attain that end, and he always feels pain over his actions when they fail to attain that end.

With these arguments Aristotle thus establishes an analogy between our friendship with another and our friendship with ourself. He does so by proving that the marks of a friendship with another are the same as the marks of a friendship with oneself. He argues that a good man exhibits each mark in his friendship with himself because he exists both as someone who is a friend and as someone who is befriended. He lives, lives well, and lives with himself—the first three marks of friendship—and he agrees with himself and grieves and rejoices with himself—the last two marks—because at one time he exists as someone who is a friend and at another time he exists as someone who is befriended.

When he introduces his discussion of the object of these friendships, Aristotle suggests why the marks of a friendship with oneself are not only the same as the marks of a friendship with another but also the source of these marks. Aristotle's discussion proving that a friendship with oneself has the same five marks as a friendship with another implies that both friendships might have objects of the same kind, for we would not unreasonably expect friendships essentially the same to have objects essentially the same. And if they have objects the same, we would expect that these friendships would have motives the same. But we might expect that a friendship with oneself would present the motive more strongly that a friendship with another and, consequently, that a friendship with oneself would be the source of a friendship with another.

When he discusses their objects, Aristotle does indicate that these friendships have the same object, and he also implies that they have the same motive. He introduces his conception of the object of friendship into this discussion with two remarks made in passing. He neither makes these remarks obvious nor does he pause to explain them. The first remark comes in a passage concluding the arguments analyzed above:

> Each of these marks of friendship belongs then to a good man
> in his relationship with himself. He has the same relationship
> with himself as he has with his friend, for his friend is another
> self. (*Eth.* 9.4.1166a29–32)

Aristotle implies that the object of friendship is another self, but he gives us only two clues to discover what another self is. These clues are the fact that the marks of friendship belong to the relationship of a good man with himself as well as to his relationship with his friend and the fact that a good man has the same relationship with himself as with his friend.

But we can see that another self would appear to be someone who is numerically different than we are and yet morally the same as we are. A friend is someone who is obviously an individual locally distinct from us; but a friend is also someone who shares the same moral principle with us, for we share a principle of happiness. Another self would thus be someone who is a locally different individual but who shares a similar conception of happiness and virtue.

Could we be another self to ourself? If we exhibit the marks of friendship in a relationship with ourself and have the same relationship with ourself as with a friend, we would appear to be somehow different from ourself and also somehow the same as ourself. We exist both as someone who is a friend and as someone who is befriended. And yet we could not be locally different from ourself, for we are each only a single individual. But we would be temporally different from ourself, for the actions that we perform as a friend occur at a different time than those that we perform as someone befriended. We would be morally the same as ourself, for the actions that we perform as a friend are actions of the same kind as those that we would perform as someone befriended. These actions are ones that lead to happiness for ourself.

Now consider Aristotle's second remark about the object of friendship:

> Whether or not there is a friendship between a man and himself we may dismiss for the present. From what we have said, there would seem to be a friendship insofar as a man is two or more, and from the fact that an excess of friendship is similar to a relationship of a man with himself. (*Eth.* 9.4.1166a33–1166b2)

The difficulty is how a man may be "two or more." But consider the first remark together with this one. If he is another self to himself, we can see that a man would clearly be two or more. He is both a self and another self. For he acts out of practical wisdom and moral virtue both as a friend and as someone befriended. He acts as a friend at one time and at another time as someone befriended. He would thus appear to be at least two if he acts at one time as a friend and as someone befriended at another time. But he would also be more than two if he acts as a friend or as someone befriended at more than one time.[5]

Another self thus appears to be an embodiment of happiness in a locally or temporally distinct individual. A self is happiness and virtue embodied in someone who befriends, another self is this same activity and virtue embodied in someone who is befriended. And a self is happiness and virtue embodied in ourself as in a friend, another self is this same activity and virtue embodied in ourself as in someone befriended.

We see therefore that our friendship with ourself and our friendship with another have the same object—another self. Our friendships with ourself and with another would therefore appear likely to have the same motive. And if the one friendship has this motive more strongly than the other, a friendship with oneself would most likely be the source of a friendship with another.[6]

When he begins his discussion of the motive of friendship, Aristotle appears at once to confirm our conjecture concerning the motive for good friendship:

> If we look deeper into the nature of things, we shall see that a virtuous friend seems to be naturally choiceworthy for a virtu-

ous man. For what is good by nature is said to be good and
pleasant in itself for a virtuous man. (*Eth.* 9.9.1170a13–16)

He argues that one virtuous man finds another virtuous man choiceworthy because he finds that what is good by nature is good and pleasant
in itself. He thus implies not only that a virtuous man finds that another
virtuous man is good by nature but also that a virtuous man finds that what
is good and pleasant in itself is choiceworthy. Put more explicitly, his argument is: What is good and pleasant in itself is choiceworthy; what is good
by nature is good and pleasant in itself; a virtuous man is good by nature;
therefore, a virtuous man is choiceworthy. The first sentence states the conclusion in its apodosis; the second sentence states an intermediate premise.
The major and minor premises are implicit.

Aristotle thus implies in this short passage that friendship with another has a motive in the choiceworthiness of the happiness of another, for
happiness is what human beings find good by nature. When we see that
what is good in another is choiceworthy, we see therefore that the happiness of another is choiceworthy. That the virtue and the good activity of
soul in another are choiceworthy. He thus suggests that, because we find
the happiness of another choiceworthy, we may feel a desire to act for the
sake of the happiness of another and that our desire may move us to act.
Otherwise, we would never become friends.

Aristotle confirms his suggestion about the motive of friendship in
the argument that follows. Though rather complex, the argument does divide into three obvious segments immediately distinguishable by their topics. The first segment sets out the two actualities of happiness, the second
concerns the choiceworthiness of the second actuality, and the third concerns the attainment of the second actuality.[7]

Explicitly discussing the two actualities of the soul, Aristotle defines
life in the first segment of the argument:

Life is defined in animals by the capacity for perception, in men
by the capacity for apperception or intuition. But capacity leads
to its activity, and the chief thing is to be in activity. To live
seems then to be chiefly to apperceive or to intuit. (*Eth.*
9.9.1170a16–19)

When he defines life, he obviously refers to the conception of happiness,
for he defines life as the activity of apperception or intuition, and the activity of apperception or intuition is among the chief human activities. He

does not distinguish actualities into intellectual and moral. He omits a reference to the part of the soul that only obeys a principle, apparently because his intention is to distinguish human life from other animal life.

The second segment of the argument establishes the choiceworthiness of the life of a good man. This Aristotle does by showing that the apperception of his life is pleasant. He first offers a short proof that life is good and pleasant:

> Life is one of things good and pleasant in themselves, for it is definite and the definite is naturally good. And the good by nature is good for a virtuous man, and for that very reason it seems to be pleasant for all. But it is not necessary to apply this to a life thoroughly wicked and corrupt nor to a life spent in pain, for a life of such sort is indefinite, as are its properties. (*Eth.* 9.9.1170a19–24)

He appears to assume that what has a principle is good and that what is good is pleasant, for if it is definite—or defined—life is in accordance with a principle. And we can see that a virtuous man clearly has a principled life, for he is happy. He apperceives happiness, wishes to have it, and acts to attain it. But a vicious man imagines only apparent goods, and he desires and seeks to attain them.

Aristotle continues with a proof that the life of a friend is choiceworthy. This proof is a bit tortuous:

(1) Life itself is good and pleasant, and it seems to be even from the fact that all desire it, especially a good man and a happy man, for life is most choiceworthy for these men and the life of these is most happy.

(2) Now someone seeing apperceives that he sees and someone hearing that he hears and someone walking that he walks, and similarly, with regard to other activities, there is something apperceiving that we are active so that we might apperceive that we apperceive and we might intuit that we intuit.

(3) And to apperceive that we apperceive or intuit is to apperceive that we exist, for to exist was to apperceive or intuit.

(4) But to apperceive that one lives is one of the things pleasant in itself, for by nature life is good, and to apperceive what is good belonging to oneself is pleasant.

(5) And life is choiceworthy, especially for good men, because to exist is good for them and pleasant, for apperceiving together what is good in itself, they are pleased.

(6) Now the virtuous man has the same relationship with himself and with a friend, for a friend is another self.

(7) Therefore, as to exist is itself choiceworthy for each good man, so is a friend, or nearly so.

(8) To exist was choiceworthy because of our apperception of our own good, and an apperception of such sort was pleasant in itself. (*Eth.* 9.9.1170a25–1170b10)

The eight statements in this passage, complex though they are, really assert only one proposition each: (1) life is good and pleasant; (2) we apperceive that we apperceive and intuit; (3) to apperceive that we apperceive and intuit is to apperceive that we exist; (4) to apperceive that we exist is pleasant in itself; (5) life is choiceworthy; (6) as a good man is to himself so he is to his friend; (7) as his existence is choiceworthy for each man so the existence of his friend is also choiceworthy; and (8) to exist is choiceworthy.

The first statement serves only to remind us that life is good and pleasant. The second through the sixth statements prove the seventh, that just as his own existence is choiceworthy for a good man so is the existence of his friend. The eighth statement sums up, stating very succinctly the cause of the choiceworthiness of our life. Life is choiceworthy because the apperception of it as a good belonging to us is pleasant. That is, our life is choiceworthy because it is an object of a pleasant apperception. This summary implies that the life of a friend is choiceworthy because of this same fact. That is, the life of a friend is choiceworthy because the apperception of his life as somehow our own good is also pleasant. The life of a friend is an object of pleasant apperception.

An analysis of the second through the sixth statements will confirm this implication about the life of a friend. But to grasp the statements, we would best begin in the middle of the argument. Otherwise, we might very easily lose ourselves in prosyllogisms. The next to the last premise, the fifth, is the crucial one. This premise proves that our life is choiceworthy. Aristotle argues that our life is choiceworthy because our apperception of it is pleasant. When we apperceive our life, we apperceive a good belonging to us; and when we apperceive our own good, we are pleased. He does not trouble to prove that the apperception of a good belonging to us is pleasant, but this proposition is obvious if not confused with its converse. We all can surely recall the pleasure of believing that we have done something well. We are most aware of this pleasure when we believe that we have acted well under trying circumstances. He thus implies in this statement that the apperception of happiness and virtue in ourselves is pleasant, for our goodness consists in our happiness and virtue. He adds in the eighth statement that this apperception is pleasant in itself.

The last premise, the sixth, asserts that a good man is to himself as he is to his friend. This statement appears to imply that as he apperceives his own life, so a good man may apperceive the life of a friend, for the apperception of his life is the relationship with himself under discussion in the argument. This statement also implies that another self is a different human being who is good. When he apperceives his life, what a good man apperceives is his happiness; and what a good man apperceives is the happiness of his friend when he apperceives the life of his friend. For life is happiness. We thus see again that another self is different than oneself, for we and another are numerically distinct. And that another self is the same as our self, for we and another are morally identical. We have the same human goodness. If we are both happy.

Aristotle concludes then in the seventh statement that as our life is choiceworthy, so is the life of a friend. As the apperception of happiness and virtue in ourself as a good belonging to us is pleasant, so the apperception of happiness and virtue in our friend as somehow a good belonging to us is also pleasant. He thus completes his analysis of the motive of friendship with another. He shows why one might find the life of another person viewed as happiness choiceworthy.

The fourth premise provides that our life is an object of pleasant apperception because it is our own good. The second and third premises prove in part what the fourth proves. The second proves by induction that our apperception and other activities are themselves objects of apperception. The third premise proves that our life is an object of apperception because it is apperception. Aristotle most likely asserts that life is apperception or intuition because practical intuition is the chief activity of our practical intellect. That life is good and pleasant, the first premise reminds us. This premise thus proves in part what the fifth assumes and in part what it proves. And of course we are alive—a proposition tacitly assumed.[8]

The argument of the fourth and fifth premise may be schematized with three premises and their conclusion:

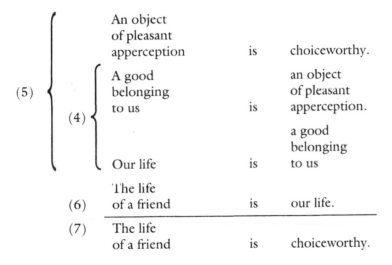

The argument of the fourth, fifth, and sixth premises and the conclusion may be schematized with four premises and their conclusion:

		An object of pleasant apperception	is	choiceworthy.
(5)	(4)	A good belonging to us	is	an object of pleasant apperception.
		Our life	is	a good belonging to us
	(6)	The life of a friend	is	our life.
	(7)	The life of a friend	is	choiceworthy.

Aristotle's premises are not completely congruent with those of our schemata. His conclusion corresponds with that of our last schema, and his last premise with that of our last schema. But his fifth premise is the conclusion of our first three premises in both schemata, and his fourth premise is the conclusion of our second and third premises in both schemata. We thus see how crucial his fifth premise is, for it encapsulates all the crucial points in this argument.[9]

The last segment of the passage under discussion clearly draws a corollary from the above argument:

A good man needs, therefore, to apperceive together the existence of a friend. This will be realized in their living together
and sharing in a principle and thought, for this is what living
together would seem to mean for man, and not, as for cattle,
grazing in the same pasture. (*Eth.* 9.9.1170b10–14)

This corollary implies that a good man wishes and acts for the sake of the
happiness of his friend, for he apperceives the existence of his friend by apperceiving the activity of his friend. That is, he apperceives that his friend
is happy.

Aristotle concludes then that a good man ought to have a friend:

If existence is choiceworthy in itself for an extremely happy
man, existence being good and pleasant by nature, and if the
existence of a friend is nearly the same, then a friend would
be a choiceworthy object. And what is choiceworthy for him,
this must belong to him or he will be deficient in it. A man
who is to be happy would therefore need good friends. (*Eth.*
9.9.1170b14–19)

In other words, a good man must have a friend because the virtue and activity of friendship has its end in the happiness of a friend.[10]

One difficulty with Aristotle's explanation of the motive of friendship may remain: Why does Aristotle say that the life of a friend is our
own good? By saying that it is, he might seem to say that one friend
does not act for the sake of another. If the life of a friend is our own
good, we might seem to advance our own happiness by acting for the life
of our friend.

The resolution of this difficulty lies in an analogy that may also serve
to make Aristotle's explanation more vivid. Aristotle develops this analogy
when he resolves the paradox that benefactors love those whom they benefit more than those benefited love them (*Eth.* 9.7.1167b16–19). He argues that a benefactor is like a craftsman:

Those who have done well by others love and feel affection for
those whom they have labored for, even if they are not useful
to them and never will be. This is the very thing which happens
with a craftsman. For everyone feels more affection for his own
work than it would feel for him if it came to life. This happens
perhaps most of all with poets, for they feel excessive affection

for their own poems, doting on them as if they were their own children. The attitude of benefactors seems to be of such sort, for what they have labored for is their work, and this they feel more affection for than the work could feel for its maker. (*Eth.* 9.7.1167b31–1168a5)

A craftsman, he continues, loves his work because he finds existence choiceworthy and he exists in his work:

The cause of this is that existence is choiceworthy and lovable for all men, and that we exist in our activity, for we exist in living and doing, and that his work is somehow the producer in activity. He is therefore fond of his work because he is fond of existence. (*Eth.* 9.7.1168a5–8)

He sums up with a general explanation:

This is natural, for that which a craftsman is in capacity, this his work manifests in activity. (*Eth.* 9.7.1168a8–9)

In the light of this distinction, we may say that we have friendships with other people because we have the capacity to help others attain and retain intellectual and moral virtues and their activities. We have the capacity to make other selves ours, for we can help someone who is numerically different than us become or remain someone morally the same as us.

We may also say that when we exercise this capacity to help someone become or remain happy, we expand our lives to include their lives, if not entirely, at least in part. We might even say that we thus obtain a taste of immortality.[11]

Though he proves that good friendship finds its motive in an object of pleasant apperception, Aristotle does not preclude the possibility that a good friendship is also useful and pleasant. We saw that, because he acts for the sake of another, a good friend is both useful and pleasant to his friend. When we act to make him happy, we do what is useful and pleasant for our friend. Aristotle, in fact, offers another proof that we find our friends useful and pleasant. This proof is noteworthy because it shows that our friend may be useful and pleasant to us even when he does not do us an overt favor.

Aristotle first proves that a friend is a useful and pleasant object for theoretical wisdom. He is an aid to this virtuous activity simply because he acts virtuously:

(1) As we said at the beginning, happiness is an activity, and an activity clearly comes into being and is not present at the start like a piece of property.

(2) Happiness is to live and to be active, and the activity of a good man is good and pleasant in itself, as we also said in the beginning, and what is our own is something pleasant.

(3) Now we are more capable of theoretical wisdom about our neighbors than ourselves and about their actions than our own, and the actions of good friends are pleasant to good men, for they are pleasant by nature for both causes.

(4) Therefore, a happy man needs such friends if he chooses to exercise theoretical wisdom about actions that are good and are his own, such actions being those of a good friend.

(5) And men do think that the happy man ought to live pleasantly. (*Eth.* 9.9.1169b28–1170a4)

The first sentence of this passage recalls Aristotle's conception of happiness—activity in accordance with virtue. The next two sentences contain the five premises of his argument, though they begin with a reiteration of the main point of the first sentence. The fourth sentence contains the conclusion and states an assumption of the whole argument in its subordinate clause. The final sentence adds a reason for the assumption.

The assumption of the argument is that a good man chooses to exercise theoretical wisdom about the activity of his friend. This assumption is not unreasonable. A good man chooses to exercise theoretical wisdom, and he may very well choose to exercise it about happiness. For to exercise theoretical wisdom itself is to act in accordance with a virtue—to be happy. And it is pleasant, as Aristotle intimates.

To say that we exercise theoretical wisdom about the activity and character of our friend is not perfectly accurate, however. We exercise theoretical wisdom about the conceptions actualized in his character and activity. We only apperceive the principle of happiness embodied in his character and action; we exercise theoretical wisdom about this principle after we separate it from its embodiment.[12]

The first sentence of Aristotle's proof implies a condition for exercising theoretical wisdom about happiness—someone must be happy. For happiness is an activity, more specifically a human activity. The second sentence explains why the exercise of theoretical wisdom about happiness is pleasant. It suggests that two causes make theoretical activity of this sort pleasant: the fact that happiness is good and the fact that it is ours. The third sentence explains why we exercise theoretical wisdom about the happiness of our friends. First, their activity and character are easier objects for the exercise of theoretical wisdom; secondly, their activity and character are pleasant objects because they are good and our own. Again, they are ours because we help our friends become or remain happy.

Aristotle thus argues that we may better exercise theoretical wisdom about happiness when we exercise theoretical wisdom about the virtuous activity of our friends. By simply acting virtuously, our friends thus become useful and pleasant for us.[13]

Aristotle also appears to generalize this conclusion to other activities, both intellectual and moral. At least, he does not distinguish between them:

> Life is difficult for a solitary man, for to be active continuously by oneself is not easy. But with others and for others life is easy. The activity is more continuous, being pleasant in itself, which it must be for a happy man. A good man, as a good man, delights in actions of virtue and detests vicious ones, just as a musician takes pleasure in beautiful melodies and feels distress over bad ones. (*Eth.* 9.9.1170a5–11)

The second sentence states the proposition to be proved— the activity of life is easy when it is undertaken with or for others. The third sentence offers a cause—such activity is more continuous, for it is pleasant. The analogy in the fourth sentence suggests why virtuous actions are pleasant.

Aristotle's assumption is that activity undertaken with others is more pleasant than solitary action. This assumption itself implies that we apperceive the activity of others better than our own when they help us or we help them. And that our apperception of their activity would yield heightened pleasure, for we apperceive their activities not only more easily but also together with our own.[14]

Almost as an afterthought, Aristotle suggests that good friendship is not only altruistic but also pluralistic. That is, friendship of this kind may exist for the sake of happiness of more than one kind. At the very end of his discussion he implies that personal friends find the happiness of others choiceworthy, whether they pursue primary or secondary happiness. He begins with an analogy between those who are friends and those who are erotic lovers. Those who are lovers prefer sight to other senses because through it their love continues:

> For those who love erotically to see is most worthy of fond-
> ness, and they choose this sense rather than the others because
> in accordance with it their erotic love is and comes to be. (*Eth.*
> 9.12.1171b29–31)

Similarly, those who are friends prefer apperception because their friendship continues through it:

> And so for friends is not to live together most choiceworthy?
> For friendship is community. And as a man is to himself, so he
> is to his friend. With respect to himself the apperception that
> he exists is choiceworthy, and with respect to his friend the ap-
> perception that he exists is choiceworthy, too. But the activity
> of this apperception comes to be in living together. And so nat-
> urally at this they aim. (*Eth.* 9.12.1171b31–1172a1)

More precisely, he ought to say that because he finds his own life and the
life of his friend choiceworthy, a man also finds the apperception of his life
and the life of his friend to be choiceworthy, too. But he does state not
only that friends find apperception choiceworthy but also that they find living together most choiceworthy.

We can see that the motive for friendship is not a pleasant apperception but rather an object of pleasant apperception. When he acts in a friendship, a man acts not for the sake of pleasant apperception but rather for the
sake of an object of such apperception—the virtue and activity of his friend.
He does enjoy a pleasant apperception when he apperceives the virtue and
activity of his friend; but he enjoys an adventitious pleasure, for he acts for
the sake of his friend. He, in fact, enjoys the apperception of the happiness
of his friend in the same way he enjoys the apperception of his own happiness. He does not strive to be happy so that he may take pleasure in apperceiving his happiness; his happiness is its own end and his pleasure in its
apperception is adventitious (see *Eth.* 10.4.1174b31–33).

Aristotle concludes that a man and his friend choose to spend their
days together doing whatever activities they enjoy most, and he gives examples of both primary and secondary happiness:

> And that which existence may be for individuals, that for the
> sake of which they choose to live, in that they wish to spend
> their lives with their friends. And therefore some drink to-
> gether, and some dice together. Others exercise together and
> hunt together, and others philosophize together. The individ-

uals spend their days together in whatever they are most fond of in life. (*Eth.* 9.12.1172a1–6)

Philosophizing together is clearly an example of primary happiness. Exercising together and hunting together are examples of secondary happiness, for these activities require courage. And drinking together ought to be an example of secondary happiness, too, for drinking in moderation is temperance. But, I confess, I am not entirely sure what virtue we exercise when gambling. Perhaps, we might consider it a subspecies of distributive justice.

We also see why good friendship is more common than one might have thought. To enter a good friendship, one need not be perfectly happy or virtuous, of course. Aristotle himself admits as much (see again *Eth.* 9.4.1166a11). But one may also share different principles of happiness, for we may act for the sake of either primary or secondary happiness, and we may act for the sake of primary or secondary happiness of different sorts. Thus, good friendship is not the exclusive province of only a few perfectly good people—if there are any such people. Those who are imperfectly good can also enjoy friendship of this kind.[15]

We thus see that we establish and maintain good personal friendships because we find the happiness of other people to be choiceworthy. And we find both the primary and the secondary happiness of others choiceworthy.

POLITICAL FRIENDSHIP

So far our analysis of Aristotelian friendship has shown what personal friendship is and why it is. The analysis has also shown that personal friendship is both altruistic and pluralistic. I now wish to ask what Aristotelian political friendship is and why it is and whether political friendship, too, is altruistic and pluralistic. What we shall see is that political friendship of the good kind is altruistic, for fellow citizens in healthy constitutions act for the sake of one another. And that political friendship of this sort is also pluralistic, for healthy constitutions include kingships, aristocracies, and polities. We shall also see that political friendship is more practicable than one might have thought. Though kingship and aristocracy are not, polity is a constitution within the reach of most societies.

Aristotle discusses political friendship most explicitly when he discusses unanimity. He argues that unanimity is political friendship:

> Unanimity appears to be political friendship, as is said. For it concerns our interests and things pertaining to our life. (*Eth.* 9.6.1167b2–4).

He uses two middle terms in this argument. Fully stated, the argument would be: What concerns our interests and things pertaining to our life is political friendship; unanimity concerns our interests and things pertaining to our life; therefore, unanimity is political friendship.

In this argument Aristotle does not explain very fully why unanimity is friendship of the political kind. He does not indicate why a relationship is friendship of this kind if it concerns our interests and our lives. Surely not any relationship concerned with our interests and lives is. A faction is not, for example. And if unanimity is friendship, Aristotle still leaves crucial questions about political friendship unanswered. He does not state whose interest or whose life unanimity concerns: Is unanimity altruistic or egoistic friendship? Nor does he state what interest or what life unanimity concerns: Does unanimity concern happiness in a primary or a secondary sense? Does it concern happiness at all?

We shall see more clearly what Aristotle means by asserting that unanimity concerns our interests and our lives if we examine his other arguments in support of his conclusion. These other arguments imply that people who are unanimous are political friends of the good kind because they exhibit two marks of friendship. The arguments show that unanimous people exhibit the first mark of friendship—to act for the sake of the happiness of another (see *Eth.* 9.4.1166a2–4)—and that they exhibit the fourth mark—to have the same tastes as another (see 1166a6–7). Because they exhibit these marks of friendship, those who are unanimous would also appear to act altruistically, rather than egoistically, and they would appear to act for the sake of the happiness of one another. From other arguments we shall confirm that these people do indeed act altruistically and that they do promote the happiness of one another.

Though he concludes that it is political friendship, Aristotle begins his discussion with the weaker proposition that unanimity is a mark of friendship. He argues that unanimity is neither similarity of opinion nor agreement about any matters but agreement about moral matters:

> Unanimity appears to be a mark of friendship. It is therefore not similarity of opinion, for this may belong to those who are unaware of one another. Nor do they say that those who agree about any matters are unanimous, such as those who agree about heavenly bodies. For unanimity concerning these things is not a mark of friendship. But they say that cities are unanimous when they agree about their interests and choose the same things and do what they believe in common. (*Eth.* 9.6.1167a21–28)

Though he does not state so, he does imply that citizens who are unanimous exhibit the fourth mark of friendship—to have the same tastes as one another. He uses almost the very same argument that he uses to establish the fourth mark for personal friendship. He argues that citizens are unanimous because they agree about moral matters and they choose and do the same things. But those who choose and do the same things and who are in agreement have the same tastes as one another (see *Eth.* 9.4.1166a13–14).

When he explains who are unanimous, Aristotle also implies that unanimous people exhibit the first mark—to wish and to do what is good for another. He argues that good men are unanimous because only they agree with one another:

> Unanimity of such sort occurs among good men. For they are unanimous both with themselves and with one another, being of the same intellect, so to speak. The wishes of such men are steadfast and do not shift like the currents of Euripos. They wish for what is just and for what is in their interests, and they seek these things by common consent. (*Eth.* 9.6.1167b4–9)

He argues that men who are unanimous are good men. To do so, he implies again that unanimous men have the same tastes as one another. But he also implies that unanimous men very probably wish for and do what is good for another, for he asserts that these men wish for and seek what is just and what is in their interest. But what is in their interest is happiness, for they are good, and justice is "another's good," for what is just is the happiness of another. At least justice defined as what is lawful is the happiness of another, as we shall see (see *Eth.* 5.1.1129b11–1130a5). Unanimous men therefore appear to wish for and to seek happiness for each other, for they are good, and they would exhibit lawfulness.

People who are not unanimous do not exhibit the first mark of friendship:

> Bad men are not capable of being unanimous, except slightly, just as they are not capable of being friends. They aim at greediness in things which are advantageous and fall short in labor and public service. Wishing the same things for himself, each man scrutinizes his neighbors and hinders him, for if they are not on their guard, their common interest soon perishes. Faction then springs up among them and they put compulsion on one another, themselves not wishing to do what is just. (*Eth.* 9.6.1167b9–16)

Aristotle explicitly asserts that bad men cannot be unanimous. He also implies that these men do not seek happiness for one another, for they are greedy about what is advantageous and avoid private disadvantages. By hindering each other they are even apt to destroy what is in their common interest, but their common interest is, of course, their happiness (see again *Eth.* 5.1.1129b14–19). Nor do they seek to do justice to one another. With their factions and manipulations they would appear to establish coerced relationships, at best.

We would conclude, then, that people who are unanimous are most probably good political friends, for unanimous people exhibit the first and the fourth mark of friendship. But people who exhibit the marks of friendship become friends with time and familiarity (see *Eth.* 8.3.1156b25–32). We would note, too, that the first mark of friendship is the key element in the definition of good friendship (see *Eth.* 8.2.1156a3–5). For the first mark is to wish and to do what is good for another.[1]

We can indeed see that unanimous people do act for the sake of the happiness of others if we examine unanimity in cities. Aristotle invites us to make this examination by presenting two examples of cities with unanimity. These examples suggest that cities are unanimous about a principle of justice for their constitution. The one example suggests that citizens may be unanimous about a principle appropriate for an aristocracy: "When each wishes the same thing for himself, like the captains in the *Phoenician Women*, they are in faction. For unanimity is not that each have in mind the same thing, whatever that may be, but that each have in mind the same thing in the same hands, as when both the populace and the good men have in mind that the best men should rule. Thus all attain that which they seek" (*Eth.* 9.6.1167a32–1167b2). He argues that faction arises when citizens disagree on who ought to hold office and that unanimity occurs when they agree on their office holders. And he implies that citizens are unanimous about an aristocratic principle, for he asserts that unanimity occurs when citizens agree that offices should be based on merit.

The other example suggests that citizens may be unanimous about a principle of justice appropriate for a democracy: "Cities are unanimous about practical matters, and of these about matters of magnitude and things possible for both or all parties. Cities are unanimous when all believe that the offices ought to be elective, or that they should form an alliance with the Lacedaemonians, or that Pittacus should rule when he himself also is willing" (*Eth.* 9.6.1167a28–32). He asserts that cities have unanimity about practical matters of magnitude, and he argues again that unanimity occurs when citizens agree on who ought to hold office. He implies that cities can be unanimous about a democratic principle. For he asserts that their citizens may agree that offices should be filled by election. He adds that they may also agree about applications of their principle for a policy and for an election.

If we consider Aristotle's discussion of constitutions themselves, we can see rather clearly that unanimity is essentially altruistic and accidentally egoistic. When he distinguishes them, Aristotle explains why some constitutions are healthy and why some are corrupt. He differentiates healthy constitutions from corrupt ones by the interests that their rulers advance. Rulers in healthy constitutions act essentially for the sake of other citizens and accidentally for the sake of themselves. They thus advance an interest the same as that of altruistic friends. Citizens in an aristocracy do, for example. But rulers in corrupt constitutions act accidentally for the sake of others and essentially for their own sake. They thus advance an interest the same as that of egoistic friends. For example, citizens in a democracy do.

Aristotle, of course, divides constitutions into six species. Or rather into three healthy species and three corruptions. The healthy constitutions, which he simply lists, are kingship, aristocracy, and polity:

> The constitutions are both kingship and aristocracy and thirdly that based on a property qualification, which appears to be properly said to be timocracy, though most people are accustomed to call it polity. (*Eth.* 8.10.1160a32–35).

He fails to explain why these constitutions are healthy.

He does not offer a simple list of corrupt constitutions. He rather takes them up one by one and explains why they are corrupt. By comparison he also indicates why the healthy species are healthy. He begins with kingship and tyranny:

> Tyranny is the corruption of kingship. Both constitutions are monarchies, but they differ very greatly, for the tyrant aims at his own interest, the king at the interest of his subjects. (*Eth.* 8.10.1160a36–1160b3)

A kingship appears to be a healthy constitution because a king acts as an altruistic friend acts. That is, he acts for the sake of others. A tyranny appears to be corrupt because a tyrant acts as an egoistic friend acts. He acts for his own sake.

Aristotle suggests that an aristocracy is an altruistic constitution when he explains that an oligarchy is egoistic:

> Aristocracy changes to oligarchy through the vice of the rulers, who distribute the goods of the city contrary to merit. They distribute all or most of the goods to themselves and offices always to the same people, taking the most care to make money. The few and the wicked thus rule instead of the best. (*Eth.* 8.10.1160b12–16)

Aristocrats appear to be concerned with the good of those whom they rule, for they apparently distribute goods according to merit. Oligarchs, however, are not concerned with the good of those under their rule, for they distribute goods contrary to merit for the sake of their own gain.

He does not explicitly argue that citizens of a polity rule for the sake of others, nor does he argue that democrats rule for their own sake:

> From timocracy, a constitution changes into democracy, for these constitutions are twins. Timocracy wishes to be associated with the people, and those who have the property qualification are equal in a timocracy. (*Eth.* 8.10.1160b16–19)

But he does imply that timocracy is altruistic and democracy egoistic, for the other constitutions were altruistic and their corruptions egoistic.

We thus see that political friends in healthy constitutions act altruistically. Those who rule in these constitutions act essentially for those whom they rule. But political friends in corrupt constitutions act egoistically. These rulers act only accidentally for the sake of those ruled. They act essentially for the sake of themselves.

In this discussion Aristotle also indicates what interests unanimous people advance when they act for the sake of others. They pursue the same interests that people pursue in altruistic personal friendships. They advance the happiness of others. Aristotle's purpose is to show that political friendship and justice occur together in constitutions (*Eth.* 8.11.1161a10–11). But when he indicates how friendship occurs in each constitution, he also shows us what interest political friendship concerns.

Aristotle begins again with kingship. He implies that friendship exists in kingship because a king cares that his subjects do well:

> A king rules his subjects with a superiority of beneficial activity. For he does well by his subjects if being a good man he cares for them, that they should fare well, as a shepherd does for his sheep. Whence Homer called Agamemnon the shepherd of the people. (*Eth.* 8.11.1161a11–15)

He clearly implies that a king is concerned with the happiness of his people, for a king desires that his subjects fare well, and to fare well is to be happy.

He also argues that the friendship of a king is like that of a father:

> Fatherhood is a relationship of such sort. But a father differs in the magnitude of benefits performed for his children. For

he is the cause of their existence, which seems to be the greatest benefit, and of their upbringing and education. (*Eth.* 8.11.1161a15–17)

Because he causes them to be brought up and educated, a father would appear to care that his children do well, for their education and upbringing would include intellectual and moral activities (also see *Eth.* 8.10.1160b22–32).

When he draws an analogy between aristocracy and marriage, Aristotle shows that the citizens of an aristocracy advance the happiness of others:

> The friendship of husband and wife is the same as that found in an aristocracy, for it is in accordance with virtue. More of what is good belongs to the better, and what is appropriate belongs to each. (*Eth.* 8.11.1161a22–25).

Aristocrats appear to distribute goods for the sake of the happiness of those ruled, for they distribute goods in accordance with virtue, as do husband and wife (also see *Eth.* 8.10.1160b33–35).

With an analogy to brotherhood, Aristotle implies that citizens of a polity, too, act for the happiness of those ruled:

> The friendship of brothers seems to be like that of comrades, for they are equal and of similar age, and such persons for the most part have similar feelings and similar characters. The friendship in accordance with timocracy seems to be like this, for the citizens wish to be equal and good. They rule in turn and on an equal basis. And thus is their friendship. (*Eth.* 8.11.1161a25–30)

Like comradeship, brotherhood is an excellent example of good friendship, for brothers most often have very similar virtues and activities, and they are most likely to act for the sake of the happiness of one another.

We thus see that the three healthy constitutions have rulers who are altruistic. A king, an aristocrat, and a citizen of a polity wish and do what makes other citizens happy. They all act for the sake of the virtues and virtuous activities of those ruled.[2]

Aristotle does not discuss all the corrupt constitutions to show what interest they concern. Instead, he asserts only that where there is little justice there is little friendship (*Eth.* 8.11.1161a30-31). He appears to mean that corrupt constitutions have little altruistic friendship, for when he explains why tyranny is not friendship, he argues that a tyrant exhibits no justice toward those under his rule:

> In tyranny, there is little or no friendship. In those relationships in which there is no common interest for ruler and ruled, there is no friendship either, for there is no justice. These relationships are like the relationships of craftsman to instrument, of soul to body, and of master to slave. For all these are benefited by being used, but there is neither friendship for lifeless things nor justice. (*Eth.* 8.11.1161a32–1161b2)

He argues, in effect, that tyranny is only an egoistic friendship—if a friendship at all. For he implies that a tyrant benefits his subjects merely as he might an instrument. That is, he benefits them for his own sake.

He does not explicitly state why oligarchy and democracy are not altruistic friendships. He asserts only that tyranny has less friendship than democracy (*Eth.* 8.11.1161b8–10). We might surmise that oligarchy and democracy are again egoistic friendships, for rulers in all corrupt constitutions act for their own benefit.

But we can see that oligarchs and democrats act for the sake of their own wealth or pleasure. With an analogy to household management, Aristotle reminds us that oligarchs pursue wealth:

> If the husband is chief in everything, the relationship changes into an oligarchy, for he does so contrary to his worth and not as being better. Sometimes women rule, being heiresses. Their rule arises not in accordance with worth either, but for the sake of wealth and power, as in an oligarchy. (*Eth.* 8.10.1160b35–1161a3)

His analogy clearly implies that oligarchs ignore worth and pursue wealth (and see again *Eth.* 8.10.1160b12–16).

A democracy would tend toward the end of pleasure. When he compares democracy with masterless households, Aristotle suggests that democrats desire to pursue pleasure:

> Democracy seems to exist most of all in masterless households, for in such households all are equal. And in those households in which the ruler is weak and the authority for rule falls to everyone. (*Eth.* 8.10.1161a6–9)

To allow all to rule on all household matters is to invite licentiousness, for to do so is to disregard worth and wealth both.

Aristotle does not indicate what end a tyrant advances. His analogy to fatherhood only suggests that a tyrant is mistaken:

> The community of a father in relation to his sons takes the shape of kingship. For a father cares for his children. Hence Homer called Zeus father, for kingship wishes to be a paternal rule. But among the Persians the rule of the father is tyranni-cal, for they use their sons as slaves. And the rule of a master in relation to his slaves is tyrannical, for the interest of the master is brought about in it. The first relationship alone appears to be right, and the Persian relationship to be mistaken. For the rule of different relationships is different. (*Eth.* 8.10.1160b24–32)

He does assert elsewhere that tyranny is an extreme constitution for the sake of utility and pleasure (see *Pol.* 5.10.1310b2–7, 1310b40–1311a11).

We see, then, that healthy and corrupt constitutions are political friendships quite similar to personal friendships, for constitutions and their corruptions are altruistic and egoistic friendships. We also see again that rulers in healthy constitutions pursue happiness for the sake of others. And that corrupt rulers pursue utility or pleasure for the sake of themselves.[3]

If he had wished, Aristotle might have explicitly defined political friendship of the good kind with a definition quite similar to his definition of good personal friendship. Good political friendship would appear to be good wishes and actions for the sake of the happiness of others—when re-ciprocated and recognized. Aristotle does show that good citizens wish and do what is good for the sake of each other. These citizens would also be likely to reciprocate and to recognize their good wishes and actions, for they take turns at ruling, and they would recognize that they do (see *Pol.* 7.4.1326b14–18).[4]

Political friendship of the good kind also appears to be a virtue. Because they are good men, citizens in healthy constitutions would most likely bear good wishes and actions toward stable characters (see *Eth.* 8.3.1156b7–12, 17–21). And they would be likely to bear these wishes and action with equality, for they have similar characters (see *Eth.* 8.5.1157b33–1158a1; *Eth.* 8.3.1156b12–17, 21–23).

Aristotle might even have argued that political friendship has an ob-ject and motive very similar to the object and motive of personal friend-ship. We saw that the object of personal friendship is another self and that another self is an individual who is different than ourself in one sense but the same as ourself in another sense. Other selves are numerically different than we are, for they are different individuals than we are. And other selves are morally the same as we are, for they engage in the same actions that we do and have the same habits. But fellow citizens appear to be other selves to one another, too. Obviously, fellow citizens are numerically different than one another. For they are different individuals. But fellow citizens are also morally the same as one another. Because they share a principle of happiness, they engage in the same actions and acquire the same virtues.

Though other selves, political friends do not, however, appear to define their principle of happiness in the same way that personal friends do. Political friends define their conception of happiness politically rather than personally. For they define their principle through a constitution and its laws. They would thus most likely define a principle more general than that of personal friends because their principle is one common to a whole city. Aristotle, in fact, argues that political friendship is less extensive than personal friendship; political friends have fewer things in common than do personal friends (see *Eth.* 8.9.1159b29–35).

But if they have an object so similar to the object of personal friendship, would not political friends also have a motive very similar to that of personal friendship? We saw that personal friends find the happiness of each other choiceworthy because the happiness of another is an object of pleasant apperception. Political friends would also appear to find the happiness of one another choiceworthy because they, too, find it to be an object of pleasant apperception. For they find that the happiness of another is a good belonging to them. The happiness of another is obviously good, and it also belongs to them because they make the happiness of others theirs when they rule.

Yet the happiness of a political friend would appear to present an object of apperception less pleasant than the happiness of a personal friend, though not unpleasant, to be sure. For the happiness of a political friend appears to be a happiness more general than that of a personal friend. And Aristotle himself implies that friendship is less intense in political relationships than in personal ones (*Eth.* 8.9.1159b35–1160a7).[5]

We thus see that political friendship of the good kind is a relationship with great similarities to personal friendship of the same kind. We can see, too, that good political friendship is not only altruistic but that friendship of this kind is also pluralistic. Aristotle shows that political friendship is pluralistic when he discusses constitutions and their species in the *Politics*. Not only do citizens in a healthy constitution advance the happiness of others, but these citizens also advance the happiness of others in either a primary or a secondary sense. Aristotle's discussion thus permits us to see that his pluralistic political friendship is practicable. Kingship and aristocracy are extremely rare, for these constitutions promote primary happiness. But polity can be moderately common, for it promotes secondary happiness.

When he discusses their species in the *Politics*, Aristotle at once confirms our inference that constitutions may be altruistic or egoistic. He implies that men by nature seek to establish a constitution that is altruistic:

> As we said according to our first arguments, in which we discussed household management and slave management, man is by nature a political animal. Therefore, even when they do not need help from one another, men nonetheless desire to live together. Not but that the common interest also brings them together to the extent that a portion of living well falls to each. (*Pol.* 3.6.1278b17–23)

With the first sentence he implies that men are political animals because they seek to establish altruistic constitutions. For this sentence calls to mind the family and its origin. As we have seen, a family originates in the fact that men and women have a natural desire to create other selves—"to leave behind another of the same sort as themselves" (*Pol.* 1.2.1252a29–30). He makes this implication more explicit with his second sentence, for he states that, without seeking help from one another, men still desire to live together. But with the last sentence, he does concede that men may also live together for their own benefit.

Aristotle indeed argues quite adamantly that a constitution is an altruistic relationship. To prove that it is, he presents a comparison of political rule, household management, and slave management. Slave management exists for the sake of the master rather than the slave:

> Although the slave by nature and the master by nature have in truth the same interests, slave management rules nevertheless for the interest of the master. It rules for that of the slave accidentally, for if the slave perishes, the master is unable to be secure. (*Pol.* 3.6.1278b32–37)

Slave management is obviously an egoistic friendship. A master acts only accidentally for the sake of his slave because he desires that his slave serve him.

But household management exists essentially for the sake of those ruled:

> The rule over children and a wife and a whole household, which we call household management, is either for the sake of those

ruled or for the sake of some interest common to both. Essentially it is for the sake of those ruled, just as we see that the other
arts, for example, medicine and athletics, are accidentally for
the sake of themselves. (*Pol.* 3.6.1278b37–1279a2)

Household management is clearly an altruistic friendship, for the head of
a household essentially rules for the sake of the members of the household.
But the head of a household does accidentally benefit himself because he
happens to be a member of his own household. He is like a coach who is
also a member of his team, or a pilot, who is always a member of his crew
(*Pol.* 3.6.1279a2–8).

Aristotle argues that political rule is similar to household management. Or rather, he argues that it was once similar, though in his time it
no longer is. Rulers once sought to advance only the interest of those ruled;
but by his time they seek to advance both the interest that they have in
common with others and their own private interest:

That is why, when a city is organized in accordance with equality and in accordance with similarity, the citizens believe that
they ought to hold political offices by turns. Formerly, as is natural, everyone thought that he ought to perform public service
by turns and that others would look after his good in turn, just
as he looked after their interest while he himself ruled. Now for
the sake of advantages—both those of the common interest and
those to be gained from office—they wish to rule continuously.
As if they are sick, they become healthy by always being in office, for perhaps thus they seek office. (*Pol.* 3.6.1279a8–16)

He asserts, in effect, that political rule is naturally altruistic, for rulers once
thought that they ought to advance the interest of one another by turns.
But he also argues that political rulers are at times corrupt because they
now seek to advance not only the common interest but also their own private interest. These men would thus appear to seek even the common interest essentially for the sake of themselves and accidentally for the sake of
others.

As he suggests that altruistic constitutions are natural, so he again argues that egoistic constitutions are perverse:

Obviously to the extent that they look to the common interest,
constitutions succeed in being right, being in accordance with
absolute justice. To the extent that they look to the interest

only of the rulers, all constitutions are mistaken and perverted
from right constitutions, for they are slavery. But a city is a community of free men. (*Pol.* 3.6.1279a17–21)

Opposing the common interest to private interest, he implies that rulers in
right constitutions advance the common interest altruistically and that
rulers in perverse constitutions obviously advance their private interest egoistically. Indeed, he calls corrupt constitutions slavery.[6]

Aristotle thus maintains that healthy constitutions are altruistic relationships of some kind. But when he specifies their ends, Aristotle also indicates for us that healthy constitutions are pluralistic. He argues that
citizens in these constitutions may be unanimous about principles of both
primary and secondary happiness. As he begins to discuss their species, he
suggests again that people possessing sovereignty in these constitutions exhibit unanimity of the good kind. He argues that the citizens in healthy constitutions pursue their common interest rather than their private interests:

Since constitution and constituency signify the same thing, and
the constituency is the chief part of a city, the chief part must
be one, few, or many. When the one, the few, or the many rule
for the common interest, the constitution must be right. Those
ruling for private interest, either of the one, the few, or the
many, are corrupt. For either those sharing in the constitution
ought not to be called citizens, or they ought to share in its interest. (*Pol.* 3.7.1279a25–32)

He may say that constitution and constituency are the same, for he discusses constitutions that have rulers who are constitutive of the constitution and not those that have rulers who are representatives of others (*Pol.*
3.6.1278b10–14).

Aristotle then goes on to imply that kings and aristocrats rule for primary happiness:

Of monarchies, we call that regarding the common interest
kingship. Of the constitutions of the few or of more than one
aristocracy, either because the best men rule or because they
rule for the best interest of a city and its community. (*Pol.*
3.7.1279a33–37)

He appears to imply that an aristocracy, at least, has the end of happiness
in the primary sense. For he argues that either aristocrats rule for the best

interest, which could only be primary happiness, or aristocrats are the best men, who could only have the virtue of primary happiness (but see *Pol.* 7.1–3).

He only asserts without explanation that a king rules for the common interest. But he also implies that kings and aristocrats rule for the sake of the same end, which again appears to be primary happiness:

> We assert that there are three right constitutions, that it is nec-
> essary that the best of these be managed by the best men, and
> that a constitution of such sort is one in which there happens
> to be some one man or a whole family or several men surpass-
> ing all others together in accordance with virtue, but in which
> both ruled and rulers have a capacity for the most choicewor-
> thy life. (*Pol.* 3.18.1288a32–37)

Clearly the most choiceworthy life would be one of theoretic wisdom (but also see *Pol.* 3.18.1288a37–1288b2; and again *Pol.* 7.1–3).

The citizens of a polity, however, rule for the sake of secondary happiness, for these citizens rule for military virtue—courage:

> And when the citizens at large make up a constituency for the
> common interest, we call it by the common name of all consti-
> tutions, a polity. And this name happens to be rightly applied,
> for one man or a few men are able to excel in virtue. But the
> people have difficulty in attaining perfection in all virtue,
> though they can best attain military virtue, for this virtue arises
> in the masses. (*Pol.* 3.7.1279a37–1279b2)

If they act on their military virtue, these citizens would of course act for the sake of secondary happiness because they would engage in courageous activity, which is an activity of a moral virtue.

He even argues that their citizens may define their common interest as merely living:

> But men also come together and keep together the political
> community for the sake of life itself. For perhaps there is some
> part of nobility also in accordance with only life itself if it is not
> overbalanced too much by hardships. Even at the cost of en-
> during many ills, many men are eager about life, as though

there were some cheerfulness in it and some natural sweetness.
(*Pol.* 3.6.1278b24–30)

He thus suggests that those who establish a constitution for the sake of
mere life might preserve and promote other activities besides intellectual
and moral ones. They appear to promote merely natural activities.[7]

Incidentally, he asserts again that oligarchs are rich men who aim at
wealth, and he implies that the poor democrats aim at pleasure: "Whenever men rule for the sake of wealth, whether few or many, their constitution will necessarily be an oligarchy. Whenever the poor rule, their
constitution will be a democracy. But it so happens, as we said, that the
rich are few and the poor many. For few are wealthy, but all share in freedom" (*Pol.* 3.8.1280a1–5). He may say that democrats espouse freedom
rather than pleasure if they have no virtue, for freedom without virtue
could only be the pursuit of pleasure.[8]

We thus see that kings and aristocrats rule for the sake of the primary
happiness of those ruled, and citizens of a polity rule for the sake of secondary happiness.

With a more detailed examination, we can see why kingship and aristocracy are very rare. And why polity need not be nearly so rare. Aristotle's
discussion shows that, though it is altruistic, kingship is either an infrequent constitution or a transitional constitution. He argues that a king
must fulfill the function of a statesman, and he implies that he may also fulfill the function of an assemblyman. But most of all a king ought to be a
statesman. He ought to lay down a set of laws for his subjects:

> The best man clearly ought to be a statesman, and he ought to
> lay down laws. (*Pol.* 3.15.1286a21–22)

He ought to rule with law because law implies a principle, and a principle
is free from passion:

> The king ought to have the principle of written law, the uni-
> versal. The better is generally that to which passion does not
> belong rather than that to which it belongs by nature. (*Pol.*
> 3.15.1286a16–18)

Aristotle actually compares the rule of law to divine rule, and human rule
to the rule of a beast (*Pol.* 3.16.1287a28–32).

But a king who fulfills the function of lawgiving is not common. Aristotle, in fact, argues that kingships most probably arose in ancient times only because few people were of outstanding virtue:

> Because of this, the first constitutions were kingships, because then, when inhabited cities were also small, men greatly distinguished in virtue were few to be found. And they were made kings because of their beneficial deeds, the very thing which is the work of good men. (*Pol.* 3.15.1286b8–11)

When they are more virtuous, people apparently do need to have recourse to a king for their constitution; in fact, they prefer not to have recourse to one (*Pol.* 3.15.1286b11–22).

Aristotle implies that a king may also fulfill the function of an assemblyman when he argues that a king sometimes ought to rule over all matters:

> When a whole family or some individual happens to be so distinguished in accordance with virtue that their virtue is superior to that of all others, then this family would justly be the royal family and have sovereignty over all, or this one man would justly be king. (*Pol.* 3.17.1288a6–19)

If he has sovereignty over all, a man or family of this sort most likely has sovereignty over matters concerned not only with making law but also with applying it.

In support of kingship of this kind, Aristotle argues that a king may be someone so distinguished in virtue that he has all the virtues that his people have piecemeal:

> Neither is it proper to kill or to exile or to ostracize a man of this sort. Nor to require him to be ruled in turn. For by nature the part does not rise above the whole, and this would happen to be the case with him who has so great a superiority. And so there remains only to obey a man of such sort and to make this man sovereign not in turn but always. (*Pol.* 3.17.1288a24–29; see also *Pol.* 3.13.1284a3–1284b34)

He may, in other words, be a political genius of some sort. At least in comparison with the other people in his city.

But a king who fulfills the function of applying the law is not common either. Aristotle notes that in his time the people decided the issues that the law cannot decide:

> To the extent that law is not able to judge, either generally or well, shall the one best man or all rule? Today assemblies adjudicate, deliberate, and judge, and all their judgments relate to matters concerning particulars. (*Pol.* 3.15.1286a24–28)

He recommends this practice because the people collectively are usually superior to any one individual about particular matters:

> Separately any man in the assembly is perhaps inferior. But a city is made up of many men. And as a feast to which many guests contribute is better than a banquet furnished by a single man, because of this, the population judges many things better than any one man. (*Pol.* 3.15.1286a28–31)

He assumes that one man who has many virtues is more corruptible than many men who each have only few virtues (*Pol.* 3.15.1286a38–1286b3).

Even if he were superior to them, a king would soon do well to surrender his rule to his subjects, for he creates a new political friendship with his rule. His laws educate his subjects:

> As many things as the law is unable to define, so many might a human being be unable to understand. But educating them for this purpose, the law sets up rulers to judge the remaining matters and manage them by their understanding of justice. (*Pol.* 3.16.1287a23–27)

But by educating them, he makes his subjects his political friends:

> Even now monarchs make many eyes and ears and hands and feet for themselves. For they make fellow rulers of those who are friends of their rule and of themselves. If they were not his friends, they would not act in accordance with his choice. If they are friends of him and of his rule, they are equals and similar to him. And thus if he thinks that they must rule, a monarch thinks that those who are equal and similar to him must similarly rule. (*Pol.* 3.16.1287b29–35)

As friends may help a king rule because they are equal and similar to him, so those equal and similar to him may help him rule because they are his friends.[9]

We thus see that a kingship is an altruistic but rare constitution, one that is either infrequent or transitional. But an aristocracy appears to be equally rare. Aristocrats must fulfill four functions, and these functions require virtue of a very high standard. At the end of their lives, aristocrats appear to exercise theoretical wisdom. At least, Aristotle argues that they fulfill priestly functions:

> Since the citizens divide into two parts, the soldiers and the counselors, and since to worship the gods is appropriate and also to provide a rest for those who retire because of their age, to the older soldiers and counselors the priesthood ought to be assigned. (*Pol.* 7.9.1329a31–34)

But presumably they fulfill philosophical functions, too, for they attain their intellectual prime at age fifty (see *Pol.* 7.16.1335b32–35).

Aristocrats also fulfill the functions of assemblymen and of soldiers. Before becoming priests, they must be assemblymen, for they must fulfill the functions of deliberating and adjudicating when they have attained practical wisdom. And before they are assemblymen, these citizens must be soldiers, for they must fulfill their military function while they still have the strength of their youth:

> There are soldiers and those who deliberate about the interest of the city and those who judge about its justice. And these seem to be the best parts of the city. Ought these men to be different or ought both these functions to be given to the same men? But this is obvious. In one way, some functions belong to the same men, in another way, to different men. They belong to different men, as each of these functions is appropriate to a different time in life, for the one requires practical wisdom and the other strength. They belong to the same men, as those who have the strength to use and to resist force would perhaps not always endure being ruled. For those who hold sovereignty over arms hold sovereignty to support or not to support the constitution. The result is thus that the constitution gives both functions to the same men. However, not at the same time, but as nature gives strength to youth and practical wisdom to age. (*Pol.* 7.9.1329a2–16)

Finally, these men also possess wealth (*Pol.* 7.9.1329a17–19).

But to fulfill these four functions, aristocrats require an extraordinary character and extraordinary resources. These citizens must possess all the virtues required for both peace and war, including theoretical wisdom, justice, courage, and temperance:

> Courage and endurance too are necessary for unleisurely times. Philosophy is necessary for leisurely times. And temperance and justice for both times, but especially when men have peace and leisure. For war makes justice and temperance necessary, but the enjoyment of good fortune and the leisure of peace make men rather licentious. (*Pol.* 7.15.1334a22–28)

To have these virtues, the citizens must lay down laws for their intellectual and moral education (*Pol.* 8); they must have the proper natural qualities of character to take advantage of their education (*Pol.* 7.7); and they must make laws for the care of the young (*Pol.* 7.17) and for reproduction and marriage (*Pol.* 7.16).

Yet citizens of an aristocracy are able to acquire and to maintain these virtues only if they also have sufficient leisure. They must be free from the necessity of fulfilling the functions of tradesmen, craftsmen, and farmers:

> It is obvious that in a city best constituted and possessed of men who are just absolutely, and not merely relative to the hypothesis of a constitution, the citizens clearly must not lead the life of craftsmen nor of businessmen. For such a life is low and opposed to virtue. Neither must those intending to live in this city be farmers, for leisure is necessary both for the development of virtue and for political action. (*Pol.* 7.9.1328b37–1329a2)

They thus require many slaves to fulfill these unleisurely functions. And these slaves do not belong to their constitution except as conditions of it (*Pol.* 7.9.1329a19–26; also *Pol.* 7.8.1328a21–37).

But who is of sufficient virtue to warrant a continual rule over others as a master over slaves? Aristotle himself doubts that the upper castes of India are as different from the lower castes as he had heard:

> If some men differed from others to the extent that we say gods and heroes differ from men—having at once a great superiority in body and also in soul, there would be no disputing that the superiority of the rulers over the ruled would be obvious. And

once and for all that the same men ought always to rule and the others to be ruled would clearly be better. But this thought is not easy to entertain. Kings have no such superiority over their subjects, as Scylax says they do in India. Because of many causes, all men obviously are of necessity to share similarly in ruling and in being ruled by turns. (*Pol.* 7.14.1332b16–27)

Though they are altruistic, we thus see that aristocracies, too, are extremely rare; very few Greek cities ever had so many blessings of good foresight and good fortune. Even Aristotle himself doubts that they are natural.[10]

Polity remains, then. A polity is an altruistic constitution and a practicable constitution. Unlike aristocracy, a polity does not require virtue of the highest standard nor an education of the best sort:

What is the best constitution and what is the best life for most cities and for most human beings? The best not by the measure of a virtue above ordinary humans, nor of an education in need of fortunate nature and nurture, nor of a constitution resting on a prayer. (*Pol.* 4.11.1295a25–29)

Aristotle argues that citizens in a polity aim at a virtue attainable by most men:

If the happy life is the unimpeded life of virtue, and if virtue is a mean, as was rightly said in the *Ethics,* then the best life must be a mean—a mean attainable by each man. (*Pol.* 4.11.1295a35-39)

He indicates that these citizens aim at a life of moral virtue, for he identifies these men as heavy infantrymen and their virtue as military virtue:

But the people have difficulty in attaining perfection in all virtue, though they can best attain military virtue, for this virtue arises in the masses. That is why those who fight in the heavy infantry possess the most sovereignty in accordance with their military virtue, and those who possess armor share in it. (*Pol.* 3.7.1279a40–1279b4)

He does characterize them as not merely virtuous but also wealthy. But if they are to act virtuously, they clearly must have some wealth, for their courageous activity requires armor.

A polity thus appears to be more practicable than a kingship or an aristocracy because citizens of a polity aim not at a life of intellectual virtue but at a life of moral virtue. Aristotle himself explains why citizens of this kind most likely find political friendship easier to attain. That is, he explains why these citizens find moral virtue easier to attain. Men with virtue of this sort apparently require only moderate wealth, and men with moderate wealth tend to obey principle:

> In all cities, there are three parts of the city—those who are excessively rich, those who are excessively poor, and, thirdly, those who have a mean between these. Since moderation and the mean are agreed to be best, obviously moderation in the possession of the goods of fortune is best of all. For moderation easily obeys a principle. (*Pol.* 4.11.1295b1–6)

If they easily obey a principle, men with moderate wealth make good political friends easily, for good friends must obey a principle of happiness. Friends of this kind act for the sake of the happiness of one another and take pleasure in apperceiving the happiness of each other.

Aristotle also explains that men with extreme wealth and men in extreme poverty tend to disobey principle:

> But superiority in handsomeness, strength, birth, or wealth, and the opposite of these, inferiority in poverty or strength or excessive dishonor, has difficulty listening to principle. The former men turn licentious and become great criminals, the latter turn vicious and become petty criminals. (*Pol.* 4.11.1295b6–10)

He appears to imply that too much wealth tempts men to vice and that too little forces them to it.

He further explains that men with too much or too little wealth are not good political friends. Men who are extremely wealthy or extremely poor can rule or be ruled only with difficulty:

> Those who have an excess of the goods of fortune—strength and wealth and friends and other things of such sort—they do not wish nor know how to be ruled. This first begins at home, when they are boys. And because of their luxury, they never develop a habit of being ruled at school either. But those who are in extreme need are very abject. The latter thus do not know how to rule but only how to be ruled as slaves are. But the for-

mer do not know how to be ruled at all but only how to rule as slave masters do. Therefore, a city of slaves and slave masters arises, not a city of free men, but one of envy and spite. (*Pol.* 4.11.1295b13–23)

These men certainly do not have good political friendship. They have, at best, only political friendship of utility or pleasure because the rich can only rule like masters, and the poor can only be ruled like slaves.

Aristotle, in fact, explicitly asserts that the rich can rule the poor only without political friendship:

This city is a far cry from having friendship and a political community, for community is a mark of friendship. Men do not even wish to share a road with those whom they hate. A city wishes to be of equals and similars as much as possible. And these qualities belong most of all to those who have moderate fortunes. (*Pol.* 4.11.1295b23–27)

He apparently means that these men lack good political friendship. For they cannot easily have altruistic friendship—they are neither equal nor similar.[11]

We see thus that political friendship of the good kind includes kingship, aristocracy, and polity. We see also that kingship and aristocracy are altruistic constitutions that are more difficult to attain. For kingship and aristocracy aim at intellectual virtue and its activity. But polity is an altruistic constitution which is easier to attain, for polity aims at the activity of moral virtue.

POLITICAL JUSTICE

We shall now ask what kinship political friendship might have with justice of the political variety. Aristotle implies that political friendship and justice of this sort have a very close relationship. For he asserts that friendship occurs in a constitution only when there is justice:

> Friendship appears to exist in accordance with each of the constitutions to the extent that there is justice. (*Eth.* 8.11.1161a10–11)

But he implies that friendship need not occur when there is justice. For he also asserts that those who have friendship no longer need justice, but those who have justice still need friendship:

> When men are friends, there is no need of justice, but when they are just, they still need friendship. (*Eth.* 8.1.1155a26–27)

Friendship thus appears to rest necessarily on justice, but justice does not appear to lead necessarily to friendship.

What we shall see is that justice is a mark of political friendship. Indeed, Aristotle himself asserts that it is:

> The best of justice seems to be a mark of friendship.(*Eth.* 8.1.1155a28)

Justice turns out to be the first mark of friendship—to wish and to do what is good for the sake of another (see *Eth.* 9.4.1166a2–5).

The fact that it is the first mark will enable us to see why justice might give rise to friendship. To wish and to do what is good for the sake of another is an element in Aristotle's definition of friendship (see *Eth.* 8.2.1156a3–5). And people who exhibit this mark of friendship can easily become friends, for friends wish and do what is good for the sake of one another with reciprocity and recognition (1155b32–1156a3).

We shall also be able to see why friendship need not arise out of justice. Even people who bear good wishes and actions for each other with recognition and reciprocity do not always become friends. For those who exhibit a mark of friendship only wish to be friends, but those who wish a friendship do not yet have it (see *Eth.* 8.3.1156b29–32).

We ought to be cautious, however. We might feel a temptation to argue that political friendship and justice can become the very same relationship. Or we might think that friendship can include justice as part of itself—good wishes and good actions. What we shall see is that friendship does indeed include justice in one sense but that justice in another sense remains distinct from friendship. People who are friends and just people perform the same activities, but they perform their actions out of virtues concerned with different emotions.

With that caution we turn to Aristotle's definition of justice. No one would deny that Aristotle conceives of justice as both a virtue and an activity. Without defining justice completely, he asserts quite plainly that justice is a habit productive of just wishes and actions:

> We see that all men wish to say that justice is a habit of the kind
> through which people have the capacity to perform acts of jus-
> tice and through which they both act justly and wish for justice.
> (*Eth.* 5.1.1129a6–9)

He also thinks that this habit is a virtue, for he takes some care to define a mean embodied in it and its activity (*Eth.* 5.3–4).

But we might naturally ask: What actions are just actions? Does a just individual act for the sake of others or for the sake of himself? Does he act for the sake of happiness or not? To determine what these actions are, Aristotle divides justice into two species. He does this with an unusual induction. His induction consists of the instances of subjects exhibiting the vice contrary to this virtue—unjust men (*Eth.* 5.1.1129a17–23). These subjects are apparently better known to us. He finds that unjust men are lawless men and greedy and unfair men and that just men are lawful men and fair men. He concludes that justice is the lawful and the fair, injustice the unlawful and the unfair:

> Let us grasp how many ways a man is said to be unjust. Both the lawless man and the greedy and unfair man seem to be unjust. That the just man is both the lawful man and the fair man is thus clear. And justice is therefore the lawful and the fair, injustice the unlawful and the unfair. (*Eth.* 5.1.1129a31–1129b1)

The greedy and unfair man is of course one and the same, for greed causes unfairness (*Eth.* 5.1.1129b1–11).

Aristotle defines the end of the lawful man first. He discovers that his end is the promotion of happiness. Just actions, he argues, are lawful actions:

> Since a lawless man is unjust and a lawful man just, all lawful actions are clearly somehow just. For the actions defined by statesmanship are lawful, and each of these we say is just. (*Eth.* 5.1.1129b11–14)

And the law aims at the happiness of men in a political community:

> The laws in their enactments concerning all actions aim at the common interest of all or of the best, either of those having sovereignty in accordance with virtue or in accordance with some other ground of such sort. We thus say that justice in some way produces and preserves happiness and its elements in a political community. (*Eth.* 5.1.1129b14–19)

This argument might be put in a more explicit form: The common interest is the production and the preservation of happiness for men in a political community; lawful actions aim at the common interest; justice includes lawful actions; therefore, justice aims at the happiness of those in a political community. By referring to all men or the best men, he appears to refer not only to kingship and aristocracy but also to polity, for in a kingship or an aristocracy only the best men rule, but all virtuous men rule in a polity.[1]

Aristotle also adds examples showing that the law requires the performance of actions required by the virtues:

The law bids us perform both the functions of a courageous man, such as not deserting our post nor taking flight nor throwing away armor, and those of a temperate man, such as not committing adultery nor running riot, and those of a good-tempered man, such as not doing violence nor speaking evil, and similarly with regard to the other virtues and vices, prescribing some functions and proscribing others. (*Eth.* 5.1.1129b19–24)

These examples show that the laws require courage, temperance, and good-temperedness.

Justice thus appears to have the same end that political friendship has. Someone who is just aims at happiness when he abides by the law, for the law aims at the common good in a political community, and the common good is its happiness. But does Aristotle argue that justice is altruistic? Does someone who is just aim at the happiness of others essentially or accidentally? That is, does he aim at the happiness of others for their sake or for his own?

When he explains that justice is complete virtue, Aristotle implies that someone who is just acts for the sake of another. He argues that justice is complete virtue not only because it includes the other virtues and their exercise (*Eth.* 5.1.1129b25–31). Justice is also complete virtue because it includes the exercise of virtues in a relationship with another:

Justice is also complete because someone possessing it is able to exercise virtue in a relationship with another and not only in relation to himself. For many are able to exercise virtue in their own actions but they are not able to exercise it in the actions of a relationship with another. (*Eth.* 5.1.1129b31–1130a1)

This argument is the crucial argument for our purpose. Aristotle cites ancient opinion to prove that justice is the exercise of virtue for the sake of another:

Because of this, the saying of Bias seems to be rightly said, that rule will prove the man, for a ruler rules in a relationship with other men already in a community. And because of this, because it is in a relationship with another, justice alone of the virtues seems to be another's good, for it does what is in the interest of another, either someone ruling or someone in the community. (*Eth.* 5.1.1130a1–5)

More explicitly his argument is: What is in the interest of another is another's good; justice is in the interest of another; therefore, justice is another's good.

He does add that a ruler acts for the sake of those who rule as well as for the sake of those who are ruled. But this addition appears to indicate that a ruler acts for the sake of those who rule with him. For he clearly asserts that a ruler does what is in the interest of others. And those who rule with him would at times also be among those whom he rules, for they rule by turns (see *Pol.* 3.6.1278b30–1279a21).

We would conclude, then, that justice is a mark of friendship. Aristotle appears to imply that justice is to wish and to do what is good for the sake of another, for he argues that those who are just act essentially for the sake of the goodness of other citizens. He would thus refer to those who rule in kingships, aristocracies, and polities, for rulers in these constitutions act essentially for the sake of the happiness of those whom they rule.

But we have considered only Aristotle's conception of justice as what is lawful. Does his conception of justice as what is fair support the same conclusion about justice? Are acts of fairness also marks of friendship? They are. The key to seeing that they are lies in the relationship between the lawful and the fair. Aristotle argues that the lawful and the fair are related to one another as whole to part and that the unlawful and the unfair are similarly related. He begins with the unlawful and unfair:

> The unfair and the unlawful are not the same but are different
> as a part is from a whole, for all the unfair is unlawful, but not
> all the unlawful is unfair. And the unjustness and injustice of the
> unfair are not the same but different than the unjustness and
> injustice of the unlawful. The one is like a part, and the other
> like a whole. For the injustice of unfairness itself is a part of
> whole injustice. And similarly the former justice is a part of
> whole justice. (*Eth.* 5.2.1130b10–16)

In this convoluted manner he argues that the unlawful and the unfair differ from one another as a whole from a part because the unlawful is wider than the unfair. He also argues that the injustice and the unjustness of the unlawful and the unfair differ in the same way and that the justice of the lawful and the fair also differ as whole and part. Presumably the justness of the lawful and the fair do, too.

But we might note that the lawful and the fair appear to stand in this relation of whole and part because they supply different means for the attainment of happiness. What is lawful aims at the happiness of others through requiring appropriate actions; but what is fair aims at the happiness of others only by providing and securing the resources necessary for action.[2]

What is fair, indeed, divides into distributive and corrective justice, and justice of both kinds concerns the resources necessary for happiness. Distributive justice concerns the provision of the external goods necessary for the happiness of others. It concerns an equal distribution of these goods among citizens:

> Of partial justice and what is just in the same sense, one species
> is that concerned with the distribution of honor or money
> or other things to the extent that they are to be divided
> among those sharing in a constitution, for of these, someone
> may have a portion unequal or equal to that of another. (*Eth.*
> 5.2.1130b30–33)

Justice of this kind aims at a proportion between the goods distributed and the people to whom they are distributed:

> Justice therefore necessarily involves at least four things. For
> those for whom there is justice are two, and those about which
> there is justice, the things, are also two. And the same equal-
> ity exists for those for whom justice exists and about those
> things about which it exists also. As the latter have equality, the
> things about which it exists, thus do the former too, for if the
> former are not equal, they will not have what is equal. (*Eth.*
> 5.3.1131a15–22)

As one person is to another, so what one person receives is to what another receives. In a word, this proportion is what mathematicians call a geometric proportion (*Eth.* 5.3.1131b12–15).

But different conceptions of the worth of the persons serve as principles for determining the distribution of things:

> All men agree that justice in distribution must be according
> to some worth. However, all do not espouse the same worth.
> Democrats espouse freedom, oligarchs money or good birth,
> and aristocrats virtue. (*Eth.* 5.3.1131a25–29)

Incidentally, these conceptions of worth imply that justice can be not only altruistic but also egoistic. Not only do aristocrats use virtue and, presumably, happiness as a principle for the distribution of things, but oligarchs use wealth, and democrats use pleasure as a principle of distribution. For freedom without virtue would be merely pleasure.

Corrective justice concerns the security of external goods necessary for happiness. Justice of this kind applies to voluntary and involuntary transactions, and these transactions concern bodily goods as well as external goods:

> Of transactions, some are voluntary, some involuntary. Voluntary transactions are such as selling, buying, loaning, pledging, lending, depositing, and hiring. They are said to be voluntary because the beginning of the transaction is voluntary. Of involuntary transactions, some are fraudulent, such as stealing, committing adultery, drugging, tricking, enticing slaves, assassination, and perjury. Other involuntary transactions are forceful, such as assault, imprisonment, murder, robbery, mutilation, slander, and libel. (*Eth.* 5.2.1131a2–9)

Corrective justice aims at a proportion in rectifying these transactions. Justice of this kind does not consider the worth of the persons but treats them as equal. It considers only the inequality resulting from the harm inflicted by one person and suffered by another:

> There is no difference whether a good man defrauds a bad man or a bad man a good man, or whether a good man commits adultery or a bad man. The law looks only to the difference in the harm and treats the persons as equal whether one acted unjustly or one suffered unjustly or whether one inflicted harm or received harm. (*Eth.* 5.4.1132a1–6)

It tries to restore equality by taking the gain away from the perpetrator and returning it to the victim:

> This injustice being an inequality, the judge tries to equalize it. For when one man wounds another or is wounded by another, or when one man kills another or is killed by another, the suffering and the action are distributed unequally. The judge tries to equalize things with a punishment and to take away the gain from the perpetrator. (*Eth.* 5.4.1132a6–10)

This proportion is not geometric but arithmetic (*Eth.* 5.4.1131b32–1132a2).

Corrective justice thus aims at preserving what happiness was present before a fraudulent or forceful transaction; it attempts to restore the balance of goods previously distributed for the sake of happiness.[3]

We see, then, that justice both as the lawful and as the fair is a mark of political friendship. Both lawful men and fair men wish for and act for the happiness of others. And to wish and to act for the happiness of others is the first mark of friendship. What is lawful aims at the actions required for the happiness of others, and what is fair aims at the distribution of goods necessary for the happiness of others or at the rectification of the distribution of these goods. At least in healthy constitutions they do.[4]

The fact that people who are just aim at the happiness of others, suggests two noteworthy similarities with political friendship, though Aristotle himself does not discuss them. These similarities concern the object of justice and its motive. Justice appears to have an object quite similar to the object of political friendship. As are political friends, so just people are especially those who are good. They accordingly share the same or very similar moral and intellectual virtues and activities. Just people are thus other selves to one another. They are numerically different than one another, for they are different individuals; but they are also morally the same as one another, for they share the same moral and intellectual virtues and activities.

Justice therefore appears to have a motive very similar to that of political friendship. Justice very probably takes for its motive an object of mental pleasure because just people would find the happiness of one another to be an object of pleasant apperception. They would find the happiness of one another to be a good belonging to them. For they find one another to be happy, and they help one another retain or attain their happiness.

But just people, like political friends, define their conception of another self politically, rather than personally, for they, too, define their principle of happiness through a constitution and its laws (see *Eth.* 5.6.1134a24–32). They would thus define a principle more general than that of personal friendship. And as political friends do, they probably would find the pleasure of apperceiving the happiness of their fellow citizens weaker than that of apperceiving the happiness of a personal friend.

We cannot, of course, overlook the fact that people who are just may treat unjust people justly. Yet unjust people are hardly good, so they cannot be other selves. But Aristotle appears to imply that just people may regard those who are unjust as potentially other selves. He does so when he discusses punishment, for it has the purpose of making others better. Punishment, he says, is therapy (*Eth.* 2.3.1104b13–18).

We must remind ourselves to be cautious, however. Political friendship and justice might seem to be the same, for these activities and their virtues have still other significant similarities. Justice not only has the same end and the same object and motive, but it also involves reciprocity and recognition of good wishes and good actions for the sake of another. Lawfulness apparently entails both reciprocity and recognition. Lawful men in healthy constitutions enact laws for the sake of those whom they rule. And taking turns at ruling, these men reciprocate their legislative actions and must recognize that they do. Similar considerations apply to fairness, for the rulers distribute their offices and honors among themselves by turn and again know that they do. They are also likely to rectify voluntary and involuntary transactions with reciprocity and recognition.

Though he apparently does not discuss its recognition, Aristotle indicates that some justice at least entails reciprocity. When he comments on the Pythagorean conception of reciprocity, he does not discuss lawfulness but he does discuss fairness. He implies that fairness entails reciprocity, but not strict reciprocity. Its reciprocity is, of course, arithmetic. He argues from common opinion that corrective justice is reciprocity: "Reciprocity coincides neither with distributive justice nor with corrective justice. Yet men wish to say that the justice of Rhadamanthus is thus: 'Should a man suffer what he did, right justice would be done'" (*Eth.* 5.5.1132b23–27). He explains why justice of this kind is not strict reciprocity: "Often reciprocity and justice disagree. For example, if he wounds someone, an official must not be wounded in return, and if he wounds an official, someone must not be wounded but only punished. And the voluntary and the involuntary also differ greatly" (*Eth.* 5.5.1132b28–31). He notes two differences between corrective justice and strict reciprocity. Strict reciprocity requires an identical return of harm done to another, and it would not require any distinction between voluntary and involuntary harms.

Aristotle also explains that distributive justice entails reciprocity in accordance with a proportion: "In communities for exchange, justice of reciprocity keeps men together—reciprocity in accordance with proportion and not in accordance with equality. For by proportionate reciprocity, the city keeps together" (*Eth.* 5.5.1132b31–34). Distributive justice, of course, has reciprocity in accordance with a proportion that is geometric.[5]

Besides its reciprocity and recognition, justice also has a mean similar to the mean of friendship. Both lawfulness and fairness have a mean of reciprocity. That is, their mean lies in an exchange of good wishes and actions or of rewards and punishments, for when they act for one another, those who are just rule by turns.

Though he again fails to discuss lawfulness, Aristotle does explicitly indicate that fairness concerns a mean of reciprocity. When he summarizes what fairness is, he states that justice of this kind has a mean in a way different than the other virtues: "Justice is a mean. It is not a mean in the same way as the other virtues, but it is concerned with an intermediate" (*Eth.* 5.5.1133b32–33). He also explains how distributive justice has a mean in a different way: "Having defined what is unjust and what is just, clearly a just action is an intermediate between doing what is unjust and suffering what is unjust. For the one is to have too much, the other to have too little" (*Eth.* 5.5.1133b30–32). He implies that distributive justice has a mean of reciprocity, for its mean is a mean between taking too much and receiving too little. Corrective justice also appears to have a mean of reciprocity, one that rectifies maldistributions.

One might object to this similarity, for Aristotle remarks that justice has a mean primarily geometric and that friendship has a mean primarily arithmetic: "Equality does not appear to be similar in just relationships and in friendships. For in just relationships, equality is primarily in accordance with worth and equality in accordance with number is secondary. But in friendship, equality in accordance with number is primary and that in accordance with worth secondary" (*Eth.* 8.7.1158b29–33). To establish this difference, he implies that justice can exist between people who have virtues that differ greatly and that friendship cannot exist between people who differ greatly in virtue: "This difference is clear if a great interval of virtue or vice or wealth or anything else arises between friends. For then they are no longer friends nor do they expect to be. And this is most manifest with the gods, for they are most decisively our superior in all good things. It is also clear with kings, for with them, men who are much their inferior do not expect to be friends. Nor do worthless men expect to be friends with the best of men or with the wisest" (*Eth.* 8.7.1158b33–1159a3). This difference in their means might lead one to think that friendship and justice are not so similar, after all.

But though he distinguishes means of two kinds, Aristotle does not deny that justice and friendship have means of both kinds. He asserts only that justice has a geometric mean primarily and that friendship has an arithmetic mean primarily. He thus leaves open the possibility that justice also has an arithmetic mean secondarily. And we have seen that corrective justice has a mean of this sort.

He also allows for the possibility that friendship has a geometric mean secondarily. In fact, he shows that it does, for he admits that his distinction is not hard and fast. It is obvious only in extreme cases: "There is no accurate definition of the point where friends can remain friends. For much can be taken away and the friendship remain. Yet when there is a great difference, as with a god, the friendship ceases" (*Eth.* 8.7.1158b33–1159a3). This concession thus allows for some differences between friends. His argument also appears to concern only personal friendship, for we can have a political friendship with a king or with others who are greatly superior to us.

We thus see how similar Aristotle's conception of friendship and his conception of justice are. Justice is for the sake of the happiness of others, it is also reciprocated and recognized, and it has a mean similar to that of friendship.

But political friendship and justice do have a significant difference. For they do not concern the same emotion. Aristotle argues that friendship concerns the emotion of love (see *Eth.* 8.8.1159a27–33). But he does not explicitly address the problem of what the emotion of justice is. He does, however, imply that justice concerns two emotions. Lawfulness concerns one emotion, and fairness another.

Unfortunately we may offer only a conjecture about what emotion lawfulness concerns. Aristotle says very little about it. But when he discusses friendship and good will, he suggests that lawfulness might concern good will. He asserts that to impart good will is to do what is just:

> The man who has been benefited imparts good will in return
> for what has been done to him. But he is doing what is just.
> (*Eth.* 9.5.1167a14–15)

He also argues that good will has two properties similar to those of justice. Good will is a mark of friendship (see *Eth.* 9.5.1166b30), and it is the beginning of friendship (1167a3–5).

Aristotle thus suggests both that political friendship and justice of the lawful kind entail the same activities and yet that they are not the same relationships. Those who are friends and those who are just do what is good for one another. But friends do so out of love, and just people do so out of good will. Also, love and good will are not the same:

> But good will is not love. For it does not involve tension or desire, but these attend love. And love arises with familiarity, but good will arises suddenly, as it does toward competitors. For good will comes to be for them, and people share their wishes, but they do not do anything with them. (see *Eth.* 9.5.1166b32–1167a2)

He may overemphasize the inactivity of good will, for we can act out of good will. Someone who is just clearly does (see again *Eth.* 9.5.1167a14–15).

Aristotle also suggests how friendship can arise out of justice when he argues that friendship can arise out of good will. He draws an analogy between friendship and erotic love:

> Good will seems to be the beginning of friendship, as the pleasure of sight is the beginning of erotic love. For no one loves erotically unless he has been carried away by the form of his beloved. (*Eth.* 9.5.1167a3–5)

What appears to happen is that good will can become love with time and familiarity. For when it is prolonged, good will becomes friendship:

> Therefore someone might say metaphorically that good will is idle friendship, and that when it is prolonged and has arrived at familiarity, good will becomes friendship. (*Eth.* 9.5.1167a10–12)

He also implies that good will becomes good friendship, for it does not become friendship of a useful or pleasant sort (*Eth.* 9.5.1167a12–14).

However, good will need not give rise to friendship, for those who are friends must feel good will, but those who feel good will are not yet friends:

> And thus it is not possible for people to be friends unless they come to have good will, but those who feel good will are not yet friends. For they wish only what is good for those for whom they have good will, but they would do nothing with them and they would not trouble themselves for them. (*Eth.* 9.5.1167a7–10)

But again he must allow that good will can be active, for those who feel it cannot become friends without acting.

We thus see that friendship has no need of justice but that justice still has need of friendship (see again *Eth.* 8.1.1155a26–27). Those who are friends initially feel good will for one another; but those who feel good will for each other are not always friends. We also see that friendship can occur when justice occurs (see again *Eth.* 8.11.1161a10–11). People who are friends concern themselves with the same actions that just people do. They both wish and do what is good for one another. But friends and just people act out of different emotions. Friends act out of love, but just people out of good will. We might say that friendship occurs with justice of an intensified kind, for love is more intense, and it arises out of good will.

Yet we cannot deny that justice may be done even without good will. But then, justice may be done without virtue either. And even involuntarily. We would more properly say that these activities are not acts of justice but merely just actions (see *Eth.* 5.8.1135a15–19, 1135b2–8). Even friendly actions may be performed without proper motivation. Useful and pleasant friends, for example, may perform the same actions as good friends, but friends of these sorts do not love one another essentially (see *Eth.* 8.3.1156a10–19, 1156b7–11).

Aristotle is more explicit about fairness and its emotion. When he distinguishes the lawless man from the unfair man, he clearly implies that fairness concerns an acquisitive emotion:

> Partial injustice is concerned with honor or money or security or, if we had any one name for it, that which includes all these things. And it exists for the sake of the pleasure that arises from gain. (*Eth.* 5.2.1130b2–4)

He suggests that unfairness concerns an acquisitive emotion, for he asserts that it exists for the sake of pleasure arising from gain. If so, fairness, too, would concern an acquisitive emotion, for it exists for the sake of moderating the emotion of its vice.

But friendship appears to include fairness as a part, too. Friendship includes lawfulness, and lawfulness fairness, for the lawful and the fair are related as whole and part (see again *Eth.* 5.2.1130b10–16). Either friendship or lawfulness could thus set limits to our acquisitiveness. And perhaps either love or good will could supplant acquisitiveness.

If we wished, we could also analyze personal friendship and its justice in a similar manner. When he defines friendship, Aristotle, in fact, defines personal friendship, and his definition obviously includes the first mark of friendship (see again *Eth.* 8.2.1156a3–5). Again, this mark is to wish and to do what is good for the sake of another (see *Eth.* 9.4.1166a2–5). But justice, too, is to wish and to do what is good for another, for it is to have and to exercise virtue for the sake of another (see *Eth.* 5.1.1129b31–1130a5).

Indeed, Aristotle implies that all friendship exists where there is justice. He argues that friendship and justice are coextensive by citing examples of friendships that are not political: "As was said in the beginning, friendship and justice seem to concern the same things and to be between the same people. For in all communities there seems to be some justice and friendship too. At least, men approach as friends fellow sailors and fellow soldiers and similarly those in all other communities" (*Eth.* 8.9.1159b25–29). He apparently refers to his statement that states-men care about friendship as well as justice in their cities (*Eth.* 8.1.1155a22–26; but see *Eth.* 8.11.1161a10–11). But he generalizes this proposition to all communities, and the relationships cited by him are villagelike relationships.

He explains more explicitly that friendship and justice occur together to the extent that people have things in common: "To whatever extent people have things in common, to that extent there is friendship between them. For to that extent, too, there is justice" (*Eth.* 8.9.1159b29–31). And he cites examples of personal friendship to show that friends have different things in common: "Between brothers and comrades, everything is com-mon. But between others, definite things are common—between some more, between others less. For of friendships, some are more friendships, some are less friendships" (*Eth.* 8.9.1159b32–35). He also uses examples of both personal and political relationships to show that different friend-ships have different justices: "And justices differ, too. For that of parents to children is not the same as that of brothers to one another nor is it the same as that of comrades or as that of fellow citizens, and similarly with the other friendships" (*Eth.* 8.9.1159b35–1160a3). Finally, he uses similar ex-amples to show that friendship and justice increase and decrease together: "And an increase of injustice arises from being between those who are more friends. For example, it is more terrible to defraud a comrade than a fellow citizen, more terrible not to help a brother than a stranger, and more terrible to wound a father than anyone else. And the justice naturally increases together with an increase in friendship" (*Eth.* 8.9.1160a3–8). Fellow citizens apparently have less justice than family members because family members have more in common.[6]

We thus see that as political friendship exists together with political justice, so personal friendship exists together with personal justice. But there remains a difference between political and personal justice. We de-fine our obligations to our fellow citizens by means of a constitution and laws and set legal penalties for failing to meet these obligations. But we hardly define our obligations to our personal friends and penalize them in this way.

We can see, finally, that friendship with oneself occurs with justice for oneself. Paradigmatically, friendship with oneself includes all five marks of friendship (see *Eth.* 9.4.1166a1–9). And we do wish and do what is good for the sake of ourself (see 1166a14–17). For we act as someone who is a friend and as someone who is befriended. We are another self to ourself.

To argue that friendship with oneself includes justice might seem troublesome, however. Aristotle himself asserts only that we have justice for ourself metaphorically. Justice of this sort exists between the parts of our soul: "According to metaphor and similarity, there is justice not in the relationship of a man with himself but in the relationship of a man with certain elements of himself" (*Eth.* 5.11.1138b5–7). He explains that this metaphorical justice is like that between master and slave or among members of a household: "Yet this is not justice of every kind but that of a master or that of a household. For on principles of such sort, stands the part of the soul having a principle to the unprincipled part" (*Eth.* 5.11.1138b7–9). But when he speaks of injustice of this sort, he generalizes with an analogy to the justice of ruler and ruled: "With a view to these parts, there would also seem to be injustice in the relationship of a man with himself because between these parts there is suffering contrary to their desires. Between them there would therefore seem to be some justice in their relationship with one another as between ruler and ruled" (*Eth.* 5.11.1138b9–13). To have justice for oneself is apparently to have justice within oneself. And this justice can be either altruistic or egoistic, for it can resemble the rule of a slave master or that of a head of a household.

Though he speaks of a metaphorical justice, Aristotle does not, however, deny that we may also have justice with ourself in some other way. He states only that "according to metaphor" we do not have justice with ourself. We would note that, if he would apply his conception of another self, Aristotle could argue that we have justice for ourself, for we can act both as someone who acts justly and as someone who is treated justly. But not at the same time. We would also note that Aristotle's metaphorical justice is not entirely inept. When we do what is good for ourself, we often use the rational part of our soul as a means to our moral virtue and its activity; and when we receive what is good from ourself, we often aim at the virtue and activity of the irrational part of our soul as an end.

We can see, then, that political justice is a mark of political friendship, for justice is wishes and actions for the sake of the happiness of another. We see, too, that political justice appears to have an object and motive the same as that of political friendship. Justice of the political kind is also reciprocated and recognized, and it has a mean similar to that of friendship. However, justice of this kind appears to concern two emotions different than that of friendship.

CONCLUSION

To summarize and to conclude, I suggest that we reflect on our discovery that Aristotelian friendship contains a number of species. We have, in fact, found nine readily identifiable kinds. Our analysis was primarily restricted to two genera—personal friendship and political friendship—with two other genera considered only incidentally—kinship and village friendship. I explored personal and political friendship to see what the consequences might be if we could successfully apply Aristotle's conception of personal friendship to his discussion of political friendship.

We found that friendship of the personal kind contains three significant species. Aristotle himself focuses his analysis of personal friendship on them. They are good friendship, useful friendship, and pleasant friendship. He distinguishes these species by distinguishing among their objects. Good friends, useful friends, and pleasant friends all feel good will and have good wishes for another person, but they do so for the sake of different qualities and activities of others. A good friend acts for the sake of the good qualities and activities of another; a useful friend acts for the sake of the useful qualities and activities; and a pleasant friend for the sake of pleasant qualities and activities.

We also saw that good friendship differs from useful and pleasant friendship as altruistic friendship from egoistic friendship. Good friends feel good will and have good wishes for others for their sake; they act for the sake of the good qualities and activities of others—for the sake of their virtues and their happiness. Useful friends or pleasant friends feel good will and have good wishes for others for their own sake; they act for the sake of the useful or pleasant qualities and activities of others but only because these activities are ultimately conducive to their own happiness or what they believe to be their happiness.

We may thus say that altruistic friendship has one species and egoistic friendship has two species. Altruistic friendship is that for the sake of the happiness of others, and egoistic friendships are those for the sake of the happiness of oneself. We also saw that altruistic friendship itself divides into two subspecies, for good friends act for the sake of the primary happiness or the secondary happiness of others.

We found that political friendship is unanimity and that unanimity concerns the constitution of a city. People who are unanimous agree on a principle for a constitution and its laws. Aristotle, of course, divides constitutions into six species—three healthy species and three corrupt ones. Like those of personal friendship, the species of political friendship are altruistic or egoistic, and they, too, are distinguished by their objects. Kingship, aristocracy, and polity—the healthy species—are altruistic. Rulers in these constitutions rule for the sake of the good qualities and activities of their fellow citizens. Kings and aristocrats attempt to do so for the sake of happiness in a primary sense—the activity of theoretical wisdom; rulers in a polity do so for the sake of happiness in a secondary sense—the activity of moral virtue.

Tyranny, oligarchy, and democracy—the corrupt species—are egoistic. An oligarch acts to develop useful qualities and activities in fellow citizens for the sake of increasing his own wealth, and a democrat develops pleasant qualities and activities in other citizens for the sake of his own pleasure. But tyranny compounds. A tyrant advances both the useful and the pleasant qualities of his subjects for the sake of obtaining profits and pleasure for himself.

Aristotle thus suggests that friendship has nine important species (Figure 7.1). Personal friendship has three species, and political friendship has six. For personal friendship has one altruistic species and two species that are egoistic. Political friendship has three altruistic species and three egoistic species. But remember, too, that altruistic personal friendship can be divided into two subspecies and that tyranny combines two egoistic supraspecies.

We also found that, whether personal or political, all altruistic friendship has the same foundation—human psychology itself. We sometimes feel a desire to act for the sake of another person. We have this desire because we apperceive that another person has qualities and activities that are choiceworthy. We may then satisfy our desire by acting with good will and good wishes for the sake of that other person. We may find that the other

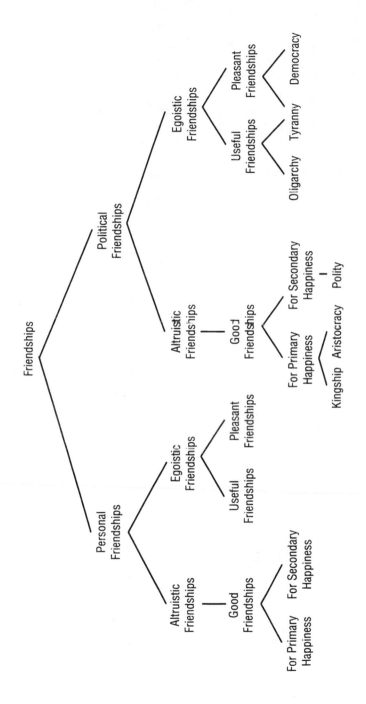

Figure 7.1

person reciprocates with good will and good wishes for our sake. And when we recognize our reciprocal good will, we have a friendship.

We find that another person is choiceworthy because he is another self, and another self is an object of pleasant apperception. Much as we take pleasure in apperceiving our own character and activity, we also take pleasure in apperceiving the character and activity of another self. Another self is a pleasant object of apperception because he is a good belonging to us. He is a good because he embodies a conception of happiness in his character and activity. But he also belongs to us because we help him embody happiness in his character and activity. And by helping him, we make his happiness ours. At least in part.

We do divide altruistic friendships into different species, but we do so because we find that our good friends are different from one another. All lovable people are other selves, but another self may embody a conception of happiness that is either personal or political. For a friend may define happiness personally or he may define happiness politically if he accepts a constitution and its laws. And another self may also embody happiness in either a primary or a secondary sense. But another self of any kind is an object of pleasant apperception—both a personal friend and a political friend and both a friend who is happy in a primary sense and one who is happy in a secondary sense.

We thus see that all altruistic friendships, both personal and political, arise from the choiceworthiness of other selves. And we can now see that the Aristotelian theory of friendship holds more than one advantage for political philosophy. Not the least advantage of Aristotle's conception of friendship is that good political friendship is a stable relationship. Aristotle explicitly discusses this advantage of good friendship only when he discusses personal friendship. He argues that good friendship endures because friends of this kind act for the sake of the activities and characters of one another, and their characters are stable (*Eth.* 8.3.1156b7–24). Useful and pleasant friendships are unstable because friends of these sorts act for the sake of their own utility or pleasure, and what is useful or pleasant soon changes (*Eth.* 8.3.1156a21–1156b6).

Though he does not discuss political friendship and its stability, Aristotle does make some observations about corrupt constitutions and their instability. These observations are consistent with what he says about friendships of the useful and pleasant sort and their instability. He asserts that tyranny, extreme oligarchy, and extreme democracy are very short lived (*Pol.* 5.12.1315b11–12; *Pol.* 6.6.1320b29–1321a4; *Pol.* 6.4.1319b1–4), and he recommends that these constitutions not carry their pursuit of wealth or pleasure too far (*Pol.* 5.10.1314a31–35, *Pol.* 5.1.1301b35–1302a8, *Pol.* 5.9.1309b18–35). The implication is obvious. The more a constitution seeks utility or pleasure, the less stable it is.

Other noteworthy advantages stem from the fact that Aristotle's conception of political friendship is altruistic. Because they rule for others, political friends are themselves active rather than passive; they prefer to do what is good for others, rather than have others do what is good for them. Aristotle does not explicitly discuss this advantage as an advantage of political friendship, either. But he does draw a similar conclusion about personal friendship. He does so when he asks whether we need friends more in good fortune or in bad fortune. He concludes that we need friends in fortune of both kinds (*Eth.* 9.11.1171a21–24). But he also observes that we do not feel the same way about our friends in both circumstances. When we are in good fortune we enjoy our friends and their company (1171b12–14). But we have mixed feeling about seeing our friends when we are in bad fortune:

> The presence of friends seems to cause mixed emotions. To see our friends is itself pleasant both in bad fortune and otherwise, and to see them is a help against grief. A friend is encouraging both by the sight of him and by his word if he is tactful. For he knows our character and by what things we are pleased and pained. But to see our friend pained at our bad fortune is itself painful. For we all shun being a cause of pain to our friends. (*Eth.* 9.11.1171a34–1171b6)

We consequently prefer not to call friends to our aid in circumstances of this sort (1171b6–10).

Someone who is good readily calls friends together when he has good luck, but when his luck is bad, he does so only with reluctance:

> One therefore apparently ought to call together friends when in good fortune. For to be given to good deeds is noble. But one ought to hesitate to do so when in bad fortune. For one ought to give them as little evil as possible. Hence, the proverb "my own bad luck is enough." (*Eth.* 9.11.1171b15–18)

The rule is to call friends when causing them the least pain can do us the most good:

Most of all we ought to summon our friends when by being
troubled a little they are likely to give us a great advantage. (*Eth.*
9.11.1171b18–19)

This rule would appear to be the opposite of one followed by an egoist.
An egoistic person would probably prefer to trouble his friends a lot even
when he would gain a little. He would, in that way, gain as much as possible for himself.

In general a good person also desires to help his friends as much as
possible and to be helped by them as little as possible:

To go unasked and readily to friends when they are in bad fortune is perhaps appropriate. To do well is part of being a friend,
most of all to those who are in need but do not seek aid. For
these deeds are more noble and pleasant for both. And when
they are in good fortune, we readily ought to join together in
their activities, for they need friends for this too. But we ought
to be tardy to accept their kindness, for to be eager to accept
advantages is not noble. (*Eth.* 9.11.1171b20–25)

Again, a person who is egoistic would prefer the opposite. He would prefer to help his friends as little as possible and to take advantage of them as
much as possible.[1]

But Aristotelian friendship also promotes activity rather than passiv-
ity in others. Because they rule for the sake of others, the citizens who rule
in a healthy constitution promote happiness in the citizens whom they rule.
Through a constitution and its laws they do what they can to help others
with their virtue and its exercise. Happiness is a common good shared by
all citizens with one another.[2]

And because it promotes activity, Aristotle's conception of political
friendship has two additional advantages. The one advantage is that it provides control for the emotions. This advantage arises from the fact that
friendship exists for the sake of happiness of others. And happiness includes
moderation of emotion, for secondary happiness is activity in accordance
with a mean between extremes of emotion.

Aristotle also touches on these advantages when he discusses friendship with oneself. He argues that someone may be a lover of self in a good
way or in a bad way. In a good way we strive to treat ourself as another self,
for we try to act in accordance with virtue:

If someone were always anxious that he himself should most of
all do what is just or temperate or in accordance with any other

virtue, and in general if he were always to try to secure for himself what is noble, no one would call a man of this sort a lover
of self or blame him. But such a man would seem more a lover
of self than the other. (*Eth.* 9.8.1168b25–29)

This man would not be called a lover of self because the term is most preva-
lent in its pejorative sense (*Eth.* 9.8.1168b19–23).

Someone who loves himself in a good way acts for the sake of his intellect:

> Just as a city and any other system seems to be its chief part so
> is a man. And therefore the man who is fond of this element
> and pleases it is most of all a lover of self. A man is also said to
> be strong-willed or weak-willed depending on whether or not
> his intuition controls him as if this were each man. And those
> things done most from principle men themselves seem to have
> done and to have done voluntarily. That each man is this ele-
> ment, or most so, is no longer unclear, and that the good man
> is fond of this element most of all. (*Eth.* 9.8.1168b34–1169a3)

Our intuition is, of course, the chief part of our practical intellect, and our
practical intellect includes intellectual virtues as well as moral virtues. For
with its principle, this intellect informs desire and makes it rational (see *Eth.*
6.2.1139a31–1139b5, *Eth.* 1.13.1103a1–3).

The other advantage of Aristotle's conception of political friendship
is that it limits acquisition of external goods. This advantage also arises
from the fact that friendship exists for the sake of the happiness of others.
The citizens who rule in a healthy constitution make other citizens happy
rather than simply provide them with material goods; and the other citizens need only concern themselves with material goods sufficient for their
virtues and activities. They thus have no need for an excess of these goods,
for we may be happy with only a moderate amount of property.

Aristotle considers this advantage, too, when he discusses personal
friendship with oneself. He implies that a good friendship with oneself will
lessen competition for external goods. When we love ourselves in a bad
way, we become preoccupied with external goods:

> Those using the term of self-love as one of reproach ascribe
> self-love to those assigning to themselves the greater share of
> wealth, honor, and bodily pleasure. For most people desire
> these and busy themselves about them as though they were the

best of things. That is why they become competitive goods.
(*Eth.* 9.8.1171a34–1171b6)

Indeed, a man who loves himself in a bad way makes external goods competitive goods.

Because his conception is pluralistic, Aristotle's conception of friendship entails additional advantages for political philosophy. Aristotle argues that kingship is rare in the extreme. Kingship is so rare because one person almost never has all the qualities necessary to rule for the sake of primary happiness, and other people seldom have the qualities necessary to be ruled for the sake of primary happiness. Nor does he offer any example of aristocracy. He thus appears to admit that a few people may only seldom, if ever, establish a constitution for the sake of primary happiness.

However, Aristotle does argue that a polity is a constitution within the reach of most people. If they eschew primary virtue and happiness, many people may yet rule and be ruled for the sake of secondary happiness. And he recommends a constitution for the sake of moral virtue and its activity. He thus implies that only very few people have the capacity to philosophize and that most people have the capacity to act morally. We can easily see why. Philosophy and the other theoretical activities require intellectual skills of a different kind than do moral activities.

Aristotle, however, recommends that we establish polities for the sake of courage and its activity. He commends the virtue and activity of the heavy infantry for the ancient world. Today we might wish rather to establish polities for the sake of other moral activities. Temperance and its activity might be appropriate, for example. The contemporary world contains many societies that embody intemperance and its various extremes. Some societies consume inordinate amounts of food and drink, but some societies have hardly enough to survive. And, of course, I need not mention the population explosion.

Aristotle's pluralism appears to hold the greatest advantage for his theory of friendship. By including the activity of moral virtue in his conception of another self, Aristotle allows the other advantages of his theory the widest application possible. Rulers in a polity may extend altruistic friendship to those who are not capable of happiness in its highest sense. They accordingly extend limitations on the indulgence of emotion and on the acquisition of wealth, too.

Aristotle probably thought that this last advantage of this conception of political friendship was the greatest. When discussing polity, he argues that polity is the most practicable constitution. Polity can eliminate factions caused by oligarchic and democratic parties, and it can eliminate the tyranny resulting from the domination by either party:

> Their good fortune is great when the ruling citizens have moderate and sufficient property. Where some citizens possess many things in excess and some nothing, there comes to be an extreme democracy or an unmitigated oligarchy. Or a tyranny from either extreme. For from rampant democracy or from oligarchy tyranny comes to be. But tyranny arises much less from moderate constitutions and constitutions akin to them. (*Pol.* 4.11.1295b39–1296a5)

Because they are able to establish an altruistic political friendship, citizens with moderate wealth are thus able to avoid egoistic political friendship and its excesses.

We can also see that the pluralism of Aristotle's conception of political friendship might be advantageous even today. Aristotle gives us cause to fear that oligarchic and democratic factions are not limited to the political arena of ancient Greece. He lists three causes—each with a ring of eternity to it—to explain why constitutions can become oligarchic or democratic. The middle class may be small and the contending factions may neglect to develop it.

> Because the middle class frequently has only a few men, whoever proves superior, whether the ones having wealth or the populace, they overstep the mean and draw the constitution their way. The populace thus rises or an oligarchy. (*Eth.* 4.11.1296a23–27)

Or the one contending faction may feel that their victory over the other justifies the exclusion of the other:

> Besides this, because faction arises and the populace and the rich fight with one another, whichever side happens to better the other does not establish a common constitution nor a fair one but seizes superiority in the constitution as the prize of victory. The one side establishes a democracy, the other an oligarchy. (*Pol.* 4.11.1296a27–32)

Or each faction may aim at hegemony:

> Having become leaders in Hellas, each faction keeps an eye on their own constitution. And the one establishes democracies in cities, the other oligarchies. They do not aim at the interest of these cities but at the interest of themselves. (*Pol.* 4.11.1296a32–36)

Surely, we need not remind ourselves of the political factions contending in our world. At least until quite recently. The extreme oligarchies and the extreme democracies of today only extend the factional conflicts of ancient Greece on a global scale. And when they attain dominance, these oligarchies and democracies corrupt the constitutions of those societies with a small middle class in an attempt to expand their own political hegemony.

We thus see that Aristotelian political friendship is both altruistic and pluralistic. And that Aristotelian altruistic pluralism holds more advantages than one might have supposed.

LAWRENCE BLUM

In this appendix I wish to examine a contemporary theory of personal friendship. Lawrence Blum appears to have discovered a conception of friendship in many respects very similar to Aristotle's conception of good friendship. Yet he denies that his conception is Aristotelian, and, indeed, in some respects he does develop a theory quite distinct from Aristotle's. Because it is in some basic ways almost identical to Aristotle's theory and yet in some ways so different, Blum provides us with a theory very useful for comparison. Blum's conception of friendship especially reflects some contemporary notions helpful for highlighting aspects of Aristotle's conception. His conception allows us to see by contrast how Aristotelian friendship is at once partial and impartial and also personal and impersonal.

We can best see what affinities Blum's conception has with Aristotle's if we examine his argument showing that friendship has moral value. This argument offers an extended example of what friendship is. If we consider it closely, we can see that his example embodies Aristotelian friendship at its best.

Blum develops an example of two women who are the best of friends by discussing some characteristics of their relationship. He states that these two women care about each other very much:

> Kate cares very much for Sue. Sue has a tendency to get depressed quite often. Kate has learned now to make Sue feel better when she is in such moods. Sue is not naturally or readily open about what is bothering her; but Kate has learned how to

draw her out when she feels that Sue wants to talk. (Blum, chap. 4, p. 68)

Though he does not say so, Blum presumably would agree that Sue performs similar favors for Kate, too.[1]

Blum also states that these two women go to great lengths to help one another:

> Kate and Sue are willing to go to great lengths to help each other out. They readily do favors for each other—helping shop, picking up something at the cleaners, making excuses and covering for each other at work, taking care of each other's children. (Blum, chap. 4, p. 69)

Kate and Sue thus appear to have a very close relationship and to live very close lives.

We can see already that these two people exhibit the first and second marks of friendship—to wish and to do well for one another and to wish one another to live (see chap. 4, pp. 54–55, 56–59). The fact that they wish one another well is more clearly present than the fact that they wish one another to live. However, to go to the lengths that they do in their relationship is almost to maintain the lives of one another, for they help each other with their household chores and even with their livelihoods.

But these two friends also appear to make similar choices about things. At least, Blum asserts that they can help each other with personal matters and, consequently, that they care about each other deeply:

> They know each other well and know how to be helpful to the other in discussing intimate personal matters. They care deeply for each other, and they know this about each other, though they do not express it to each other explicitly. (Blum, chap. 4, pp. 68–69)

They even share a closer outlook with each other than they share with their husbands (Blum, chap. 4, pp. 68–69).

These two also enjoy doing things together and sharing some common experiences:

> Sue and Kate enjoy each other's company. They enjoy talking about people they know and events that take place in the office. (Blum, chap. 4, p. 68)

They might very well enjoy doing other things together besides conversing about their work, for they also appreciate qualities seen in one another (Blum, chap. 4, p. 68).

These friends obviously share their feelings with one another, too:

> When Kate is troubled about something Sue is concerned too; and vice versa. Sue thinks about how to help Kate out. For example, she helps her to think about how to deal with her horrible boss. (Blum, chap. 4, p. 69)

The fact that they share their feelings apparently prompts them to help one another.

Blum thus describes two friends who also exhibit the third, fourth, and fifth marks of friendship—to live together, to choose the same things, and to grieve and rejoice together (see chap. 4, pp. 54–55, 55–56, 59–60). They live together, for they at least enjoy common activities of their work. They appear to choose the same things as each other, for they can even help each other with intimate matters. And they grieve and rejoice together. At least, they feel what each other feels at work.

But we ought not to forget, of course, that the first mark of friendship is the crucial mark. When reciprocated and recognized, good wishes for the sake of another are friendship itself (see chap. 3, pp. 35–37). We assume that the good will is essentially good will (pp. 37–40). But Blum is very clear that the good wishes felt for another in a friendship are to be done not for the sake of oneself but for the sake of the other. He asserts that friendship seems to lose its moral significance if we see our friend as an extension of ourself:

> Another conception of friendship which conduces to failing to see its moral significance pictures friendship, or rather doing good for one's friends, as a kind of extension of the self, so that when one acts for the other one is simply promoting what is in a sense one's own good. (Blum, chap. 4, p. 75)

He appears to view a relationship of this sort somewhat askance, for he adds that someone in a friendship of this sort has no clear conception of a separate self (Blum, chap. 4, p. 75).

He continues to argue that we do not act for another because we see an extension of ourself in another but rather that we act for another for the sake of him:

> Our discussion can help us to see what is wrong with this con-
> ception as a general characterization of friendship. For a gen-
> uine friend truly cares for the other for his own sake. He is
> willing to give of himself to promote the other's good. . . .
> (Blum, chap. 4, p. 75)

He also rules out any combination of altruistic and egoistic motives. For
example, we do not act both for the sake of our friend and for the sake of
our own activity of friendship. Neither do we act for the sake of the friendly
activity of our friend and its benefits nor for the sake of any future benefits
(Blum, chap. 4, p. 76).

Blum even appears to advance a conception of another self, though
he does not use the term. He argues that a friend recognizes that another
is distinct and also that he shares an interest with another:

> . . . he understands the other in his own being and interests,
> and can distinguish the other's interests from his own, even
> while he is able to care deeply for their realization and in that
> sense identify with the friend and his good. (Blum, chap. 4,
> p. 75)

To see another person as another self is, of course, to see another as both
different than oneself and the same as oneself. For another self is a different individual than we are; but another self has the same or very similar
moral and intellectual qualities. And if he has the same qualities, another
self engages in the same activities (see chap. 2, pp. 28–29; chap. 1, pp.
6–13).

As if these similarities were not enough, Blum also appears to have
captured Aristotle's conception of the motive for good friendship. He implies that when we act for the sake of another, we take pleasure in seeing
another succeed:

> Even in the non-egoistic sense described above, the one who
> identifies gets pleasure from the good accruing to the one with
> whom he identifies. But this pleasure is not the motive of his
> beneficent action; in fact it is a sign of the degree to which he
> cares for the other as other than himself and in his own right.
> (Blum, chap. 4, p. 75)

But Aristotle argues that we find another lovable because the other is an
object of pleasant apperception (see chap. 4, pp. 64–68). Notice, too, that
Blum suggests that the pleasure of seeing another succeed is an adventitious pleasure (see pp. 71–72).

Yet Blum denies that his conception is Aristotelian. His reason for doing so is important for us. He denies that this conception is Aristotelian on the grounds that to care for others is not to care for their moral virtue:

> To make the friend's moral character the central feature of friendship is to neglect too much the shared liking and caring (and mutual recognition of these by the friends) and the shared activities in which these are expressed. These features, though not unrelated to a person's moral character, are not primarily grounded in them either. (Blum, chap. 4, p. 82)

Blum thus fails to see that we are our moral virtues and their activities. What makes us good is an activity of our rationality in accordance with virtue (see chap. 4, pp. 57–58). And what we can share most of all are the activities of our virtues.

Though he appears to use a conception of another self, Blum would thus appear to define another self without Aristotle's principle of happiness. And, perhaps, without any moral principle. He does argue that we and a friend share an identity of interest (see again Blum, chap. 4, p. 75). But he indicates that whatever interest we share, our interest is not an activity in accordance with virtue. At least, it is not in accordance with moral virtue (see again Blum, chap. 4, p. 82).

That Blum neglects Aristotle's conception of happiness appears to account for some significant differences that exist between Blum's conception of friendship and Aristotle's conception—despite the near identity of Blum's example and Aristotle's definition. Because he does not make use of a rational moral principle, Blum argues that a good friendship is emotional and that it is personal and partial. His arguments will allow us to see better how Aristotle argues that good friendship is rational and how Aristotle might argue that good friendship is personal and impersonal as well as partial and impartial.

We shall begin with the question of rationality and emotionality. Blum wants to argue against the view that a moral character includes only what is an outcome of practical rationality, which is presumably active (Blum, chap. 8, p. 172). He argues instead that moral character includes emotionality, which is passive:

> . . . I will argue that the moral self cannot plausibly be conceived to exclude phenomena with regard to which we are passive, of which we are not the initiators or authors. Hence it is no argument against emotions and feelings being objects of moral assessment that we are passive with respect to them, that

they are not within the province of the will. (Blum, chap. 8, pp. 172–73)

He even argues that we ought not to identify moral character with the will:

> It is therefore also mistaken to identify the moral self with the will, or with deliberative reason, decision, and choice. The moral self must include emotions and feelings. (Blum, chap. 8, p. 173)

He adds that our emotions reflect on us morally as much as our will does (Blum, chap. 8, p. 173).

Blum also presents some instances of emotional attitudes that are relevant to moral character and judgments about it. For example, he cites racial attitudes that regard persons of one race as superior to those of another race. He mentions social and economic attitudes that find expression in life-styles indicative of high social position and great wealth. And he cites an academic orientation that entails being unsympathetic to students and their problems (Blum, chap. 8, p. 172).

I think that Aristotle would reject the proposition that the moral self is passive about emotions, but he would accept the proposition that the moral self includes emotions. Aristotle would not agree that moral character is partly active and partly passive. He argues that our practical intellect is active, for it can control our emotions and make them rational. Recall how Aristotle asserts that we are our intellect and even that our practical intellect makes our emotions part of itself (see chap. 4, pp. 57–58; chap. 2, pp. 20–21). When he discusses self-love, he also identifies ourself with our practical intuition, which grasps a practical principle (chap. 7, pp. 119; chap. 2, p. 23).

But Aristotle would nonetheless agree that moral character contains an emotional part. He does not argue that when we make them rational, we extirpate our emotions. Instead, he maintains that the efficient cause of our action is a combination of rationality and emotionality. Human beings are either thoughtful desire or desireful thought. This combination of thought and desire is moral virtue (see again chap. 4, pp. 57–58).

Of course, Aristotle could only agree that Blum cites examples of emotional attitudes that do reflect on the moral character of those who hold them. These attitudes reflect a bad moral character because they are instances of irrational attitudes. They are attitudes that the practical intellect has yet to control and to develop into virtues.

Blum presents two arguments in favor of his position. These arguments are worth examining because they show more precisely what his conception of moral character lacks. He asserts that his arguments rest on three propositions:

> . . . I will argue, (1) these phenomena—i.e., what it is to have a certain attitude or to hold a certain value—cannot be seen as the outcome of decision and choice, something which we will; (2) other-directed values and attitudes cannot be understood purely cognitively, as the outcome of a process of conscious rational thought, to which we give our assent; (3) they cannot be understood purely behaviourally, as a disposition to initiate certain actions. (Blum, chap. 8, p. 173)

The difference between the first two propositions is slight. The first appears to concern an assent arrived at by means of deliberation; the second an assent arrived at by means of some other rational process (see Blum, chap. 8, pp. 173, 175).

Blum uses his first two propositions together in his first argument (Blum, chap. 8, p. 173). He asserts that, according to these propositions, our rationality establishes our attitudes:

> According to them a person's values and attitudes can be portrayed in this way: the person chooses the values, or decides to adopt them. He weighs the various considerations for and against, and plumps for those values and attitudes most worthy of assent. The values and attitudes are then the result of conscious and deliberate thought and reason. (Blum, chap. 8, p. 173)

But he claims that rationality by itself cannot cause us to accept an attitude:

> . . . even if it is possible, through rational processes alone, to regard a value or attitude as worthy of being held, and even if it is possible to choose or decide to assent to the value, it is not possible to come to hold or have the value or attitude in this way. It is thus not correct to see the values and attitudes as grounded in decision, choice, and reason. (Blum, chap. 8, p. 174)

In other words, he wishes to distinguish between the assessment of an attitude and the possession of it (Blum, chap. 8, p. 174).

To support his claim, Blum offers an example, which concerns someone who comes to view that people of different races are equal:

> Let us envisage someone who through rational deliberation
> comes to the view that blacks and whites are, and should be re-
> garded and treated as, moral and social equals. He thinks it
> through, agrees that this moral view point is worthy of assent,
> and gives his assent to it. (Blum, chap. 8, p. 174)

But the fact that he assents to his view is not sufficient to show that he actually holds the attitude that the different races are equal:

> Let us suppose, for example, that the man makes disparaging
> remarks about blacks. He supports policies which prevent
> blacks from achieving social equality. He is upset when blacks
> move into his neighborhood, and when his children associate
> with blacks in school. (Blum, chap. 8, p. 174)

These reactions, he concludes, would lead us to doubt that this person
truly holds the attitude that whites and blacks are equal (Blum, chap. 8, p.
174).

Aristotle would have to disagree that practical rationality is not sufficient to establish a virtue. He would argue that Blum appears to miscon-
ceive the practical intellect and its functions. The practical intellect not only
grasps practical truth but also controls desire. Its ability to control desire is
what enables us to attain and to maintain moral virtue (see again chap. 2,
pp. 20–21).

But Aristotle would also have to agree that the practical intellect cannot by a simple act establish a virtue or eradicate a vice. To create a virtue,
we must first perform good actions. Only after repeating these actions will
we create a good habit (see chap. 2, pp. 24–25). He also argues we may
perform bad actions, and if we repeat them, we will form bad habits. These
habits we may have great difficulty changing. In fact, we may be unable to
do so (see *Eth.* 3.5.1114a11–21).

Blum's second argument rests on his third proposition. He argues
that an attitude is not merely a disposition to act. An attitude consists in
certain thoughts and feelings, and these thoughts and feelings need not ini-
tiate an action (Blum, chap. 8, p. 178). Aristotle would certainly agree with
this argument. Moral virtue not only disposes us to act in certain ways but
also prevents us from acting in certain ways. Also, moral virtue disposes us

to feel certain emotions, for virtue concerns both actions and passions (see chap. 2, p. 26).

Blum's arguments thus allow us to see quite clearly how Aristotelian friendship is essentially rational. Friendship is a moral virtue and a moral activity. We can use our practical rationality to perform friendly actions, and we find that these actions in turn create a virtue in us. Our virtue is, in fact, a form given to our emotion of love (see chap. 3, pp. 42–47). We can exercise this virtue in friendly activity, but of course we need not always do so.

The fact that friendship is rational is especially important for a consideration of other qualities that it has. Blum attempts to show that friendship differs from our common moral perspective in two significant respects. Friendship, as he conceives it, has both a personal aspect and an aspect of partiality. He argues that friendship is personal because we have an emotional attachment to our friends:

> While desiring to avoid simplistic accounts of it there are two aspects of friendship which will be important for the discussion. One is the personal importance which our friends have to us— the fact that friends are people we like, enjoy being with, trust and rely on, that they are part of what in our lives is valued by us. (Blum, chap. 3, p. 43)

Friendship involves partiality, too, because we feel an altruistic emotion for our friend solely because he is our friend:

> The other aspect is that friendship (or, anyway, most genuine friendship) involves a substantial concern for the good of the friend for his own sake, and a disposition to act to foster that good, simply because the other is one's friend. (Blum, chap. 3, pp. 43–44)

He notes that the personal aspect implies the aspect of partiality (Blum, chap. 3, p. 44). Presumably, our emotional attachments cause us to benefit a friend because he is a friend.

Blum argues that our common conception of morality has both an impersonal aspect and an aspect of impartiality. Morality of this sort is impartial because it demands that we not give any weight to our own preferences:

> So taking the moral point of view in one's actions and judgments means regarding them from an impartial standpoint, not

giving weight to one's own, but rather giving equal weight to
the interests of all. (Blum, chap. 3, p. 44)

This morality is also impersonal because we must take into account all persons:

> The viewpoint is impersonal because it gives due consideration
> to all, favoring none simply because of personal preference, but
> only according to principles which can be vindicated from that
> impartial perspective. (Blum, chap. 3, p. 44)

Again the two aspects are closely linked. He observes that if we act in a
manner which is not impersonal, then we also violate impartiality (Blum,
chap. 3, pp. 44–45).

   I submit that Aristotle might well be puzzled by the distinction between personal and impersonal and that between partial and impartial. He
could easily argue that all friendship is both personal and impersonal. Blum
argues that an emotional attachment is what makes a relationship personal.
But Aristotle would argue that all friendship involves an emotional attachment to another self (see chap. 1, pp. 7–13; chap. 3, pp. 46–47; chap. 4,
pp. 62–69; chap. 5, p. 84). Aristotle would also argue that all friendship is
impersonal. Blum argues that equal consideration based on a principle
makes a relationship impersonal. But we have to give equal consideration
to other selves in all friendships, both personal and political. And our consideration rests on moral principles because conceptions of happiness define other selves (see chap. 2, pp. 28–30; chap. 4, pp. 60–62; chap. 5, pp.
83–84).

   Most probably Aristotle could also argue that all friendship is both
partial and impartial. All friendship is obviously partial, for we act for the
sake of all friends because they are our friends. We do so because our
friends, whether personal or political, are choiceworthy objects. We find
them to be objects of pleasant apperception (see again chap. 4, pp. 62–69;
chap. 5, p. 84). But all friendship is also impartial. For we give equal
weight, or nearly equal, to our own interests and to those of our friends
(see *Eth.* 9.9.1170b7–8). The weight that we give to our interests and
those of our friends also rests on principles, for other selves are defined by
principles of happiness.

   Now Blum might object that in our own analysis we distinguish personal friendship from political friendship and that this distinction implies a
difference between personal and impersonal friendship. I would answer that
we do not base our distinction on whether the friends feel emotional at-

tachments to one another or use a principle in their relationship. Aristotle would argue that the difference between personal and political friends rests on what principle of happiness friends use to define their activities and characters. Personal friends use a private conception, which is very rich (see chap. 2, pp. 28–29; chap. 4, pp. 61–62, 72–73); political friends use a public conception, which is less rich and is also a legal one (chap. 2, pp. 29–30; chap. 5, p. 84). But whatever principle they use, friends in these different relationships find one another to be a source of emotional attachment.

Because he distinguishes them, Blum also faces the problem of showing that morality and friendship are compatible. To show that they are, he tries to argue that morality does not often conflict with friendship. He contends that morality requires impartiality only in certain situations and that friendship does not usually involve us in these situations (Blum, chap. 3, p. 46). He adduces some examples both to concede that friendship can lead us to violate impartiality and to show that friendship does not generally conflict with impartiality (pp. 46–47).

More importantly, he argues that his examples indicate to us what situations require us to be impartial. We must be impartial in official capacities within public institutions or practices:

> The examples so far given point to one of the primary sorts of situations in which such impartiality is demanded—namely, an official capacity within some public institution or practice. (Blum, chap. 3, pp. 46–47)

He offers more examples to show that officials within public institutions must be impartial:

> A judge, a captain of a ship, a doctor, a nurse, and a teacher all occupy roles or positions in which a certain kind of impartiality is demanded of them regarding the interests of certain parties whom they serve or for whom they have some responsibility. (Blum, chap. 3, pp. 46–47)

He adds that these officials must also extend their impartiality even to those for whom they have some personal attachment (Blum, chap. 3, pp. 46–47).

Blum would thus separate institutional roles, which require impartiality, from noninstitutional roles, which do not:

> Institutional roles and positions are an obvious arena of life in which a certain kind of impartiality between the interests of all,

including those to whom we are personally connected and attached, is demanded of us. Equally obvious is the fact that situations covered by such roles are very untypical of those in
which we interact with and benefit our friends. (Blum, chap. 3,
p. 48)

He consequently finds that impartiality does not lead to a fundamental
conflict with friendship:

And so the existence of such roles does not betoken a common,
much less a fundamental, moral problem regarding the beneficence dispensed to our friends. (Blum, chap. 3, p. 48)

He also offers more examples to show that after they meet the demands of
impartiality, even officials may provide extra assistance to those for whom
they have personal attachments (Blum, chap. 3, p. 48).

But Blum thinks not only that institutional roles demand impartiality but also that the demand for impartiality is limited to institutional roles:

I have claimed that institutional-role contexts are ones in which
impartiality is demanded of us. What I have not yet done is to
show that the demand of impartiality is limited to such institutional-role contexts. Nor, related to this, have I given a general
characterization of the conditions in which such a demand is an
appropriate one, from a moral point of view. (Blum, chap. 3,
p. 49)

His last sentence suggests, however, that institutions and practices may rest
on certain conditions that demand impartiality.

What Blum appears to favor is the position that institutional roles demand total or strict impartiality, for he argues that noninstitutional situations require us to act with some impartiality:

To help gain some clarity regarding the non-institutional contexts in which impartiality is incumbent upon us, it is necessary
to make an important distinction. The fact that impartiality
does not demand that we constantly appraise our potential
beneficence to our friends by an impartial standard does not
mean that we are justified in totally disregarding the interests
of others when the good of our friends is at stake, even out-

side contexts in which strict impartiality is demanded. (Blum, chap. 3, p. 49)

He presents an extended example of a situation that requires some impartiality but also allows for only some partiality:

> To take an extreme example, suppose that I am in a train crash in which many people are injured, including my best friend (but not myself). I am certainly generally justified in giving my first attention to my friend. But it seems also required for me to give some attention to others. Some weighting is evidently called for here. The point is that strict impartiality is not required or appropriate, but neither is ignoring the interests of others simply because the weal and woe of one's friend is at stake. (Blum, chap. 3, p. 49)

He also gives a snow storm as another example (Blum, chap. 3, p. 49).

Blum accordingly concludes by distinguishing situations of three types:

> We then have three different sorts of situations. In the first we are required to treat the interests of the relevant parties from a strictly impartial perspective, even if one of the parties is our friend. Personal attachment must be entirely overlooked (though only up to a certain point). In the second, we are required to give some attention to the interests of others, but are not required to regard those interests strictly impartially or as having equal weight to the interests of friends who are involved. In the third type of situation consideration to the interests of others is not at all appropriate or relevant. In such situations it is morally permissible to act solely for the benefit of one's friend. (Blum, chap. 3, p. 50)

The first situation would be an institutional one. This situation requires strict impartiality, for we must act on the basis of an official role. We may, however, act partially after fulfilling our impartial obligations. The third situation is that of friendship. In this situation we may apparently be as partial as we please to our friends. The second situation requires what we may call weak impartiality. We must exhibit some concern for others, but we may give more attention to our friends. What criterion we might use for dividing our attention Blum does not say (Blum, chap. 3, p. 49).

Aristotle would agree with Blum that conflicts arise between our obligations to different persons and that these conflict arise because we have different relationships with these persons. He might even accept Blum's division of conflicts into their types. But Aristotle would argue that we need not characterize these relationships as moral relationships and friendships; nor need we characterize them as entailing impartial obligations and partial ones. For all these relationships are moral ones and they are all friendships. Our obligations in different relationships differ because our friendships differ, for they concern different other selves.

Perhaps I might best present Aristotle's point of view by considering what Blum calls the basis of impartiality. He quotes Sidgwick to define what justice is:

> Here the definition given by Sidgwick seems to me close to the mark:
>
> > What then do we mean by a just man in matters where law-observance does not enter? It is natural to reply that we mean an impartial man, one who seeks with equal care to satisfy all claims which he recognizes as valid and does not let himself be unduly influenced by personal preferences. (Blum, chap. 3, p. 52)

Blum generalizes this definition to include matters of law observance as well, for he applies it to institutional contexts as well as noninstitutional ones (Blum, chap. 3, p. 52).

But what especially appeals to Blum about this definition is that it defines justice by preexistent claims and makes claims of this sort define impartial obligations (Blum, chap. 3, p. 52). Blum concludes that only preexistent claims create a demand for impartiality:

> . . . the application of impartiality depends on the pre-existence of claims on the part of persons involved (though the claim need not actually be made, or even recognized as existing, by the person who has it). It is only when someone has a certain claim on a benefit that it is a matter of impartiality to give due regard to his interest in that benefit. If he has no claim to it then such regard is no longer a matter relevant to impartiality. (Blum, chap. 3, pp. 52–53)

He also gives an example of settling a dispute between a friend and another person:

> For example, suppose I am helping to settle a dispute between two persons, one of whom is a friend. Both persons are looking to me for mediation in the quarrel. This is a circumstance where justice or impartiality is required, or appropriate. We are to overlook our personal attachment and consider only the factors relevant to the dispute. Hearing the claims made on both sides, it might turn out that I feel that the non-friend's claim has more merit, and that he is more deserving of the benefit regarding which there is a dispute. (Blum, chap. 3, p. 52)

This example explicitly rests both justice and impartiality on preexistent claims.

Aristotle would agree that justice is impartial, but he could not agree that justice completely distinguishes other moral relationships from friendships. He would argue that justice is a mark of good friendship. Justice is, in fact, a mark of good friendship of every kind, for it is to do what is good for the sake of another, and to act in this way is the first mark of friendship (see chap. 6, pp. 97–98, 98–104).

Aristotle would also argue that all friends make what Blum calls preexistent claims on us, for we can define our obligations to our friends only by means of the principle of happiness shared with them. Our friends differ only because we share different principles of happiness with them (see again chap. 1, pp. 6–13; chap. 2, pp. 28–30). But these principles define their needs for us; they tell us what activities they value as ends and what virtues are the means to these ends (see chap. 6, pp. 109–110).

So, I conclude that Blum presents some arguments that are very helpful for us. His arguments allow us to supplement our analysis of Aristotelian friendship with some contemporary conceptions about friendship. As a result, we can see that Aristotelian friendship is at once partial and impartial as well as personal and impersonal.

JOHN RAWLS

This appendix examines a contemporary philosophical theory concerned with justice and society. John Rawls, of course, explicitly states very little about political friendship, but what he says about a just society and about friendship indicates that he espouses a theory of political society significantly different from Aristotle's theory of political friendship. Our interest in him stems from the fact that Rawls might seem to develop a political theory quite similar to Aristotle's theory, for he seems to develop an altruistic conception of society, though he actually advances an egoistic one. And because it seems to be altruistic, Rawls's conception of society especially allows us to see how Aristotle's conception of political friendship differs from some contemporary political thought. We shall see as well how Rawls's conception could adversely influence an interpretation of Aristotle.

Without going into great detail, we might first recall how Rawls establishes his political principles and what they are. We shall then be able to see the implications of his political theory for his conception of friendship. To establish his principles, Rawls, of course, has recourse to what he calls the original position. The original position is a hypothetical situation designed to express what he believes to be conditions reasonable to impose on agents who are to choose principles of justice (Rawls, sec. 20, pp. 120–22).[1] In this situation, the agents act under two circumstances that occasion disputes about justice. The one circumstance is that the agents are mutually disinterested. They have an interest in their own plan of life, yet they take no interest in the plans of others. The other circumstance is that the agents act under a condition of moderate scarcity. They find the resources available to them to be neither so abundant nor so rare that cooperation becomes infeasible (Rawls, sec. 22, pp. 126–28).

Rawls also assumes that the agents are rational. They know that they have a plan of life, but they do not know what it is. They consequently choose to advance their plan by preferring more of what he refers to as primary goods rather than less (Rawls, sec. 24, pp. 142–43). Their rationality is merely that of social and economic theory (p. 143, p. 143 n. 14). Their primary goods are goods that, he asserts, anyone would want to have in order to carry out whatever ends one might have. They include rights and liberties, opportunities and powers, and income and wealth (Rawls, sec. 15, p. 92). The agents also act behind a veil of ignorance. This veil allows them to have general knowledge about human society but not to have knowledge about certain particulars. They especially do not know how their choice of principles will affect themselves (Rawls, sec. 24, pp. 136–37).

The agents in the original position follow the maximin rule of choosing their principles of justice. This rule is a decision rule for situations of uncertainty. It requires that the agents rank possible alternatives by their worst outcomes and choose the alternative with the worst outcome that would be best. The agents choose an alternative that would allow them to be satisfied with their positions in society and with the primary goods allotted to their positions, even if an enemy were to assign their positions to them (Rawls, sec. 26, pp. 152–54).

These agents choose two principles of justice for themselves—the principle of equal liberty and the difference principle. The principle of equal liberty asserts that every person is to have an equal right to the most extensive liberty compatible with a similar liberty for all. This principle applies to the distribution civic liberties, such as the freedom to vote and to hold office as well as the freedom of speech and assembly (Rawls, sec. 11, pp. 60–61). The difference principle states that social and economic inequalities are to be arranged to everyone's advantage and attached to offices open to all. This principle applies to the distribution of power and opportunity and of income and wealth (pp. 60–61). That the distribution works to the advantage of everyone means that higher expectations for those better off must improve expectations for those worse off (Rawls, sec. 13, pp. 75–78).

We can see already that Aristotle would regard the agents in the original position as essentially egoistic. He would probably argue that political friends who are altruistic would choose a principle of happiness for others for their sake, because he implies that an altruistic political friend does what is good for others for their sake (see chap. 5, pp. 76–78; chap. 3, pp. 37–83, 39). He would also argue that political friends who are egoistic would choose a principle for others for their own sake, for an egoistic political friend does what is good for others for his own sake (see chap. 5, pp. 78–83, 85–87; chap. 3, pp. 37–39). But the agents in the original position clearly choose their principles of justice for the sake of themselves. They do not choose the principle of liberty and the difference principle so that others will find themselves in positions satisfactorily equipped with primary goods; instead, they choose these two principles so that they will not end up in positions that are unsatisfactory to themselves.

Aristotle might even characterize these agents as egoistic in a pejorative sense. He argues that those who love themselves in a praiseworthy sense exhibit a rationality that grasps a conception of happiness and that they use their rationality to care for their virtue and its activity (see chap. 7, pp. 118–19). More importantly, their pursuit of happiness puts a limit on their desire for other goods. But those who love themselves in a blameworthy sense pursue material gain or mere pleasure, and they try to secure more external goods rather than fewer (pp. 119–20).

Aristotle would thus find that the agents in the original position do not love themselves in a laudatory sense. At least, they do not act as people who love themselves in this way would act. Though they have a conception of happiness, they do not use their conception correctly when they choose their principles. If they did, they would not always prefer to have more rather than fewer material goods.

From Aristotle's point of view the assumption that the agents act behind a veil of ignorance has a flaw. Rawls assumes that, because they do not know what plan of life they have, the agents in the original position have a rationality not of goodness but of utility or pleasure and that they accordingly try only to obtain more rather than less liberty, power, income, and wealth. But the agents ought to know that if they have a conception of happiness, they would not always want more and more external goods. To be happy, they would need only sufficient goods to act in accordance with virtue.

Rawls himself, of course, denies that his theory is an egoistic one. He argues that though they do not do so in the original position, the agents in his hypothetical society do take into account the interests of other agents after they choose their principles. Indeed, he argues that the principles chosen require them to do so (for example, see Rawls, sec. 25, pp. 147–48). Rawls might even seem to claim that the agents in the original position become altruistic, for he maintains that his hypothetical agents find a common interest in their social institutions and activities. And a common interest of this sort seems to allow them to take an interest in the activity of others for their sake. He also argues that these agents wish others to have and to exercise moral virtues. They thus seem to wish others to be happy for their sake, too.

To show that the agents change their attitude about others, Rawls distinguishes what he calls the thin theory of goodness from what he calls the full theory. The thin theory is no more than the assumptions made about those who decide on the principles of justice in the original position:

> But to establish these principles it is necessary to rely on some notion of goodness, for we need assumptions about the parties' motives in the original position. Since these assumptions must not jeopardize the prior place of the conception of right, the theory of the good used in arguing for the principles of justice is restricted to the bare essentials. This account of the good I call the thin theory: its purpose is to secure the premises about primary goods required to arrive at the principles of justice. (Rawls, sec. 60, pp. 395–96)

We have already seen that this theory of the good explains how the agents try to secure equal liberty and more rather than less of other primary goods (but see also Rawls, sec. 60, p. 397).

The full theory adds to the thin theory other moral conceptions, such as that of moral virtue:

> The characteristic feature of this full theory, as I have said, is that it takes the principles of justice as already secured, and then uses these principles in defining the other moral concepts in which the notion of goodness is involved. Once the principles of right are on hand, we may appeal to them in explaining the concept of moral worth and the good of the moral virtues. (Rawls, sec. 60, pp. 397–98)

The full theory seems to be what we usually think of as a moral theory. This theory even seems to contain a conception of happiness, for it contains a conception of moral virtue and its goodness.

The problem of using the thin theory to establish the full theory Rawls terms the congruence problem. He wishes to solve this problem by using the principles of justice established in the original position to account for the goodness of social institutions in themselves as well as for the goodness of moral virtue, especially justice (Rawls, sec. 60, pp. 398–99).

But we might well harbor a doubt about the success of Rawls's attempt to solve the congruence problem. To show that they are not egoistic, one must do more than show that the agents take into account the interests of others, for those who are egoistic do take the interests of others into account. They do so, however, not for the sake of others but only for their own sake (see chap. 5, pp. 85–87; chap. 3, pp. 37–39). But we saw that the agents in the original position choose the principles of justice for their own sake. Would they not also apply these principles for their own sake? And so we might wonder whether the agents consider the interests of others for the sake of others or for the sake of themselves.

When he discusses the good of their social institutions, Rawls especially seems to show that the agents of his hypothetical society are altruistic. He argues that the citizens of a well-ordered society value their common institutions and activities as ends, and that they also value the activities of other citizens as ends. To show that they do, he even appeals to the principles of justice indirectly through what he dubs the Aristotelian principle.

Rawls asserts that the citizens of his society have final ends that they share, and he implies that these ends include common institutions and activities:

> Thus human beings have in fact shared final ends and they value their common institutions and activities as good in themselves. We need one another as partners in ways of life that are engaged in for their own sake, and the successes and enjoyments of others are necessary for and compl[e]mentary to our own good. (Rawls, sec. 79, pp. 522–23)

When he describes their cooperation, he seems to imply that those who act for the sake of a common end also act for the sake of one another:

> Different persons with similar or complementary capacities may cooperate so to speak in realizing their common or matching nature. When men are secure in the enjoyment of the exercise of their own powers, they are disposed to appreciate the perfections of others, especially when their several excellences have an agreed place in a form of life the aims of which all accept. (Rawls, sec. 79, pp. 522–23)

He thus suggests that people find happiness in a common end, and also that they appreciate the happiness of others who share their common end.

Following von Humboldt, Rawls calls this shared common end a social union (Rawls, sec. 79, pp. 523–25). He compares a social union to a baseball game and points out that, among other ends, the game has a shared end:

> This shared end can be realized only if the game is played fairly according to the rules, if the sides are more or less evenly matched, and if the players all sense that they are playing well. But when this aim is attained, everyone takes pleasure and satisfaction in the very same thing. A good play of the game is, so to speak, a collective achievement requiring the cooperation of all. (Rawls, sec. 79, pp. 525–26)

He also explains that a shared end is a scheme of conduct in which each person can take pleasure in the actions of others as they jointly carry out their plan:

> There must be an agreed scheme of conduct in which the excellences and enjoyments of each are complementary to the good of all. Each can then take pleasure in the actions of the others as they jointly execute a plan acceptable to everyone. (Rawls, sec. 79, p. 526)

Because they take pleasure in the activities of others, each person seems to take an interest in his own activities and in those of others as well.

Rawls continues to argue that a social union includes what he calls a well-ordered society:

> The main idea is simply that a well-ordered society (corresponding to justice as fairness) is itself a form of social union. Indeed, it is a social union of social unions. (Rawls, sec. 79, p. 527)

He explains that a well-ordered society has the chief characteristics of a social union:

> Both characteristic features are present: the successful carrying out of just institutions is the shared final end of all the members of society, and these institutional forms are prized as good in themselves. (Rawls, sec. 79, p. 527)

That is, a well-ordered society is itself a shared final end and is itself valued as an end.

He uses an analogy to explain the first feature further. He appears to imply again that the members of a well-ordered society take an interest in one another for the sake of the other:

> In much the same way that players have the shared end to execute a good and fair play of the game, so the members of a well-ordered society have the common aim of cooperating together to realize their own and another's nature in ways allowed by the principles of justice. (Rawls, sec. 79, p. 527)

Through cooperation, they seem to develop their own capacities and the capacities of others. Rawls adds that each wants not only himself but also others to have the virtue of justice:

> This collective intention is the consequence of everyone's having an effective sense of justice. Each citizen wants everyone (including himself) to act from principles to which all would agree in an initial situation of equality. (Rawls, sec. 79, p. 527)

Each person would again seem to care for others as well as for himself.

Rawls thus argues that the people in a well-ordered society take an interest in their common institutions and in other people. But do they take this interest in their institutions and in others for the sake of others or for the sake of themselves? Rawls presents three considerations to prove that the people in a well-ordered society will regard it as a social union. But these considerations each show that they take an interest in others for the sake of themselves.

The consideration most relevant for our purpose rests on Rawls's Aristotelian principle. This principle asserts that we enjoy the realizations of our capacities and that we enjoy these realizations more when they are more complex (Rawls, sec. 65, pp. 426–27, p. 426 n. 20). The principle also has a companion effect. This effect is that we enjoy the exercise of the abilities of others and desire to do the same as they do (pp. 427–28).

When he applies the Aristotelian principle, Rawls argues that because it is a social union, a well-ordered society allows us to develop better our own capacities:

> Because such a society is a social union of social unions, it realizes to a preeminent degree the various forms of human activ-

ity; and given the social nature of human kind, the fact that our potentialities and inclinations far surpass what can be expressed in any one life, we depend upon the cooperative endeavors of others not only for the means of well-being but to bring to fruition our latent powers. (Rawls, sec. 86, p. 571–72)

The Aristotelian principle also allows us to take pleasure in the greater complexity of this new realization of our powers:

And with a certain success all around, each enjoys the greater richness and diversity of the collective activity. (Rawls, sec. 86, pp. 571–72)

More important for us is the fact that we thus realize not merely social goods but individual goods of others:

What binds a society's efforts into one social union is the mutual recognition and acceptance of the principles of justice; it is this general affirmation which extends the ties of identification over the whole community and permits the Aristotelian Principle to have its wider effect. Individual and group accomplishments are no longer seen as just so many separate personal goods. (Rawls, sec. 86, pp. 571–72)

If we identify with our common activity, we also appear to identify with others and their individual activities.

Rawls thus seems to use his Aristotelian principle to argue that citizens in a well-ordered society are altruistic. This principle suggests that a social union allows individuals to develop a capacity for a new activity, and this new activity is a common end that they value for its sake. The principle also suggests that they enjoy the richness of their shared end and the richness of the activities performed by others who share their end. And so they seem to value the activities of others for their sake, too.

But Aristotle would probably not agree that these citizens are altruistic. He could admit that citizens of a society can participate in a social union for the sake of others; but he would maintain that citizens in Rawls's society enter a social union for their own sake. Aristotle does not explicitly argue that a political ruler might act for his own sake when he acts for the sake of his own rule, but he does imply that we engage in egoistic personal friendship when we engage in a friendship for the sake of friendship itself. We act merely for the sake of our own happiness (see chap. 3, pp. 49–51). What Rawls argues, in effect, is that citizens in a well-ordered society act for the sake of their social relationship itself; they participate in a social union for its own sake. Because they do, these citizens enjoy a political relationship for its own sake. They thus promote their own happiness, for they act for the sake of their own activity.

Aristotle would argue, too, that citizens in Rawls's society benefit themselves in other ways. Rawls's citizens engage in a social union so that they can develop their capacities for new activities through cooperation with others and so that they can enhance their enjoyment of these new cooperative activities. Aristotle would agree that we can increase our activities and their enjoyment by acting together with others; we can better engage in both theoretical and practical activities with others (see chap. 4, pp. 69–71). However, if we engage in activities with others so that we might increase our activities and enjoyment, we engage in what is an egoistic friendship because we value the activities of others for our own sake.

We thus see that Rawls's citizens participate in their social union with an egoistic motive. But perhaps these citizens have an altruistic motive for wanting others to have moral virtue. Rawls does try to show that his citizens want others to have moral virtues and their goods. To do this, he argues that they want others to have properties that he refers to as broadly based. Properties of this sort are desirable with respect to almost any role (Rawls, sec. 66, p. 435). He argues that we prefer people to have virtues because these virtues are broadly based:

> I note straightway that the fundamental moral virtues, that is, the strong and normally effective desires to act on the basic principles of right, are undoubtedly among the broadly based properties. (Rawls, sec. 66, pp. 435–36)

He also argues that we especially want moral qualities to accompany other qualities, such as intelligence and imagination or strength and endurance (pp. 436–37).

However, Rawls immediately places a condition on his argument. Its conclusion holds true only in a society that is just or nearly just:

> At any rate, this seems bound to be true so long as we suppose that we are considering a well-ordered society, or one in a state of near justice, as I shall indeed take to be the case. Now since the basic structure of such a society is just, and these arrange-

ments are stable with respect to the society's public conception of justice, its members will in general have the appropriate sense of justice and a desire to see their institutions affirmed. (Rawls, sec. 66, pp. 435–36)

When he refers to a well-ordered society, he of course refers to a social union (see again Rawls, sec. 75, p. 527).

Rawls places his argument under this condition in an attempt to forestall an objection. He recognizes that other philosophers argue that one cannot use a conception of instrumental rationality to derive moral qualities (Rawls, sec. 66, pp. 434–35). But he claims that he can make a derivation of this sort through the original position:

The reason why the so-called instrumental or economic theory fails is that what is in effect the thin theory is applied directly to the problem of moral worth. What we must do instead is to use this theory only as a part of the description of the original position from which the principles of right and justice are derived. We can then apply the full theory of the good without restriction and are free to use it for the two basic cases of a good person and a good society. Developing the thin into the full theory via the original position is the essential step. (Rawls, sec. 66, pp. 434–35)

That is, his answer to the objection is merely to apply rationality of this sort not directly but indirectly.

Because of this condition, Rawls's attempt to use instrumental rationality to establish morality shows again that his theory is egoistic. We saw that the people in the original position choose their principles of justice not for the sake of others but for the sake of themselves. If they use these principles to establish virtue, they would also choose moral virtue for others not for their sake but for their own sake.

Rawls, in fact, points out that people in society act on principles of justice only if other people do the same:

But it is also true that it is rational for each person to act on the principles of justice only on the assumption that for the most part these principles are recognized and similarly acted upon by others. Therefore the representative member of a well-ordered society will find that he wants others to have the basic virtues, and in particular a sense of justice. (Rawls, sec. 66, pp. 435–36)

Each person thus appears to act egoistically, for each apparently acts justly with the expectation that others will reciprocate.

If we examine how he explains our acquisition of a sense of justice, we find that Rawls indeed argues explicitly that we act justly only because we are treated justly by others. He distinguishes three psychological laws of moral development in a well-ordered society. The first law concerns the stage of moral development occurring within a family:

> First Law: given that family institutions are just, and that the parents love the child and manifestly express their love by caring for his good, then the child, recognizing their evident love of him, comes to love them. (Rawls, sec. 75, p. 490)

Rawls explains that a child initially has a self-interest that is rational, but restricted to certain desires and instincts, and that his love is a new desire brought about by benefiting from the actions of his parents (Rawls, sec. 70, pp. 463–64).

But this first law suggests that a child loves his parents in an egoistic manner, for he loves them only for the sake of the benefits received from them. His love arises from connecting his parents with his success in sustaining his world and with his sense of worth (Rawls, sec. 70, p. 464).

Rawls does deny that we can use instrumental rationality to explain why a child loves its parents. He explicitly states that a child does not love his parents as a means to his initial self-interested ends (Rawls, sec. 70, pp. 463–64). But he rules out only instrumental rationality in a rather narrow sense, for he explains that instrumental rationality would entail that a child act as if he loved his parents (pp. 463–64). That is, he thinks of rationality of this sort as deceptive. But we can feel affection for another as a means to an end without being deceptive.

Rawls's second law of moral psychology concerns development within an association larger than a family but smaller than a society:

> Second Law: given that a person's capacity for fellow feeling has been realized by acquiring attachments in accordance with the first law, and given that a social arrangement is just and publicly known by all to be just, then this person develops ties of friendly feeling and trust toward others in the association as they with evident intention comply with their duties and obligations, and live up to the ideals of their station. (Rawls, sec. 75, p. 490)

The statement of his law explicitly mentions friendly feeling, though it does not state very clearly why this feeling arises. Does a person develop friendly feeling for others because their compliance with their obligations benefits him or not?

When he explains how the second law takes effect, Rawls argues that people in an association find other people in it to be of benefit to themselves. He assumes that the association is just and that its justice assures that each member benefits from it:

> Since the arrangements of an association are recognized to be just (and in the more complex roles the principles of justice are understood and serve to define the ideal appropriate), thereby insuring that all of its members benefit and know that they benefit from its activities, the conduct of others in doing their part is taken to be to the advantage of each. (Rawls, sec. 71, pp. 471–72)

He thus acknowledges that people choose the principle of liberty and the difference principle for the sake of themselves.

Rawls also adds that good will is the intention to honor an obligation and that the recognition of good will in turn arouses feelings of friendship (Rawls, sec. 71, pp. 471–72). But, again, friendly feeling of this sort is not altruistic but egoistic. Only because others honor their obligations do people have friendly feeling.

Finally, Rawls's third law of moral development concerns a society itself:

> Third law: given that a person's capacity for fellow feeling has been realized by his forming attachments in accordance with the first two laws, and given that a society's institutions are just and are publicly known by all to be just, then this person acquires the corresponding sense of justice as he recognizes that he and those for whom he cares are the beneficiaries of these arrangements. (Rawls, sec. 75, p. 491)

The statement of this law is explicitly self-interested. Rawls makes the very same statement when he explains how this law takes effect (Rawls, sec. 72, pp. 473–74).

Rawls also makes some observations about these psychological laws. One observation is noteworthy because it explicitly mentions both justice and friendship. He asserts that these laws are not principles of reinforced learning but rather principles of active affection:

> While they have a certain resemblance to these learning principles, they assert that the active sentiments of love and friendship, and even the sense of justice, arise from the manifest intention of other persons to act for our good. Because we recognize that they wish us well, we care for their well-being in return. Thus we acquire attachments to persons and institutions according to how we perceive our good to be affected by them. (Rawls, sec. 75, pp. 494–95)

Aristotle himself might have made this statement to show how political friendship is egoistic. Rawls states explicitly that we are friends with others in society because of their intention to act for our benefit and that we care for them only because they care for us.

We see then that Rawls seems to advance an altruistic theory of political society, for he rests his conception of a political society on his conception of social union, and a social union seems to exist for the sake of itself and for the sake of others. However, we also see that his theory is, in fact, an egoistic one. The citizens in his society do enter a cooperative scheme for its own sake, and they value the cooperative activity of others for its sake; but, by doing so, they act for the sake of their own happiness, for they develop their capacity to engage in new activities through cooperation with others. They also wish others to have and to exercise moral virtue; but, again, they do so for the sake of themselves, for they expect to benefit from the virtues of others.

I can now show how one might be tempted to use Rawls's theory of society to interpret Aristotle's conception of political friendship. There are two obvious ways in which one might try to do so. We could accept Rawls's justification of a social union through the original position and his account of moral virtue and its activity. We would then argue, in effect, that people who are in a social union act egoistically. We might even declare explicitly that moral qualities are in fact useful and pleasant qualities. We could also argue that Aristotelian political friends enter a cooperative scheme for its own sake. We would explain that they enter a scheme of this sort to develop their potential for action and to increase their pleasure in action. But we would add that political friends also develop useful and pleasant qualities in others for their own sake, for they expect to receive advantages and pleasures from those who have these qualities. If they do not, they cease to participate in the scheme.[2]

Alternatively, we could reject Rawls's use of the original position to justify a social union and to account for moral virtue. But we could nonetheless accept his conception of a social union and the role of moral virtue within it. We would then attempt to argue that people who are in a social union do act altruistically and that Aristotelian political friends participate in a cooperative scheme which has value for its own sake. We would explain that through a scheme of this kind political friends develop their potential for action and increase their pleasure in action and that they also develop the potential of others for action and increase their pleasure in action. But we would deny that political friends want others to have moral qualities for their own sake. We could explain that they do not expect to receive any advantages or pleasures from others but that they promote and appreciate the goodness of others as in part their own.[3]

Unfortunately, whichever option we prefer for an interpretation, we risk transforming Aristotelian political friendship from an altruistic relationship into an egoistic one. We cannot use the conception of a social union by itself to argue that a political relationship is altruistic. Whether or not a social union is altruistic depends on those who enter it and on their intentions. Nor can we use by itself the conception of doing what is good for another to show that a political friendship is altruistic. Again, only our intentions determine whether a relationship is altruistic or not.

When we participate in a social union for the sake of our participation itself, we enjoy our activity of political friendship for its own sake, for our intention is to pursue our own happiness. Whether we conceive of our scheme as altruistic or egoistic, we act for the sake of our own virtuous activity. We may enter a political friendship to develop moral virtue in others and to increase their happiness. But if we do so only to make their happiness part of our own, we intend to promote our own happiness. And if we argue that a cooperative scheme promotes the useful and pleasant qualities in others, we most likely act for the sake of what we receive from others.

I would once again argue that Aristotelian political friends intend to do what is good for others for their sake. Political friends of this kind enter a political relationship for the sake of the happiness of others, and they also promote moral virtue in others for the sake of the happiness of others. For their pains, Aristotelian friends receive only the adventitious pleasure of apperceiving that others are happy.

Of course, I do not deny that Aristotelian political friends can promote the happiness of others by participating in a cooperative scheme. But friends of this sort participate in a cooperative scheme for the sake of the good qualities of others and their activities. They have the intention of advancing the happiness of others, and they do not view the happiness of others as their own. But I also argue that Aristotelian friends need not cooperate with others. Political friends of this sort need only exchange favors with one another for the sake of each other. Nor do I deny that Aristotelian friends have good qualities that are also useful and pleasant to others. But I would argue that only because these qualities are useful and pleasant to each other can friends of this kind exchange favors for the sake of one another.

NOTES

CHAPTER 1. INTRODUCTION

1. Ross probably presents the most egregious example of this attitude. He speculates that we find the two books on friendship included in the *Ethics* only because of faulty editing (Ross, intro., pp. xx–xxi; also see Urmson, intro., pp. 6–7; ch. 9, pp. 109–10).

2. Cooper attempts to argue that not only good friends but also useful and pleasant friends do what is good for the sake of the qualities of one another (Cooper, "Forms," pp. 631–32).

3. Adkins argues that good friends as well as useful and pleasant friends act for the sake of their own good or pleasure (Adkins, pp. 39, 42–43).

4. Burnet offers this explanation for good friendship (Burnet, p. 430; but also see Grant, vol. 2, 301; and Robin, pt. 6, pp. 242–43).

5. For example, Hardie presents an argument of this sort (Hardie, ch. 15, pp. 327–29). But others also offer similar explanations (see, e.g., Irwin, *Principles,* ch. 18, p. 393; Kahn, pp. 22–25; or Annas, "Self-Love," pp. 6–12).

6. Cooper argues that political friends act for the sake of one another as fellow citizens (Cooper, "Forms," pp. 645–48; Cooper, "Animals," pp. 232–36). Adkins suggests that friends in their political relationships act rather for their own sake (Adkins, p. 43).

7. Those who discuss a motivation for political friendship seem to be in agreement. Cooper, Price, and Irwin all argue that political friends

do what is good for the sake of one another (Cooper, "Animals," p. 238, but also see pp. 237–38; Price, ch. 7, pp. 196–97; Irwin, *Principles,* ch. 18, p. 399; Irwin, "Good," pp. 94–95). And yet they explain that political friends so extend their happiness as to include the happiness of each other (Cooper, "Animals," p. 238; Price, ch. 7, pp. 203–4; Irwin, *Principles,* ch. 18, p. 399; Irwin, "Good," pp. 94–95). Their explanation would thus appear to be suspect, for they apparently eliminate any genuine political friendship. They all argue that we act essentially for the sake of our own happiness when we act for the sake of the happiness of others. For on their account our happiness includes that of others (Cooper, "Animals," p. 238; Price, ch. 7, pp. 196–97 or 203–4; Irwin, *Principles,* ch. 18, pp. 400–2; Irwin, "Good," pp. 94–95).

8. Newman presents this argument (Newman, vol. 2, pp. 392–93).

9. This argument Stewart presents (Stewart, vol. 2, pp. 262–64).

10. Some scholars do concern themselves with human goodness and its attainability in personal friendship. Without much difficulty we might extrapolate their concern to political friendship. For example, Cooper observes that good friendship would seem to occur only among those who are perfectly virtuous and thus that friendship of this sort could not occur among people of ordinary virtue (Cooper, "Forms," pp. 624, 625–26).

11. Some philosophers apply Aristotle's principle in a limited manner. Irwin attempts to use his principle to define what another self is and to examine what the end of good friendship is (Irwin, *Principles,* ch. 18, pp. 395–97). Yet he does not attempt to distinguish other selves of different kinds, nor does he distinguish good friendships of different kinds.

Some philosophers also use Aristotle's principle to define the character of a good friend or to examine the end of good friendship (e.g., see Price, ch. 4, pp. 105–6, also see pp. 106–8). But they do not use his principle to define what another self is or to distinguish among other selves or good friendships.

12. For example, see Grant, Stewart, or Burnet.

13. Adkins or Cooper, for example.

14. Urmson reflects this language usage. He asserts that friendship is a social relationship that falls short of citizenship (Urmson, ch. 9, p. 109).

He feels that family relationships as well are not naturally called friendships (p. 111).

Cooper expresses some concern about φιλία and its breadth of meaning, but he does not attempt to make a survey of Aristotelian friendships (Cooper, "Forms," pp. 620–21). Stewart, too, is concerned. He briefly outlines what he calls Aristotle's natural history of friendship (Stewart, vol. 2, pp. 262–64).

15. The translations are my revisions of the Oxford translation.

16. Newman worries about Aristotle's distinction between friendships in accordance with nature and those in accordance with convention. That political friendship exists by convention is especially worrisome to him because Aristotle asserts at the beginning of the *Politics* that a city is based on nature (Newman, vol. 2, app. A, pp. 394–95). But Aristotle does not deny that what exists by convention can also have a natural basis. A city, of course, ought to have a constitution and laws in accordance with human nature (see, e.g., *Pol.* 1.7.1323a14–21).

17. Kahn also recognizes that Aristotle introduces his conception of another self when he discusses parenthood, but he argues that the identity of kinship is not an identity of qualities shared but an identity of birth. Though their likeness contributes to their feelings, brothers, for example, feel an affection for each other derived from their common birth. He even suggests that Aristotle ought to take into account birth and kinship as a basis for friendship (Kahn, pp. 21–22, p. 22 n. 1). But Aristotle argues, rather, that family members feel affection for one another because they resemble each other so closely. This fact explains why brotherhood resembles comradeship (see again *Eth.* 8.12.1161b33–1162a1, 1162a9–14). He would not deny, of course, that those who are kin resemble each other because of their birth and kinship. Their natural identity obviously stems from their common birth.

Irwin argues correctly that a child and its parents are other selves because of their family connections and that the parents are concerned with the welfare of their child. He also observes that a child and its parents need not be virtuous. But he explains that a child is another self because it is dependent on its parents, and its character is developed by them and expresses their aims (Irwin, *Principles,* ch. 18, p. 398; Irwin, "Good," p. 93). Irwin thus appears to recognize that a child shares a biological identity with its parents. But he does not give sufficient weight to the fact that only after it becomes independent can a child and its parents share a moral identity as well as an intellectual one.

Irwin continues to argue that a child is another self to its parents because it is scarcely separate from them. Its parents view their thought and deliberation as closely related to its acts. But he does concede that a child is less another self because it does not freely and rationally accept its aims and goals (Irwin, *Principles,* ch. 18 n. 11). I would argue that a child is primarily a biological other self to its parents when it is immature, and that a child is primarily a moral and intellectual other self when it fully matures. That is, when it freely and rationally develops mental and moral virtues of its own. Only then does it exhibit a separate, yet similar, character.

Millgram agrees that parents and children are other selves. He argues that because of procreation parents and their children have the same being. He also appears to argue that parents love their children primarily because they procreate their children and not because their children are similar to them (Millgram, pp. 366–68). But we can see that procreation is not the primary factor. Millgram fails to explain why brothers love each other, for they obviously do not procreate one another. Brothers, however, are usually very similar to one another. Millgram also limits his discussion of kinship to natural identity.

Price apparently agrees with our analysis of childhood and parenthood. He argues that a child is a copy of its parents and implies that a child is both a biological and a moral copy (Price, ch. 6, pp. 164–65). He appears to overlook the fact that a child may be an intellectual copy as well. Citing *Metaphysics* 7.8.1033b29–32, Price also argues that a child shares with its parents a formal identity and not a numerical one. He recognizes too that brothers have a biological and a moral identity based on their family ties (pp. 165–66). Yet he does not generalize this conception of another self and apply the conception to friendships of other kinds.

Stewart partially agrees with our analysis. He asserts that other selves are different and separate individuals, and that they are yet the same. He implies that other selves have a natural identity because they are born of the same parents. But he does not consider the possibility that other selves might also have a cultural identity (Stewart, vol. 2, pp. 321–22).

Fraisse argues that Aristotle uses the family to serve as a model to show how friendship accommodates itself to natural differences (Fraisse, pt. 2, pp. 205–6). A family has an egalitarian friendship as its principle, for beyond their differences, family members also have a more intimate relationship that rests on a sense of their humanity. That is, their friendship rests on an essential identity behind their accidental differences (pp. 206–7). I would agree that a family does rest on an essential identity of its members, but I would also argue that their identity is not their humanity but rather their more specific similarities of character. The identity shared by parents and children, for example, is their natural and cultural characteristics. Fraisse does note that the friendship of parents and children is intensified and rendered more agreeable because they share the same life (Fraisse, pt. 2, pp. 207–8).

18. Newman wishes to argue that friendship has the end of living together and a city the end of living well and that friendship advances the end of living together as a means to the end of living well (Newman, vol. 3, pp. 208–9). But we shall see that friendship includes not only the end of living together but also the end of living well as well as that of merely living. At least good friendship does. Friendship of this kind has five marks, and three marks are wishes and actions for the sake of living together, living well, and living (see *Eth.* 9.4.1166a2–9). Indeed, we shall see that good friendship is wishing and doing what is good for the sake of another (see *Eth.* 8.2.1156a3–5).

Irwin agrees that Newman contrasts the end of friendship with that of a city (Irwin, *Principles,* ch. 18 n. 22; Irwin, "Good," p. 86 n. 14). Irwin himself asserts that friendship helps identify the end of a city (*Principles,* ch. 18 n. 22). It apparently exemplifies the end of living together ("Good," p. 86 n. 15). But Irwin also contends that Aristotle contrasts two forms of living together. He implies that members of small communities do not aim at living well in their own relationships and that those who live in a city do have this aim. For he argues that because they aim at happiness, those who live together in smaller communities also aim at living together in a city (*Principles,* ch. 18, pp. 402–3; also "Good," pp. 86–87). But those who are friends in smaller communities do aim at living well in their own relationships. Clearly good friends exhibit this mark of friendship (see again *Eth.* 9.4.1166a2–3).

Cooper agrees that Aristotle in this passage indicates the source and the nature of a specific bond between citizens. He explains that lesser associations give rise to the friendship specific to civic life and its activity. As personal friends take an interest in the character of one another, so civic friends also take an interest in the character of other citizens (Cooper, "Animals," pp. 232–34). I agree with Cooper's analogy. But Cooper, of course, might better say that friends wish one another to be not merely virtuous but also happy.

Annas agrees with Newman that friendship, which has the end of living together, is a means toward a city, which has the aim of a good life (Annas, "Comments," pp. 242, 246). Yet she implies that a city has the end of living together as well. She argues that people become personal friends with one another because they participate in the same political activities (pp. 246–48). Aristotle would, of course, argue that living together with others is doing something together with them, such as participating in politics (see, e.g., *Eth.* 9.12.1172a1–8). Annas herself recognizes that to live together means to share in activities (Annas, "Comments," pp. 243–44). So I would argue that we become political friends when we share a political life together. I would not deny that we may become personal friends too, but only if we share a personal life as well.

Couloubaritsis argues that friendship does not include families or cities. He asserts that families and cities result from the choice to live together, and he implies that this choice occurs without any emotion (Couloubaritsis, "Rôle," pp. 176–77). But the fact that they choose to live together does not prove that fellow citizens and family members do not feel affection for one another, and, again, one mark of friendship is to wish to live together (*Eth.* 9.4.1166a6–8, also 1166a23–24).

19. Political philosophers do, of course, recognize that Aristotle's conceptions of the family, the village, and the city and of their development depend on his conception of human nature and culture. But they fail to recognize that his conception of these relationships and their development depends in turn on his conception of another self. Barker does not, for example, (Barker, ch. 6, pp. 264–68). Yet Barker asserts that fellow citizens are other selves to one another. He argues that a city rests on a common good which is the same for each citizen and that each citizen regards another exactly as if he were himself (Barker, ch. 5, pp. 235–37).

Though he quotes it, Irwin appears to have some reservation about Barker's claim. He asserts only that Barker is right to assume some connection between political friendship and other selves (Irwin, *Principles,* ch. 18 n. 10).

CHAPTER II. HAPPINESS AND VIRTUE

1. This topic and the others that I shall discuss are of course subjects of scholarly controversies. For present purposes I do not believe that we need enter these controversies, though I shall mention one or two. I shall instead attempt to avoid detail as much as possible and to keep our discussion above the fray. Those who might wish to examine these topics in greater detail have two courses open to them. They may peruse the modern commentaries on Aristotle's *Ethics,* or they may consult contem-

porary studies of the *Ethics*. Of course, they might also consider journal articles for even closer analyses.

2. I am obliged to point out that my interpretation of practical intuition disagrees with most contemporary interpretations. Both Engberg-Pederson and Dahl present a discussion of other interpretations (Troels Engberg-Pederson, *Aristotle's Theory of Moral Insight* [Oxford: Clarendon Press, 1983], esp. ch. 7; Norman O. Dahl, *Practical Reason, Aristotle, and Weakness of the Will* [Minneapolis: University of Minnesota Press, 1984], esp. app. 1).

3. The distinction between dominant and inclusive happiness appears to originate with Hardie (Hardie, ch. 1, pp. 22–26; also see ch. 15, pp. 229–31).

4. Irwin argues that another self consists of determinate character traits associated with one piece of matter. That is, another self is a universal in a definite spatio-temporal position. We do not love rational agency by itself nor spatio-temporal uniqueness by itself; we love an agent who has developed his human capacity in the form of these human virtues (Irwin, *Principles*, ch. 18, pp. 395–96). He does not cite any textual evidence from the *Ethics* for this definition, though he does refer to its metaphysical underpinnings (Irwin, *Principles*, ch. 18 n. 8). I can agree with this metaphysical interpretation. But I would note again that Irwin neglects to distinguish friendships of different kinds in accordance with other selves of different kinds and their different activities and character traits.

Irwin also implies that a self and another self have similar character traits because they cooperate with one another. He argues that our wishes, deliberations, and decisions are ours because they are connected in a structure and that our actions are ours because they are the product of this structure. He appears to assert that we treat our friend as another self because his wishes, deliberations, and decisions taken together with ours have a similar structure and that his actions are also ours because they are products of this structure (Irwin, *Principles*, ch. 18, p. 392; Irwin, "Good," p. 91). I would argue that we need not cooperate with another for him to be another self. Without cooperation we may simply engage in similar activities and embody similar virtues. That is, we may think and act alike.

Kahn argues that other selves are identical because they share a common principle (Kahn, pp. 34–35). But he explains that the principle that other selves share is a principle of the theoretical intellect (pp. 35–37). At least, he declines to distinguish a theoretical principle from a practical one

(p. 30, and n. 1). What we and our other selves have in common is our relationship to an impersonal or superpersonal principle. Through this principle we live a life in accordance with moral and intellectual virtue (pp.
37–38). We consequently find this principle to be a principle of our common humanity and rationality; any differences between us are merely acci-
dents of individuation (pp. 38–39). But Kahn cannot use a principle so
abstract to account for friendship and its different varieties. We would have
good friendship of only one kind if we had only one principle in common
with other selves. Yet we do have different theoretical and practical principles in common with other people who have good yet different characters.
Kahn himself argues that the Greeks had little appreciation or affection for
our common humanity (Kahn, p. 20).

Irwin agrees that Kahn argues in favor of a principle shared by all
human beings, and he observes that on Kahn's view we love a feature
that all humans share, rather than a distinct individual (Irwin, *Principles,*
ch. 18 n. 9).

5. Others also use the terms "altruistic" and "egoistic" in these
senses (see, e.g., Kahn, pp. 20–21; Annas, "Friendship," pp. 537, 542–43;
or Irwin, *Principles,* ch. 18, pp. 390–91, ch. 18 n. 3).

6. On the weighing of evidence for these inferences one might consult Hirsch (E. D. Hirsch, *Validity in Interpretation* [New Haven: Yale
University Press, 1967], esp. ch. 5).

I would agree with Monan in general that Aristotle does use a reflective method of language analysis in his *Ethics* (Monan, ch. 5). But I
would argue that the *Ethics* is theoretical wisdom rather than practical wisdom. Though a practical science, the *Ethics* is nonetheless a science.

CHAPTER III. A DEFINITION OF FRIENDSHIP

1. Irwin suggests that we cannot wish wine well for its sake because
it has no desires or aims of its own. He argues that we can act for the sake
of a friend because we can help him fulfill his aims and desires (Irwin,
Ethics, p. 359). I think that we can wish wine well for the sake of its wine-
ness. Some oenophiles seem to do so with rare vintages.

2. Cooper argues that we act for the sake of the essential or accidental qualities of our friends. He explains that essential qualities are
good qualities and they are properties that a person has because he realizes his human nature. Accidental qualities are useful and pleasant quali-

ties and they are properties that a person has because he answers to the needs of another (Cooper, "Forms," pp. 634–35). I would argue that we cannot distinguish good friends from useful and pleasant friends by their essential and accidental qualities, for we may find that good qualities possessed by another are also useful and pleasant and that the useful and pleasant qualities of another are also good. People who are good do, in fact, find one another to have qualities that are at once good, useful, and pleasant (*Eth.* 8.3.1156b12–17).

Annas also argues that friends have essential or accidental qualities. She asserts that essential qualities are good qualities that belong to an individual person and that accidental qualities are useful and pleasant qualities that anyone may have (Annas, "Friendship," pp. 548–49). But we cannot distinguish essential and accidental qualities in this way, either. Good qualities may belong to anyone. Both intellectual and moral virtue are, after all, qualities that we possess because of our human nature. And, of course, only one individual may have a useful or pleasant quality, such as an idiosyncratic sense of humor.

3. Cooper believes that all friendships are altruistic. He contends that not only good friends but also useful and pleasant friends bear good wishes for the sake of their friends. Good friends bear good wishes for one another for the sake of their essential qualities, and useful and pleasant friends do so for the sake of their accidental qualities (Cooper, "Forms," pp. 631–35). He adds that good friends really love one another for the sake of the other, and useful and pleasant friends do not. For good friends recognize each other for who they actually are, and useful and pleasant friends do not (pp. 640–41). But Cooper himself eventually concedes, in effect, that useful and pleasant friends do not love the accidental qualities of one another except for the sake of their own good or pleasure, for he asserts that they dissolve their friendship if they no longer expect to receive anything from one another (Cooper, "Forms," p. 634 n. 1, pp. 635–38, p. 637 n. 14).

Price, citing the same passages, agrees that Cooper severely qualifies the good will found in useful and pleasant friendships when he states that a useful or pleasant friend must remain useful or pleasant for the friendship to continue (Price, ch. 5, pp. 150–51).

Cooper attempts to argue, nonetheless, that useful and pleasant friends do not act for the sake of some good or pleasure to be received from one another, that these friends, rather, bear good wishes for the sake of one another because of some good or pleasure already received from the other. He bases this argument on the assumption that "the most natural way" to read διά at *Eth.* 8.2.1156a3–5 and presumably at *Eth.* 8.3.1156a14–15 is not prospectively but retrospectively. That is, a person bears good wishes for another not because of any hope about what the other may be or do in the future but because of a recognition of what the other has been or done in the past (Cooper, "Forms," pp. 632–34).

Cooper, however, appears to overlook an important grammatical distinction. Aristotle uses διά with an accusative to signify an end and with a genitive to signify a means. He obviously uses it with a genitive to indicate a means at *Eth.* 8.2.1155b18–21. He asserts that the useful is δι᾽ οὗ some good or pleasure comes to be, and that goodness and pleasure are lovable ὡς τέλη. And he uses διά with an accusative at *Eth.* 8.3.1156a14–15 to indicate an end as the synonymous phrase at 1156a10–12 tells us. He says that those who love διὰ χρήσιμον love another ᾗ γίνεταί τι αὐτοῖς παρ᾽ ἀλλήλων ἀγαθόν. Unfortunately the phrase at 1156a12–14 is ambiguous. He says that those who love δι᾽ ἡδονήν love ὅτι ἡδεῖς αὐτοῖς. But at 1156a16–19 Aristotle asserts that those who love κατὰ συμβεβηκός love one another ᾗ πορίζουσιν οἳ μὲν ἀγαθόν τι οἳ δ᾽ ἡδονήν.

Price cites several passages to show that διά is interchangeable with ἕνεκα. But he concludes that διά indicates both the goal of a friendship and its ground in a friend (Price, ch. 5, pp. 151–52 and n. 27). Price, too, neglects to take into account the object of διά and its case. But in all the passages cited by him διά does take an accusative.

Irwin agrees that διά is ambiguous, but he also fails to consider the case of its object. He asserts only that the preposition may refer to either the final cause or the efficient cause, and he cites *Eth.* 8.3.1156a31 and *Eth.* 10.2.1172b21 as examples of Aristotle using it to refer to a final cause (Irwin, *Ethics,* p. 359). I would note that in both passages cited Aristotle uses διά with an accusative.

I am afraid that Cooper tries to have his friends and to turn them to good advantage, too, though he himself asserts that to do so is incoherent (Cooper, "Forms," pp. 631–32). What Cooper appears to do is to discuss mixed friendships. These friendships are partly good friendships and partly useful or pleasant ones. People in such relationships sometimes act altruistically and sometimes egoistically. Cooper himself actually describes them as acting in these ways (Cooper, "Forms," pp. 638–40). I still have to argue, however, that Cooper describes friendships that are predominately egoistic, for he states that the people in them part ways if they do not get what they want.

Price appears to agree partially. He implies that Cooper discusses mixed friendships but believes that Cooper discusses mixed friendships of the wrong kind. That Cooper believes useful and pleasant friends feel good will for the useful and pleasant qualities of another, he rightly asserts. But he himself claims, without textual evidence, that useful and pleasant friends feel good will for the human qualities of another (Price, ch. 5, pp. 158–59 and n. 36).

Citing Cooper, Kraut also argues that Aristotle discusses mixed friendships. According to Kraut, to wish and to act for others for their sake is not to benefit them as a means to another end. But he also notes that the possibility of a complex motivation is left open. That is, we can benefit another in part for his sake and in part for our sake (Kraut, *Aristotle*, ch. 2, pp. 78–79 and nn. 3, 4). Kraut thus implies that friendship is in part egoistic and in part altruistic. A son who benefits his father, for example, also gains something for himself because he performs an ethical action (pp. 84–86). But Kraut, too, describes a mixed friendship that is predominately egoistic, for he ascribes to Aristotle the view that an agent undertakes every action for the sake of his own interest, though not always for the sake of his maximal interest. A son who helps his father may forgo an opportunity to indulge in philosophical activity, but he takes advantage of an opportunity to engage in a morally virtuous activity (pp. 84–86).

4. Adkins argues that all friendships are egoistic. He contends that all friends act for the sake of their own good or pleasure. Good friends bear good wishes for the sake of essential qualities of one another in order to obtain some good or pleasure for themselves, and useful and pleasant friends bear good wishes for the sake of accidental qualities of one another in order also to obtain good or pleasure for themselves. Adkins argues that Aristotle employs a linguistic trick to suggest a false distinction between good friendship and useful and pleasant friendship. Aristotle suggests that good friendship is altruistic and that useful and pleasant friendships are egoistic when he opposes ἐκείνων ἕνεκα to κατὰ συμβεβηκός at *Eth.* 8.3.1156b7–12. For κατὰ συμβεβηκός calls to mind the earlier argument at 1156a16–19, which opposes ᾗ ἐστιν ὅσπερ ἐστὶν to ᾗ πορίζουσιν οἳ μὲν ἀγαθόν τι οἳ δ' ἡδονήν (Adkins, pp. 39, 42–43). But Aristotle's distinction—between acting for the sake of another as an end and acting for the sake of another as a means—is the same one that he used before and a true one. Aristotle in fact opposes not only ἐκείνων ἕνεκα but also διὰ with an accusative to κατὰ συμβεβηκός, for he asserts that those who wish what is good δι' αὐτοὺς do not wish what is good κατὰ συμβεβηκός at 1156b10–11.

Adkins also relies on Aristotle's argument that good friends love what is good and pleasant both absolutely and for themselves (*Eth.* 8.3.1156b12–23). He argues that a good friend bears good wishes for another for the sake of what is good and pleasant absolutely but that what is good and pleasant absolutely is what is good and presumably pleasant for himself (Adkins, p. 39 and n. 1). I have to concede that this passage is ambiguous, but to me Aristotle would appear to make his usual point that what is good and pleasant absolutely is good and pleasant relatively to good men (e.g., see *Eth.* 8.2.1155b21–26). I would argue that what is good and pleasant relatively to a good man who bears good wishes for another is also good and pleasant relatively to a good man who receives good wishes from another. Only what intention he has tells us whether a good man acts for the sake of what is good and pleasant absolutely and for himself or for the sake of what is good and pleasant absolutely and for his friend.

Adkins does cite *Eth.* 1.1.1155a1–12 (Adkins, pp. 40–41). In this passage Aristotle probably uses ordinary opinion to explain why we need friends. He argues that even rich men seem to need friends to do well by and to protect their riches, and poor men need friends to fall back on. I find this passage to be ambiguous, too, for we do not know what intentions these men have when they help their friends. And even men in good friendships at times seek help from their friends, though they do so reluctantly (see *Eth.* 9.11.1171b15–19).

What Adkins appears to do is to show that useful and pleasant friendships can exist between good men. I would not deny that good men can have useful and pleasant friendships, that these friendships can rest on their good qualities, and that these friendships can be egoistic. But I would again argue that good men can also have good friendships and that their good friendships can rest on their good qualities and be altruistic.

5. Without using the distinction between essential and accidental good will, Alpern agrees that Aristotle qualifies the element of good will in his definition of friendship. What he asserts is that Aristotle's definition is a partial and preliminary characterization of friendship. The element of good will applies to friendship in general, but after the division of friendship into its species, this requirement wholly applies to good friendship, and it applies imperfectly to useful and pleasant friendships. He also asserts that though all friendship requires good will, only good friendship has good will that is disinterested. Useful and pleasant friendships do not (Alpern, pp. 309–10).

Walker, too, agrees that friendship in all its species does not genuinely satisfy the condition of good will, though he does not discuss essential and accidental good will either. He argues that only good friends wish each other well for their own sakes and that useful and pleasant friends do not really feel affection for each other (Walker, pp. 186–87). Yet he does observe that good friendship is essentially friendship and that useful and pleasant friendships are accidentally friendship (p. 188).

Price agrees with Walker, but he prefers to speak not of a determinate definition, which is qualified, but of a determinable definition, which is presumably determined (Price, ch. 5, pp. 138–40).

6. Cooper argues that good will is present not only in good friendships but also in useful and pleasant friendships. He cites *Eth.* 9.5.1167a10–15 to the effect that Aristotle recognizes a spontaneous good will that arises toward someone with good character. He also implies that good will that arises for useful or pleasant qualities is not spontaneous (Cooper, "Forms," pp. 632, 641–43). But Aristotle does not divide good will into spontaneous and nonspontaneous types. What he does is assert that good will involves only sudden and superficial fondness and does not entail doing things together (*Eth.* 9.5.1166b34–1167a3) and that love involves tension and desire and entails familiarity (1166b32–34).

Incidentally, Cooper would have to agree that Aristotle uses διά with an accusative at *Eth.* 9.5.1167a10–14 to indicate an end, for he translates the synonymous term ἐπί as "for the sake of" (Cooper, "Forms," pp. 641–43). And at 1167a15–18 Aristotle obviously uses διά with a genitive to indicate a means.

Irwin, citing *Eth.* 9.5.1167a10–14, also argues that Aristotle restricts good will to good friendship. He asserts that good will in useful and pleasant friendship has an instrumental justification (Irwin, *Principles*, ch. 18, nn. 2, 3). Price agrees, and he also cites *Eth.* 9.5.1167a10–14 and 1167a14–18 (Price, ch. 5, pp. 152–54). Adkins is in agreement as well (Adkins, pp. 41–42).

Citing *Psy.* 2.5.417b2–7, Couloubaritsis observes in general that one passion can become another through alteration (Couloubaritsis, "Philia," pp. 41–42). Couloubaritsis also offers a specific explanation of how good will develops into friendship. Good will is an achievement of thought that reaches its end. This achievement is an immobility that disposes us favorably toward someone else. And in its immobility, good will tries to surpass itself by engendering fondness (Couloubaritsis, "Philia," pp. 51–54). I would argue not that good will itself engenders fondness but that a person toward whom we feel good will occasions it. For a person who is an object of good will is virtuous, and a virtuous person is lovable.

7. The distinction between essential and accidental friendship is the key to the solution of the problem of focal analysis. Aristotle uses the conception of focal analysis in the *Eudemian Ethics* to show how the defini-

tions of good, useful, and pleasant friendship are related to one another. The problem is whether he also uses focal analysis in the *Nicomachean Ethics* to compare the definitions of these species. The solution is that he does.

Aristotle states in the *Eudemian Ethics* that definitions are related by focal analysis when a primary definition is implied by another definition, but another definition is not implied by a primary one. He gives an example. The definition of medical doctor is implied by that of medical instrument, but the definition of medical instrument is not implied by that of medical doctor (*Eud. Eth.* 7.2.1236a15–33). Owens points out that Aristotle's reference to the primary definition is graded, for the definition of medical art is also implied by the definition of medical doctor (Owens, pp. 131–32 and n. 6).

Aristotle asserts in the *Nicomachean Ethics* that good friendship is primarily and chiefly friendship and that useful and pleasant friendships are friendship in accordance with some similarity (*Eth.* 8.4.1157a30–32). Now we can see that the definition of good friendship and those of useful and pleasant friendships are similar because all three definitions contain the element of good will. We can also see that the definition of good friendship is implied by those of useful and pleasant friendships, but the definitions of useful and pleasant friendships are not implied by that of good friendship. For good friendship entails good will essentially, but useful and pleasant friendships entail good will accidentally. Our assumption is that what is essentially good will is implied by what is good will accidentally.

Owens also asserts that focal analysis is present. He argues that the human association that is highest is imitated in lesser ways by the lower associations (Owens, pp. 132–33 n. 8). But he does not distinguish between essential good will and accidental good will. He states only that though they differ essentially from the primary instance, the secondary instances are genuinely and literally friendships (pp. 132–33 n. 8).

Gauthier, too, offers a solution similar to mine. He asserts that the conception of friendship is a conception in which unity is found only in a relationship in which the unique term that realizes it perfectly is referred to by the terms that realize it imperfectly (Gauthier and Jolif, vol. 2, p. 686). He apparently assumes that virtuous friendship is not defined in relation to useful and pleasant friendships. At least he asserts that useful and pleasant friendships are defined in relation to virtuous friendship (pp. 668–69).

Fraisse adds an interesting element to my interpretation. Arguing in favor of focal analysis, he explains that good friendship alone attains its essential unity, for only in virtuous friendship do useful and pleasant friendships find their unity. In it friendship attains its qualitative perfection, and toward it accidental friendships evolve (Fraisse, pt. 2, pp. 225–32, see also pp. 202–17, 217–26).

Fortenbaugh, however, denies that focal analysis is present in the *Nicomachean Ethics*. He attempts to argue that each species of friendship is defined by its own function. Good friends have the goal of loving each other for the sake of one another, useful friends have the goal of loving each other for the sake of personal benefits received, and pleasant friends have the goal of loving each other for the sake of the pleasure provided (Fortenbaugh, "Analysis" pp. 52–53). Accordingly, he argues that the definitions of these species are not conceptually dependent on one another (pp. 58–59). Fortenbaugh even recognizes that good friendship rests on well-wishing that is not self-interested and that useful and pleasant friendships rest on well-wishing that is self-interested (p. 55). Yet he still fails to see that good friendship is wishing what is good essentially for the sake of another and that useful and pleasant friendships are wishing what is good accidentally for the sake of another.

Walker agrees that good friends wish one another well for the sake of each other and that useful and pleasant friends do so for their own sake (Walker, pp. 186–87) He apparently would also agree that good friendship is essentially friendship and that useful and pleasant friendships are accidentally friendship (p. 188). Nonetheless, because of his rather strict conception of focal analysis, he does not believe that the definitions of these three species are amenable to focal analysis. Walker argues that an element in the primary definition would have to be implied in a secondary definition by a relative phrase and that an element in the primary definition could not be accidentally possessed by a secondary definition (Walker, pp. 192–94).

Price appears to argue that Walker does indeed present arguments to show that focal analysis is present (Price, ch. 5, pp. 141–44). Yet he, too, ultimately denies that an analysis of this sort is present, apparently doing so on only the slightest evidence. He notes only that the standard adjectives for good friendship in the *Eudemian Ethics* are "primary" or "first," and in the *Nicomachean Ethics* these adjectives are "perfect" or "complete" and that "primarily and chiefly" are opposed to "in accordance with some similarity" at *Nic. Eth.* 8.4.1157a30–32 (pp. 137–38). However, he also expresses some reservations about Aristotle's definition of focal analysis. He despairs of a decisive solution because Aristotle does not define sufficient conditions for focal analysis (pp. 134–37).

8. Gauthier agrees that Aristotle's argument concerns only good friendship. He argues that choice is an intellectual action that requires full

knowledge of the means for realizing a wish and that choice is necessary for returning love and for realizing a wish for good friendship. He, too, cites *Eth.* 8.3.1156b25–32 (Gauthier and Jolif, vol. 2, pp. 681–82).

Burnet tries to prove that all reciprocal loves arise from habit. He argues that reciprocal love must arise from choice on the grounds that no passion could be reciprocal (Burnet, p. 370). Stewart shows us where the weakness of Burnet's argument lies. Burnet's argument includes too much, for some reciprocal love may not arise from choice. In a pleasant friendship reciprocal love between weak-willed people would arise from emotion. Stewart also agrees that Aristotle's argument concerns only good friendship, but he argues that a good man forms a habit because he acts on a recognition of an orderly system of life (Stewart, vol. 2, p. 290).

9. With a general analysis of emotion and habit, Couloubaritsis also concludes that good friendship is a virtue that arises out of the emotion of love. He argues that we have true friendship when we feel love in accordance with a mean, for friendship of this sort is a virtue (Couloubaritsis, "Rôle," pp. 179–84).

Grant appears to agree, too. Commenting on *Eth.* 8.5.1157b28–31, he reminds us that a habit is a settled disposition resulting from the regulation of an emotion (Grant, vol. 2, p. 261).

Without citing Aristotle, Stocker implies that friendship requires a virtue. At least, he argues that if we act out of friendship, we must do more than act for the sake of a friend; we must also have a relationship of significant duration (Stocker, pp. 751–53). He also argues that to act out of friendship is to have not only a purpose but also a disposition to a purpose and that to have a purpose need not be to have a disposition to it. That is, to act out of friendship requires a character structure of care, concern, and liking (pp. 756–57).

10. Stocker would probably agree with my analysis. He does not distinguish what an action essentially is from what an action accidentally is. But he does argue that to act out of friendship is not to act for the sake of friendship itself and that to act for the sake of friendship is not to act out of friendship. If we act for the sake of friendship, we do not make the benefit of our friend our goal, but we make our friendship itself our goal (Stocker, pp. 754–55).

Stocker also argues that we can perform the same action both for the sake of our friendship and for the sake of our friend. He explains that by acting for the sake of our friendship we can strengthen our allegiance to our friend (Stocker, p. 762). He even tries to argue that we acquire the virtue of friendship by acting for the sake of friendship itself. After we acquire the virtue, we then act for the sake of our friend (pp. 760–62). I would argue that we strengthen our relationship with ourself when we act for the sake of our friendship, for we act for the sake of our own virtue and its activity. We would best strengthen our relationship with our friend by acting for his sake. That is, to acquire the virtue of friendship, we ought rather to act for the sake of our friend.

Several contemporary philosophers would disagree with my analysis. They almost all prefer to use self-love to account for friendship. Hardie believes that Aristotle presents an egoistic conception of good friendship. He does observe that Aristotle accepts altruistic emotions at face value (Hardie, ch. 15, pp., 325–27). But he also argues that a good man acts out of self-love when he acts for his friends, for even a man who sacrifices his life for others gains nobility for himself (pp. 327–29). Hardie thus fails to distinguish between an action essentially for the sake of another and accidentally for the sake of oneself and an action essentially for the sake of oneself and accidentally for the sake of another.

Irwin also argues that self-love and altruism do not conflict. He explains that someone who is virtuous is a rational agent and has rational plans, and his rational plans include other-regarding plans. Hence self-love requires concern for others (Irwin, *Principles*, ch. 18, p. 393). We thus see that friendship is again an action performed essentially for our own sake. Irwin argues that we fulfill our self-love by acting out of friendship. For we merely fulfill our plans by so doing.

Irwin argues, too, that a virtuous person never sacrifices himself, for a person of such sort is not entirely selfless and self-forgetful. He believes that his concern for his own happiness includes his concern for the happiness of his friend. That is why he is a self-lover without being selfish (Irwin, *Ethics*, p. 371). But a virtuous person can be selfless and self-forgetful. He can easily forget himself in a friendship with another, for he can devote himself entirely to his friend. At least for a short time. Only a virtuous person who devotes himself entirely to himself can never forget himself; he always intends to advance his own happiness even when he helps another.

Moravcsik argues that a person can so conceive of himself that he can take relational properties—including friendship—as parts of himself. We apparently act for the sake of a wider self when we act for the sake of others (Moravcsik, pp. 146–50). Moravcsik, too, would thus present a conception of friendship that is essentially egoistic, for he argues that we act essentially for the sake of our virtue and activity of friendship and not for the sake of our friend.

Kahn distinguishes between an interest which is egoistic and an objective which is altruistic. An egoistic interest is a desire or motive concerned with the welfare of an agent for his own sake. An altruistic objective is a goal or intention concerned exclusively with the welfare of another for his sake. He explains that a father who wants his daughter to have a good education has an altruistic objective, but because he desires to be proud of her or to be a successful parent, he also has an egoistic interest (Kahn, pp. 22–25). Kahn thus fails to distinguish between an action essentially for the sake of oneself and an action essentially for the sake of another. To act for the sake of being a successful and proud parent is to act for the sake of parenthood, which is friendship. At least for Aristotle it is (see especially *Eth.* 8.12.).

Kraut attempts to show that a friendship with ourself is prior to a friendship with another but yet not egoistic (Kraut, *Aristotle*, ch. 2, pp. 115, 118). He argues that a friendship of this sort is not egoistic because a genuine self-lover strives to do what is good not only for himself but also for others. He does this through what Kraut calls moral rivalry. For example, only one solo musician can win a musical contest, but the harder each musician tries to win, the better all contestants play, and the more they all enjoy their performances (Kraut, *Aristotle,* ch. 2, pp. 116–17, 118; see also Kraut, "Comments," pp. 19–20). Kraut, too, would thus fail to distinguish between what an action is essentially and what it is accidentally. He does make a similar distinction between active and passive benefits (Kraut, *Aristotle*, ch. 2, pp. 117–18). But he does not see that benefits distinguished in this way indicate what an action really is and what it is not. Our intentions tell us whether a friendship with ourself or with another is prior and thus whether we act egoistically or altruistically. If we enter a contest with the intention of developing our abilities or of winning the contest, we essentially act for our own benefit. We may accidentally benefit others by improving their performances or by increasing their enjoyment. If we enter a contest with the intention of helping others perform better or of increasing their enjoyment, we then act essentially for their benefit. And if we win, we win the contest by accident.

Kraut also asserts that the interpretation advanced by Kahn is not intelligible. He argues that we cannot benefit others for their sake for our own sake. He asks how benefiting another for our sake can be a reason for benefiting him for his sake. Our own good can provide a reason for benefiting another, but it cannot provide a reason for benefiting another for his sake (Kraut, *Aristotle*, ch. 2, pp. 136–37 and n. 53). Kraut is right to assert that we cannot have it both ways. But he himself still tries to have it both ways. He claims that a person can benefit another both for the sake of the other and also for his own sake. That is, one can have two independent reasons for acting, to benefit another and to benefit oneself (Kraut, *Aristotle,* ch. 2, p. 137; Kraut, "Comments," pp. 21–22). Kraut thus describes a mixed friendship. This friendship would be partly a good friendship with another and partly a good friendship with oneself. And he does state that though a friendship with oneself is the source of a friendship with another, a friendship with oneself is eventually supplemented by and occasionally supplanted by a friendship with another (*Aristotle,* ch. 2, pp. 137–38).

Annas argues not only that self-love is compatible with altruistic actions but also that all altruistic actions are acts of self-love (Annas, "Self-Love," pp. 6–10). She realizes that an agent who helps another cannot have both the end of helping himself for his own sake and the end of helping a friend for the sake of his friend. She also sees that though he does not aim at it, an agent does gain something for himself when he helps another. But she concludes that self-love explains and justifies what an agent does for another without being his motive. That is, his self-love is unconscious (pp. 10–12). Do we need to resort to subconscious explanations and justifications for altruistic actions? Aristotle surely would not, for he goes so far as to identify an agent with his practical intellect and its principle (see again *Eth.* 9.8.1168b29–1169a6). Annas herself asserts that he does (Annas, "Self-Love," pp. 3–4, 6, 8). What intention an agent has is sufficient to justify and to explain his actions. At least if the agent is virtuous.

Urmson seems to agree that we may truly act for the sake of a friend. Yet he appears to assume that when we act for a friend, we really wish to avoid self-despisement. He argues that we love our friend for his own sake when we sacrifice our life for his because we would despise ourself if we did not. He explains that, unless he is a true friend and not a mere acquaintance, we would do nothing sordid in not sacrificing ourself for our friend. Then he asks rhetorically why we would be unable to live with ourself if we did not value our friend and his welfare (Urmson, ch. 9, pp. 114–17). Urmson thus implies not that we wish to have a friendship with ourself but that we seek to avoid an enmity with ourself. What he fails to do is to consider what our intention might be. If we intend to advance his happiness, we act for the sake of our friend; if we intend to advance our happiness, we act for our own sake. We also act for our own sake if we attempt to avoid our own miserableness.

Price probably deserves a special prize for presenting a similar interpretation in a rather intriguing variation. He appears to agree that we can do what is noble for ourself by benefiting a friend and that we can benefit a friend by letting a friend act. Then he adds that we can let a friend act for our sake. That is, we can benefit our friend by affording him the opportunity to do something fine for us, for we allow him to act as our friend (Price, ch. 4, pp. 111–14). Now I have to admit that we might, indeed, seem to participate in a friendship with another by permitting him to act as a friend toward us. But I would think that we might be viewed with suspicion if we offered to do our friend the favor of allowing him to do us a favor. He might not think our offer genuine. We can, however, see that conduct of this sort might be appropriate for teaching another what friendship is. For example, a parent might in this way teach a child how to be a friend. And, hopefully, a parent would act for the sake of the child.

CHAPTER IV. A MOTIVATION FOR FRIENDSHIP

1. Annas appears to agree with the more general points of my analysis, but she nonetheless fails to grasp in its entirety the analogy underlying this proof and its implications. For she neglects to apply Aristotle's principle and to define another self (Annas, "Friendship," pp. 539–44).

2. Almost all modern commentators assert that a good man agrees with himself because the principled element of his soul agrees and harmonizes with the unprincipled element (e.g., see Stewart, vol. 2, pp. 352–54; or Gauthier and Jolif, vol. 2, p. 728). Indeed, we may assert that a good man agrees with himself in this way. As someone who is a friend, we appear to be primarily our principled element; and as someone who is befriended, we appear to be primarily our unprincipled element. We use our practical wisdom and its activity often as a means to attain moral virtue and its activity, for the activity of practical wisdom determines the proper activity of our emotions. We also take moral virtue and its activity often as an end, for the proper activity of our emotions we wish to attain. But a good man, in fact, has an agreement between his principled and his unprincipled elements taken together as a means and these same two elements taken together as an end. As a friend, we exercise both practical wisdom and virtue as a means for attaining happiness; and as someone befriended, we receive help in exercising both practical wisdom and virtue as ends constituting happiness.

One might object that Aristotle himself appears to draw a similar comparison between the agreement of a good man with himself and the relationship among the elements of his soul (*Eud. Eth.* 7.6.1240a15–21). But Fraisse points out that Aristotle expresses reservations about this comparison (Fraisse, pt. 2, pp. 233–34). What Aristotle states is that a friendship between the elements of the soul is a friendship by analogy only and not absolutely and that loving and being loved occur between two distinct entities (*Eud. Eth.* 7.6.1240a9–15). Fraisse argues that we can draw an analogy between the interior harmony of a good soul and the interpersonal harmony of a good friendship with another but that we cannot use the interior harmony of the soul for the derivation of the interpersonal harmony of the friendship (Fraisse, pt. 2, pp. 233–34). He asserts that even in a good friendship the one friend would hold the other friend in constant subordination (p. 237). The implication is that the one, who acts as a friend, would constantly act as the rational element, and the other, who acts as someone befriended, would constantly act as the irrational element. I would argue that we can draw an analogy between the agreement of the elements of a good soul and the agreement of good friends and that we can use a good friendship with oneself as a basis for a derivation of good friendship with another. But we do not base our derivation on the analogy. When we agree with ourselves, we have an agreement between our whole soul and itself, for our whole soul remains distinct from itself. We sometimes exhibit intellectual and moral activity as a means, and we sometimes exhibit intellectual and moral activity as an end.

Ross also believes that Aristotle attempts—but fails—to argue in favor of a friendship between the parts of the soul. He argues that we cannot have a friendship with ourself because we cannot take an interest in or sympathize with an element within ourself. Friendship requires two distinct selves (Ross, *Aristotle,* ch. 5, pp. 231–32). Thus, Ross, too, fails to distinguish between a self as virtue and action constituting the means to happiness and a self as virtue and action constituting the end of happiness.

Annas agrees with us. She asserts that Aristotle does not discuss a relationship between the parts of the soul and that what is at stake is the possibility of regarding one person in two ways (Annas, "Friendship," p. 540 n. 1).

3. Other contemporary scholars agree that we are our practical intellect. Price argues that the self is a persona realized in its choices and decisions (Price, ch. 4, pp. 106–8). Annas explains that to identify with our practical reasoning is to make decisions and commitments and to regard these as our own. Such a person is not tempted or torn by his impulses (Annas, "Self-Love," pp. 3–4). Irwin suggests that Aristotle speaks of a metaphysical self defined by its function and essence. That is, he speaks of a stable character and not mere desire, which need not be good (Irwin, *Principles,* ch. 18, pp. 390–91; see also Irwin, *Ethics,* p. 367). But Millgram puts the matter most succinctly. He asserts that we very often iden-

tify ourself with traits believed to be central to our character (Millgram, pp. 372–74).

Stewart also agrees. He argues that Aristotle does not mean a personality devoted entirely to our scientific faculties. But that he speaks in favor of a principled life, in which reason is the source of rules and relations in science and conduct, and disparages a lie of passion, in which prejudice or pleasure and pain unduly influence science and conduct (Stewart, vol. 2, p. 357).

Gauthier disagrees with Stewart. He appears to argue that Aristotle identifies our personality with our theoretical intellect, and he asserts that we ought to think of our intellect not in a very broad sense but in the most narrow sense. He cites *Eth*. 10.7.1178a2–3, where Aristotle argues that we seem to be our theoretical intellect if, indeed, it is the chief part of us. But Gauthier himself also cites *Eth*. 9.4.1166a18–23, where Aristotle explicitly refers to practical wisdom, and *Eth*. 9.8.1168b28–35, where Aristotle speaks of an intellect that we obey and that makes us strong-willed or weak-willed.

Gauthier also worries about this identification of ourself with our intellect because Aristotle makes it without the ample explications found in his psychology (Gauthier and Jolif, vol. 2, pp. 728–29). Yet Aristotle himself asserts that we may understand ethics without a full understanding of psychology (*Eth*. 1.13.1102a18–26).

Burnet argues that friendship with ourself is for the sake of our intellect, especially our theoretical intellect (Burnet, pp. 344–45). He, too, refers to *Eth*. 10.7.1178a2–3, but he refers to *Eth*. 9.8.1168b28–35, as well (p. 411).

4. Stewart is thus correct to follow Susemihl's punctuation. He adds to our analogy the thought that our wish for our own good cannot overpass our self-identity. That is, we cannot wish for what is good for ourself as having become God (Stewart, vol. 2, pp. 357–60).

Irwin puts the point succinctly when he says that my concern for myself is for me as being that which I essentially am (Irwin, *Ethics*, p. 367).

Grant, who believes that this argument applies to all men, argues that no man would relinquish his character to gain the whole world because by doing so he would not gain anything. He would no more gain than he now gains by God possessing the world (Grant, vol. 2, p. 289). But a bad man might well wish to become a better man and to rid himself of his bad character and life. Such a man would gain by changing his character; he might not gain the world, but he might well gain happiness. And I suspect that we all gain by God possessing the world.

5. Grant argues that a friendship with oneself exists insofar as two or more marks of friendship exist (Grant, vol. 2, p. 290). Stewart agrees with Grant (Stewart, vol. 2, pp. 362–63). However, Aristotle argues that all five marks exist in a friendship, not that only two or more marks exist. One might also wonder how any mark could exist without the others because anyone who is happy would exhibit all five marks.

Burnet agrees that good men exhibit all five marks of friendship, but he unfortunately argues that a friendship with ourself exists between the parts of our soul. He cites *Eud. Eth.* 7.6.1240a15–21 (Burnet, p. 413).

6. Annas argues that we come to regard our friend as we regard ourself. She explains that we may regard the desires of a friend and their fulfillment as we regard our own desires and their fulfillment (Annas, "Friendship," p. 542; Annas, "Self-Love," pp. 1–3). I agree, though I would speak not of desires and their fulfillment but of virtues and their activities. But Annas also claims that Aristotle does not show how a friendship with another is possible. She even asserts that Aristotle begs the question when he merely states that we can regard ourself and our friend in the same way (Annas, "Friendship," pp. 543–44; Annas, "Self-Love," pp. 1–2). But Aristotle does not beg the question. He proves that a friendship with ourself and with another are the same, for he argues that friendships of either kind exhibit the same marks. He does not show that a friendship with ourself is the source of a friendship with another. But the simple assumption that we might have a greater concern for ourself than for another is sufficient to establish the conclusion.

Fraisse also agrees that a friendship with ourself has an extension in a friendship with another (Fraisse, pt. 2, p. 237). But he argues that a friendship with ourself is merely a correlate to a friendship with another because we can love ourselves only in the way in which we love another (pp. 236–37). He also maintains that good friendships both with ourselves and with others derive rather from the unity of our personality through its virtue (Fraisse, pp. 234–35, 237). I, of course, admit that the unity of our character is important. So is the unity of our action. But I also argue that we wish for this unity of character and of action more strongly in our friendship with ourself and that our friendship with ourself is accordingly the source of our friendships with others.

Stewart argues that a friendship with ourself is not chronologically but logically prior to a friendship with another. Good friendship arises among good men, and good men arise only after the development of a family into a city, which renders social feelings possible (Stewart, vol. 2, pp. 352–54). Aristotle, however, allows that friendship may arise even before the development of a family into a city. He argues that a family itself is a friendship and that parents have goodness in some measure (see *Eth.* 8.10–12). And friendship does exist between those who are not perfectly good (*Eth.* 9.4.1166a11). A friendship with ourself would thus appear to be not logically but chronologically prior to a friendship with another. Friendships of both kinds are essentially the same and have motives essentially the same, but a friendship with ourself has a motive that is stronger and is felt sooner. A friendship with ourself and a friendship with another would also appear to be simultaneous logically because friendship of either kind occurs only among those who are good to some extent.

Kraut, who develops an argument similar to that advanced by Stewart, argues that we exhibit the marks of friendship most fully in a relationship with ourself and that we love ourself most of all. He concludes that a friendship with ourself accordingly provides a paradigm for a friendship with another. He thus implies that a friendship with ourself is logically prior and he asserts that a relationship with ourself is not temporally prior (Kraut, *Aristotle,* ch. 2, pp. 132–33). I concede that a friendship with ourself can exhibit the marks of friendship more fully and that a relationship with ourself is stronger. But I would argue again that a good friendship with ourself is essentially the same as a good friendship with another, for both relationships exhibit the same marks. A friendship with ourself and one with another are, therefore, logically simultaneous. And if we love ourself more than another, we would very likely form a good friendship with ourself before we form a friendship with another. Our relationship with ourself is thus temporally prior.

Kraut does, nevertheless, argue that a friendship with ourself is the source of a friendship with another. He maintains that a person who truly loves himself is virtuous and that a virtuous person wishes others, too, to be virtuous and to live. We express our self-love in moral rivalry in ways that incur no objection from others (Kraut, *Aristotle,* ch. 2, pp. 133–34). The implication is that a friendship with ourself includes a wish to develop relationships with others. But Kraut would thus allow our relationship with ourself to subsume our relationships with others, for we still act for our own sake, even though we place moral limits on our actions.

7. Cooper fails to give this argument serious consideration because he believes that the argument applies only to someone who already has a friend. That is, the argument answers not the question of why someone would desire to make a friend but the question of why someone would desire to keep a friend who is already his. Cooper assumes that only someone who is already a friend is another self (Cooper, "Good," pp. 292–94). But

does Aristotle intend to prove only that we must find another self desirable as an object actually ours? May we not find another self desirable as an object potentially ours? We surely do not feel affection only for someone who is already our friend; we also feel affection for someone who may become our friend. That is, for someone whom we see that we may help in some way. Cooper himself accepts this distinction between another self who is actually a friend and another self who is one potentially. When he explains why we enter a friendship, he argues that we are able to know ourselves better through another because the other is another self and consequently has qualities the same or very similar to ours (Cooper, "Good," pp. 298–99 and n. 12).

Hardie feels that we need not take Aristotle's argument seriously because Aristotle does not remind us that we are more directly aware of our own thoughts and actions than we are of the thoughts and actions of others. He apparently attributes to Aristotle the belief that we can be aware of the thoughts of another self in literally the same way as we are aware of our own thoughts (Hardie, ch. 15, pp. 331–32). Thus he fails to see that Aristotle distinguishes between ourself and another self as between distinct persons and that Aristotle discusses our awareness of others as an apperception of their thoughts and actions. Cooper points out that whether our self-awareness differs from our awareness of others does not matter. What matters is that we are aware of the thoughts and actions of others and find this awareness quite similar to our awareness of our own and that we also take pleasure in the thoughts and actions of others and find this pleasure similar to the pleasure that we take in our own (Cooper, "Good," p. 294 n. 6).

8. Some modern and contemporary scholars with analyses different than mine agree with my conclusion. Grant argues, without detailed analysis, that our sense of our own existence is nearly the same as our sympathetic consciousness of the existence of a friend (Grant, vol. 2, p. 301).

With a more detailed analysis, Burnet concludes that our sympathy depends upon our self-consciousness. That is, sympathy depends upon a self that distinguishes itself from its thoughts and sensations and that can relate itself to its own thoughts and sensations and to the thoughts and sensations of another in the same way (Burnet, p. 430).

Robin argues that a friend sympathizes intellectually with the joys and pains of another. He states that self-love, which is an accord of thought with itself in action, is the true principle of friendship, which is an exteriorization of self-love. The love that we feel toward ourself is the principle of disinterested friendship (Robin, pt. 6, pp. 242–43).

Without citing *Eth.* 9.9. at all, Sherman also suggests that one friend feels sympathy or empathy for another and that something like it may be the hallmark of friendship (Sherman, ch. 4; pp. 135–36).

Some modern contemporary scholars, however, disagree with my analysis and conclusion. Stewart believes that the motive for good friendship is to be better able to apperceive ourselves. He argues that through friendship we can better distinguish our apperception of our activities from our activities themselves, for we enhance our understanding of the distinction between our apperception of our activities and our activities through our understanding of the distinction between our apperception of the activities of others and their activities (Stewart, vol. 2, p. 392). But Aristotle does not argue that we are better able to apperceive ourselves because we apperceive others; he argues that as we apperceive ourselves and take pleasure in apperceiving ourselves, so we apperceive other selves and take pleasure in doing so. So far is he from proving that through friendship we apperceive ourselves better, he would appear to imply that through better apperceiving ourselves, we are better able to enter a friendship with another. Cooper agrees that our apperception of ourselves better enables us to enter a friendship with another (Cooper, "Good," pp. 295–96).

Fraisse rightly states that as we find our existence desirable, so we find the existence of a friend desirable. Unfortunately he also asserts that our existence is desirable because we have a consciousness of our existence and that our consciousness of our existence is desirable in itself. And so our consciousness of the life of a friend is also desirable (Fraisse, pt. 2, pp. 241–43). He thus suggests that our motive for friendship is to apperceive an identity that we share with another (pp. 243–45). But Aristotle does not appear to assert that we enter a friendship because we find the apperception of the life of our friend desirable nor that we wish to live because we find the apperception of our own life desirable. What Aristotle states is that we find the apperception of the life of a friend to be pleasant, and he argues that the life of a friend is choiceworthy because the apperception of his life is pleasant. But we do not act for the sake of our apperception when we enter a friendship. To do so would be to reduce good friendship to useful or pleasant friendship. Rather, we enter a friendship because we choose to act for the sake of our friend. Our apperception of our friend is what tells us that his life is choiceworthy.

Ross argues that one person may feel the pleasure or pain of another, and he speaks as if he means physical pleasure and pain. For he gives the example of a mother who feels the pain of her child as much as the pain of her own body (Ross, *Aristotle,* ch. 5, pp. 231–32). Hardie rightly corrects him for this, arguing that when she feels distress at the pain of her child, a mother feels not the pain of her child but sympathy and pity (Hardie, ch. 15, pp. 324–25). Yet Hardie appears to attribute Ross's belief to Aristotle, for he criticizes Aristotle for implying that we can be aware of the thoughts of another self in literally the same way as we are aware of our own thoughts (pp. 331–32). He thus fails to see that what he calls sympathy and pity Aristotle discusses as pleasant or painful apperception.

By suggesting that a self can be extended indefinitely, Ross also claims that Aristotle attempts to break down the distinction between egoism and altruism. He asserts that we can so extend our interests to another self that we take as direct an interest in his welfare as we do in our own (Ross, *Aristotle,* ch. 5, pp. 231–32). But for Aristotle the distinction between egoism and altruism remains. Aristotle does not argue that we can take an interest in the happiness of another as directly as we do in our own; he argues only that we take an interest in the happiness of another nearly as directly as we do in our own (see *Eth.* 9.9.1170b7–8). We cannot extend our interests so indefinitely that we become another self. Though we can embody the same principle in our actions and virtues, we and another self still remain persons who are numerically distinct from one another.

Irwin asserts rightly that we enjoy perceiving the actions that a friend performs in the same way as we enjoy perceiving our own actions. But, unfortunately, he adds that we enjoy contemplating the activity of a friend because another self is an extension of our own activity (Irwin, *Principles,* ch. 18 n. 6). He argues that we prefer more self-realization rather than less and that we realize ourself more fully when we have a friend. We especially promote self-realization when we wish what is good for the sake of our friend. In this way we can give ourself many opportunities for rational action that we would otherwise not have (Irwin, *Principles,* ch. 18, pp. 393–94; Irwin, "Good," pp. 91–92; Irwin, *Ethics,* p. 372). But Aristotle does not argue that we enjoy apperceiving the happiness of another because his happiness is an extension of our own; he argues, rather, that we enjoy apperceiving the happiness of another as we enjoy apperceiving our own. We find that the enjoyment of our happiness and the enjoyment of his happiness are the same or nearly the same. But his happiness and our happiness nonetheless remain different. If we take pleasure in the happiness of another because it is an extension of our own, we take pleasure only in an egoistic relationship.

Irwin explains that we can extend our happiness to include that of others through a shared life. That is, we cooperate in deliberation, decision, and action. My thoughts apparently are to your thoughts and actions as they are to my own. Our thoughts and actions provide one another with reasons for future thoughts and actions (Irwin, *Principles,* ch. 18, p. 392; Irwin, "Good," p. 91). But we do not need to cooperate with another in order to become friends with him; we need only reciprocate favors with him. And we must, of course, recognize that we do (see *Eth.* 8.2.1156a3–5). We may cooperate on a project with another if we wish; but if we do, we can still enjoy apperceiving our own happiness and the happiness of the other without collapsing the two.

Irwin even claims that the distinctive feature of friendship is living together (Irwin, "Good," p. 91). But wishing and doing what is good for the sake of another is the distinctive feature of friendship. In fact, Aristotle uses this very feature to define friendship (*Eth.* 8.2.1156a3–5 again). Friends do live together, rejoice and grieve together, choose the same things, and wish each other to live (see *Eth.* 9.4.1166a2–9). But these features are merely additional marks of friendship, not its defining mark.

Kahn also argues that the distinction between egoism and altruism collapses for Aristotle. This distinction collapses because the distinction between ourself and our friend collapses. The life of our friend belongs to us, and our life belongs to him. We share with our friend a principle that is one and the same (Kahn, p. 37). Kahn even argues that we cannot coherently share similar principles that are distinct. That is, we do not derive our happiness from a principle which is the same as that of our friend except for being ours and not his (p. 37 n. 1). Kahn thus explicitly rules out a principle that is the same formally but present in individuals different numerically. But Aristotle's conception of happiness clearly is a formal principle shared by individuals numerically different.

Strictly speaking, then, we cannot extend our happiness to include that of another. We may affect the actions of a friend and our joint actions with him, but we cannot perform his actions for him, for his actions can result only from his own practical intellect. We make the happiness of another ours only in the sense that we provide a formal cause. We may help another deliberate, for example. But the happiness that we help produce is not ours in the sense that we provide an efficient cause. Our friend must himself choose to accept our advice and to embody it in his action.

Sherman explicitly recognizes this distinction between ourself and our friend when she states simply that friends cannot make choices for each other (Sherman, ch. 4, p. 140). They do promote the good of one another, but they also acknowledge the rational agency of one another (pp. 138–39). She illustrates this acknowledgment with an example of self-sacrifice. The one friend may not give action itself to the other but only opportunities for acting or means for realizing ends (pp. 139–40). Unfortunately, she takes her example of self-sacrifice from a friendship with oneself and argues that a friend who sacrifices himself in a friendship of this sort secures the good of fine action for himself (pp. 139–40). She thus implies rather strongly that friendship has an egoistic motive. Aristotle would argue that a friend who sacrifices himself in friendship with another helps secure the good of action for his friend, for friendship is only thus altruistic.

Sherman rightly asserts that friendship has intrinsic worth, but she, too, implies that this worth is egoistic. She argues that friendship provides a way of realizing our own virtue and activity. That is, our happiness includes the happiness of our friends (Sherman, ch. 4, pp. 126–28). But, again, if we expand our own virtue and activity to include the virtue and activity of others, we act essentially for the sake of ourselves. Sherman, in fact, recognizes that on Aristotle's view of friendship we must not act for our virtue and presumably its activity but for the sake of our friend (Sherman, ch. 4, pp. 137–38).

Sherman attempts to explain how our happiness can include that of others. She argues that our life can be self-sufficient only when we interweave it with that of others and pursue a joint life together. Human self-sufficiency is relational (Sherman, ch. 4, pp. 128, 130–32). But we can be self-sufficient and have relationships without cooperation; we can choose to live with others without participating in a joint activity. We may merely grant each other favors, and if we are friends, we do so for the sake of one another.

Kraut argues that a boundary separates our happiness from that of our friends. My happiness consists in my virtuous activity, and your happiness in your virtuous activity. He also observes that our happiness may be affected by others; they may diminish our happiness by denying us opportunities for action. And their unhappiness may detract from ours; we may act to alleviate their misery even if to do so is not optimal for us (Kraut, *Aristotle*, ch. 2, pp. 148–49). Presumably Kraut would also agree that our friends may increase our happiness by giving us opportunities for action and that our happiness may also be enhanced by theirs as well.

Kahn argues that our happiness includes the apperception of the happiness of our friend (Kahn, p. 32). He admits that we thus take an egoistic interest in what he calls an altruistic object. That is, in the welfare of our friend (pp. 30–31, 32). But Aristotle does not argue that the pleasure of apperceiving the happiness of our friend is a motive for friendship. Our motive for friendship is the happiness itself of our friend, and our pleasure in apperceiving his happiness is merely an adventitious one. The pleasure of apperceiving that our friend is happy is similar to the pleasure of apperceiving that we are happy. Surely we do not wish to be happy so that we can apperceive that we are. Happiness is an activity valued for its own sake, and our pleasure in it is adventitious (see *Eth.* 10.4.1174b31–33). But Kahn does argue that we wish to be happy in order to apperceive our happiness. At least, he argues that we do so in part (p. 33).

Kraut presents another argument similar to that of Kahn. He states that we must take into account not only the instrumental value of our friends but also the pleasure gotten from them (Kraut, *Aristotle,* ch. 2, pp. 139–40). He explains that if a certain feature makes ourself desirable to perceive, and if the same feature belongs to our friend, then our friend is desirable for us to perceive, too. He concludes accordingly that as the perception of the goodness of ourself is desirable, so the perception of the goodness of our friends is also desirable. If we lose a friend, we lose someone whom we find desirable to observe (pp. 140–41). But Kraut fails to see that we reduce our friends to their instrumental value if we value them for the pleasure received from them. Aristotle argues that we wish to have a good friend in order to do what is good for him; our pleasure in apperceiving his goodness is accidental. He does not argue that we wish to have a good friend in order to take pleasure in apperceiving his goodness. If we do, we reduce our relationship to an egoistic friendship of pleasure, albeit an intellectual pleasure. That this intellectual pleasure is egoistic, Kahn correctly sees.

Millgram argues that we can broaden our happiness to include the happiness of our friend because the happiness of our friend is part of our own happiness (Millgram, p. 375). He cites *Eth.* 8.2.1161b18–19 and 1161b20–24, passages in which Aristotle argues that parents love their children as part of themselves. He suggests that our friend himself is part of us and belongs to us as does a tooth or a hair (pp. 375–76). He even asserts that our friend and we are one numerically. At least, that Aristotle holds this view (p. 376 n. 26). Millgram thus presents an argument that makes Aristotle sound rather like Aristophanes (see *Symposium* 189c–193e). We are obviously not numerically one with a friend; we are one only morally, for we share a common moral principle, which is happiness. The principle shared by us is not numerically one either; it is one in form only. To say that we regard our friend as part of us is only to acknowledge that we share a principle with our friend. A friend is part of us because he has the same form that we have. We share only this part of ourself with him. However, we do help our friend embody the principle shared with him, and in this way we might say that he belongs to us.

Irwin, too, asserts that a father, at least, regards his child as his own much as a tooth or hair is his own (Irwin, *Ethics,* pp. 363–64). But Price agrees that a friend is not part of us as is a tooth or a hair. He cites Aristotle's statement at *Eth.* 5.6.1134b10–11 that a child is part of its father in this sense only until it grows up and becomes separate. He argues that another self must resemble us in our entirety (Price, ch. 6, pp. 164–65).

9. Burnet and Ross agree with this analysis on the more general points, though they disagree on the more specific ones. They set out the major premises of Aristotle's argument in syllogisms and short prosyllogisms; I set out the major premises in one long syllogism. Burnet's Syllogism II appears to be a diagram of the first five premises of Aristotle's argument. But Burnet argues that the conclusion of these premises is not that life is choiceworthy but that life is an object of pleasant apperception. He fails to take the fifth premise into account. His Syllogism III diagrams Aristotle's sixth premise and his conclusion. But, again, he concludes not that the life of a friend is choiceworthy but that the life of a friend is an object of pleasant apperception. He still neglects the fifth premise. His Prosyllogism A corresponds to what we call the first segment of the argument; his Prosyllogism B and Syllogism I to the first part of the second segment (Burnet, pp. 428–30).

Ross's Prosyllogism E through his second Lemma diagrams Aristotle's first five premises. But Ross also appears to believe that this part of the argument concludes that life is an object of pleasant apperception. Though he mentions it, he, too, fails to give due consideration to the fifth premise. His Arguments I and K correspond to Aristotle's sixth premise, his conclusion, and his summary. He does try to show that this part of the argument proves that the life of a friend is desirable, but to do so, he refers back to the first segment of the argument (1170a21–22) and, of course, to the fifth premise (1170b3–5). He thus misses the conclusion of the argument and treats the summary as the conclusion. His Prosyllogism A corresponds to the first segment of the argument, his Prosyllogisms B, C, and D to the first part of the second segment, and his summary and Argument L to the conclusion of the third segment (Ross, *Ethica,* n. pag., 1170b19 n. 1).

10. Cooper believes that this argument is unsound. He argues that no one need have all the things good by nature, on the grounds that there are too many things good by nature and too many kinds of them. He offers an analogy. Even though card games are good in themselves, a person who does not play cards need not be any the less happy (Cooper, "Good," pp. 293–94 n. 5). But Aristotle does not argue that we must make friends with all desirable people nor with desirable people of every kind. He argues only that we must make friends with some desirable people, for we must

satisfy the human emotion of love in an appropriate way. If we do not, we will be defective. And though we do not have to play cards, we surely ought to engage in leisure activities of some sort. I would, nevertheless, recommend a friendly game of poker now and then.

11. Price does not attach much importance to beneficence. He claims that only a benefactor is active and that a beneficiary is only passive (Price, ch. 4, pp. 114–15). For a benefactor exercises choice in doing what is good, and a beneficiary receives a good apparently without choice (pp. 115–16). But he does cite *Eth.* 9.7.1168a7 and concede that a beneficiary can sometimes be active (pp. 114–15), especially when he receives a moral benefit (pp. 115–16). Aristotle would, of course, argue that moral benefits are what friends especially receive from one another.

Millgram attaches paramount importance to beneficence. He argues that we wish and do what is good for the sake of a friend because we make another person into another self. That is, we make another person a virtuous being (Millgram, pp. 365–66, 368–71). He draws on Aristotle's analogy to a craftsman. We love our friend as a craftsman does the product of his craft, for he loves his own being, and he shares his being with his product, though he does not share the same being with his product (pp. 367–68). He also draws on Aristotle's discussion of parenthood. We love our friend as parents love their children. For parents love their children because they are responsible for the being of their children and because they share the same being with their children (pp. 366–67).

But Millgram claims too much for beneficence. At least, he claims too much for benevolence in personal friendship. We love a personal friend not because we make another person another self but because we make another self ours. Parents do love their children because they procreate them and because their children resemble them. Craftsmen, too, love their products because they produce them and because their products share their being. But do we procreate or produce our personal friends? We cannot forget that good will is the beginning of friendship (see *Eth.* 9.5.1167a3–5). We do what is good for another because we bear good will toward him, and we bear him good will because he already has virtue (*Eth.* 9.5.1167a18–20). And so we act beneficently toward someone who already is another self. By our beneficent actions we can make another self our friend, for with our favors we can make him ours, and he can make us his with his favors. If our good will is reciprocated and recognized (see again *Eth.* 8.2.1156a3–5). Millgram himself recognizes that we do perform favors for others out of spontaneous good will (Millgram, pp. 371–72). I am however grateful to Millgram for exaggerating the role of beneficence in friendship. By so doing, he enabled me to correct a similar error in my own analysis.

Sherman appears to agree with me. Citing *Eth.* 9.12.1172a12, she argues not that friends create one another but that friends mold one another. That is, they greatly influence the lives of each other (Sherman, ch. 4, pp. 148–49). She also notes that parents have a reproductive connection to their children and an educative connection with them (pp. 148–50). But she argues that, when mature, children love their parents only for the benefits received from them (pp. 150–51). I would hope that children might eventually love their parents as their parents love them. That is, as other selves.

Moravicsik puts the point nicely. He argues that friendship entails loyalty and that we are loyal to a friend because we share a history of interaction with him. He gives examples, such as going through hard times together or working together for a common cause (Moravicsik, pp. 135–42). Price, too, argues that we identify with another self not because of a unique character but because of a series of choices and actions. We and a friend contribute to the happiness of each other in a common life (Price, ch. 4, p. 130). According to Kraut, we help shape the character of our friend over a long association, and what our friend does is partly ours because of our influence on his character (Kraut, *Aristotle,* ch. 2, p. 143).

12. Stewart appears to agree. He says that the actions contemplated must be "clearly realized in consciousness" (Stewart, vol. 2, pp. 385–86). Cooper would also agree (Cooper, "Good," p. 301 n. 13).

13. Curiously, Cooper agrees that Stewart is wrong to argue that the motive for good friendship is to apperceive ourself better (see again Cooper, "Good," pp. 295–96). Yet he attempts to argue that the motive for good friendship is to be better able to know ourselves (pp. 295–96, 300–302). He argues that we know intuitively that we have the same character as another and that we know objectively what character we have through friendship with another (pp. 298–99). But what Aristotle argues is not that through friendship we know ourselves better but that through knowing ourselves we are better able to enter a friendship. For knowledge includes apperception, apperception being intuition. Nor does Aristotle distinguish between intuitive knowledge and objective knowledge. Knowledge includes intuition (see *Eth.* 6.6. and 6.11.1143a25–1143b14), and knowledge is objective (e.g., see *Eth.* 6.1.1139a3–14). Cooper thus appears to reduce good friendship to useful or pleasant friendship or to discuss a mixture of good with useful or pleasant friendship. In fact, he claims

that the benefit of self-knowledge explains why we enter a good friendship. We cannot know ourself through a friend unless we also value our friend for his own sake (Cooper, "Good," pp. 312–15).

Cooper does attempt to distinguish between self-apperception and self-knowledge. He cites the *Magna Moralia* to show that we need a friend in order to know ourself better (*Mor.* 2.11.1213a10–26). And he argues without textual evidence that αἰσθάνεσθαι and its derivatives are not synonymous with γνῶναι, εἰδέναι, or γνωρίζειν (Cooper, "Good," pp. 295–96). But even in the *Magna Moralia* Aristotle would appear to use γνωρίζειν synonymously with αἰσθάνεσθαι. At least, he does on two occasions in his chapter on practical wisdom. He suggests that we know the objects of both intuition and apperception. He asserts that with different parts of the soul γνωρίζομεν different objects (*Mor.* 1.34.1196b23–25). He states explicitly that γνωρίζομεν both τὸ νοητὸν and τὸ αἰσθητόν (1196b25–26) and that γνωρίζομεν ψόφον ἀκοῇ, χυμὸν γεύσει, and χρῶμα ὄψει (1196b21–22). He also suggests that we know a practical principle. He asserts that we may act neither with choice οὐδὲ γνώσει τῶν καλῶν. But when we act this way, we act ὁρμῇ τινι ἀλόγῳ (*Mor.* 1.34.1198a15–18). We act better when our desire is μετὰ λόγου (1198a20–22).

Like Cooper, Price maintains that we can gain self-knowledge through friendship. He argues that we have to achieve an understanding of our own activities through a friend. When we act by ourself, we are less aware of our activities than of their objects; but when we cooperate with another, we become conscious of his activities and so of ours, too (Price, ch. 4, pp. 120–22). Thus, Price mixes good friendship with useful and pleasant friendship, for if we enter them for self-knowledge, we enter our friendships in part at least for the sake of an ulterior purpose. Yet Price expresses reservations about Cooper's claim that we intuitively know that a friend has a character similar to ours before we objectively know what character he has. He argues that we do not have to guess about his character but that we simply learn who he is by doing things with him (Price, ch. 4, pp. 122–24).

Millgram agrees with us, however. He asserts that Cooper has got things backwards, that he uses these arguments to develop an instrumental reason for friendship. Millgram himself uses them in an argument of his own to develop a noninstrumental reason. A person who helps us gain self-knowledge will have a reason to love us, for he makes us his other self (Millgram, pp. 368–71). Though Aristotle does not, Millgram is right to claim that we can give these arguments a noninstrumental interpretation. However, I would again argue that a person who helps us does not usually make us another self but, rather, makes another self his.

Irwin also argues that Aristotle presents an egoistic defense of friendship in this argument. He asserts that a friend whose actions serve to give us self-knowledge would be simply a means for us to contemplate our own actions better. Also, he asks, Why would we need a friend to know ourself better? Would not another person of virtue sufficiently similar to ours serve as well (Irwin, *Principles,* ch. 18 n. 6)? Cooper himself asks this very question of Stewart (Cooper, "Good," p. 295).

Gauthier, too, apparently believes that this argument is Aristotle's best explanation and that Aristotle's argument about the cause of friendship is less profound. He asserts that friendship has the end of perfecting our imperfect knowledge (Gauthier and Jolif, vol. 2, pp. 760–62). But, again, we do not enter good friendship with the intention of perfecting our knowledge, though we may perfect our knowledge through friendship of this sort.

Couloubaritsis argues that we can really discover who we are only in the light of another who is our friend (Couloubaritsis, "Philia," pp. 58–59). He argues further that we can better ourselves by suppressing any imperfections brought to light by knowledge gathered from a friend (pp. 59–62). I would counter that by knowing ourself and by perfecting ourself we can know our friend better and better help him perfect himself; and, of course, he can do the same for us. Otherwise, our friendship is not altruistic but egoistic.

14. Cooper attempts to argue that we also enter a good friendship with the motive of being more continuously active. He explains that we especially benefit in this way by sharing actions with others. We share actions when we perform them together with one or more people. We find that these actions are more interesting and enjoyable because they strengthen our sense of their worth, enhance our attachment to them, and expand the scope of our activity (Cooper, "Good," pp. 302–10). But Cooper again reduces good friendship to useful or pleasant friendship. If we enter them to be more continuously active, we enter our friendships with an ulterior purpose in mind. And he does admit that these psychological benefits are necessary to explain why a human being would enter a good friendship. We value friendship because only through it can we construct a continuously active life. He also implies that good friendship is a means to these benefits, for he asserts that our life cannot be more continuously active unless we share our chief interests equally with another (Cooper, "Good," pp. 312–15).

Price argues that Aristotle dissolves the dichotomy between altruism and egoism because two persons may find that one and the same action is a constituent of their happiness (Price, ch. 4, pp. 105–6). He also argues that Aristotle allows our identity to overflow and to extend into the life of another (pp. 114–15). He explains that we can especially extend ourself by cooperating with others; through cooperation our activity is at once an exercise of our own capacities and of the capacities of another (pp. 116–17). We may share in a decision only, or we may share in its execution, as well (pp. 118–20). But Price implies that good friendship thus becomes egoistic, for he asserts that each friend finds his own happiness in the cooperative activity shared with another. And he does state that good friendship is disinterested only because it excludes a selfish affection that does not include a cooperative activity (Price, ch. 4, p. 124). But good friendship is disinterested because we can help another engage in an activity of his own for his sake.

To show that Aristotle speaks about cooperative activities, Price cites *Eth.* 9.9.1170b11–12 and *Eth.* 9.12.1172a1–3, 1172a6–8, 1172a10–14 (Price, ch. 4, pp. 118–19). But what Aristotle states in these passages is that friends do various things together. And we can do things together without being engaged in a cooperative activity. Aristotle does state that friends become better by improving each other. But we can improve each other by doing what is good for one another without engaging in a cooperative activity.

Barker appears to favor a position of this sort, too. He argues that we need friends for the sake of their society if we are to have pleasure, which is part of happiness. We have more energy when working with others, and when we see it in another self, we are more conscious of our energy. And our consciousness of our energy is true happiness (Barker, ch. 5, pp. 235–37). But when we act to increase our consciousness and its pleasure, we act for the sake of an ulterior motive. And happiness is, rather, energy or activity itself; the pleasure of consciousness is adventitious (see again *Eth.* 10.4.1174b31–33).

Kahn agrees with us that Aristotle's arguments about both wisdom and activity can give only an egoistic explanation for friendship. He argues that they show not why we would wish a friend to be happy for his sake but only why we would wish a friend to be happy as a means to our own happiness (Kahn, p. 31).

15. Cooper, of course, argues that people of ordinary virtue can have a good friendship for the sake of useful or pleasant qualities (Cooper, "Forms," p. 643). But I am arguing that people of less-than-perfect virtue can have good friendship for the sake of what virtue and activity they do have in common. But I would not deny that ordinary people can

have a friendship that mixes good with useful or pleasant friendship. So can good people.

Kraut appears to agree that friendship may be for the sake of primary or secondary happiness. He asserts that we can apply two standards in our treatment of others. The one is philosophical, the other ethical (Kraut, *Aristotle,* ch. 3, p. 157). He also argues that since we may be happy in a primary or secondary sense and since, when happy, we still need friends, we need to have friends whether we live a philosophical or nonphilosophical life with them (pp. 183–84).

But Kraut continues to argue that good friendship includes friendship for the sake of philosophy because good friendship is perfect, but useful and pleasant friendships are defective. His explicit assumption is that problems with our friends cannot mar the best life (Kraut, *Aristotle,* ch. 3, pp. 175–76). I would argue, rather, that good friendship includes philosophical friendship because good friendship is for the sake of happiness and happiness includes theoretical activity. But I agree that friendship of the good kind is perfect friendship, whether or not it is for the sake of philosophizing.

Kraut also appears to assume that good friendship rests on moral virtue and its activity, for he asserts that philosophers enter good friendships because they value practical virtue. Yet he notes that philosophers value their friends not merely for their good character but also for their theoretical virtue (Kraut, *Aristotle,* ch. 3, pp. 176–77). I doubt that Aristotle would distinguish theoretical virtue from our character or that he would identify moral virtue with our character. Theoretical as well as moral virtue is part of our character, for it is a virtue. And we can have good friendship with philosophers whose moral character may have defects. We may philosophize together with them without sharing in practical activities. I shall not mention any names.

CHAPTER V. POLITICAL FRIENDSHIP

1. Though he does not discuss unanimity, Barker implies that a city is friendship. He asserts that a city aims at securing for its citizens not only life and good life but also social life, and by social life he means living together (Barker, ch. 5, pp. 235–37). These qualities are, of course, the first three marks of friendship (see *Eth.* 9.4.1166a2–7). Barker also adds that all citizens have the same preferences and feel the same pleasures and pains (Barker, ch. 5, pp. 235–37). These two qualities are the last two marks of friendship (see *Eth.* 9.4.1166a7–9). Barker thus appears to have all the marks of friendship in mind, though he does not mention them as such.

Fraisse argues that unanimity is a mark of friendship but that it is not friendship itself. He recognizes that those who are unanimous agree with one another about their interests and common actions (Fraisse, pt. 2, pp. 250–51). He thus implies that they exhibit the fourth mark. But he argues that unanimous people are not friends because they delight only in the same objects. Friends take delight in each other (Fraisse, pt. 2, pp. 250–51). The implication is that unanimous people do not exhibit the fifth mark of friendship. I would argue, first, that those who exhibit one mark of friendship are likely to exhibit all five marks. And, I would argue that those who enjoy the same virtues and activities would very likely enjoy each other, for they would most probably embody similar virtues and engage in similar activities.

Fraisse also presents another argument to show that unanimity is not friendship. He recognizes that unanimity concerns our actions and our life together, but he argues that it does not concern the present (Fraisse, pt. 2, pp. 199–201). I would have to ask how we could not concern ourselves with the present and yet act and live together.

Gauthier finds himself tempted to identify unanimity with the fourth mark of friendship—to have the same tastes as one another. But he resists on the grounds that unanimity has a narrower domain than does this mark. Its field is limited to civic interests (Gauthier and Jolif, vol. 2, pp. 737–38). We can agree that unanimity has a narrower domain than personal friendship, but political friends do agree on these narrower political interests.

Annas argues that political friends cannot exhibit any mark of friendship because friendship is a relationship that requires intimacy and living together. She asserts that one cannot live together with every other citizen as such or grieve and rejoice with them. Nor can citizens wish one another well for their sake and know that they do (Annas, "Comments," pp. 243–44). She suggests, rather, that personal friendships can arise from working together on political projects (pp. 247–48). What Annas fails to do is to distinguish the marks of personal friendship from those of political friendship. We do not share intimate activities with political friends, but we can share political activities with them. A fact that Annas herself notes (Annas, "Comments," p. 248). Thus, when we help one another with a political project, we share a political life together and can become political friends. And even without being political friends, we do know that some citizens wish and do what is good for the sake of other citizens. Our knowledge about their activities is not always perfect, but neither is our knowledge in closer relationships.

Morrall implies that unanimity can be only useful or pleasant friendship (Morrall, ch. 4, pp. 62–63). But Aristotle indicates that unanimity may be good friendship as well as useful or pleasant friendship, for he implies that unanimous men do what is good for others for their sake. Morrall also argues that Aristotle's characterization of most men as obedient to emotion degrades politics to instrumental control (Morrall, ch. 4, pp. 63–66). Aristotle does admit that most men do not listen to argument, but he also argues that politics has the end of preparing the souls of men for the seeds for wisdom by instilling good habits in them (*Eth.* 10.9.1179b20–1180a14).

Price agrees that unanimity is political friendship for the sake of goodness. He argues that political friendship for the sake of utility is too prone to complaints to be unanimity (Price, ch. 7, p. 198).

One might, of course, object that Aristotle himself asserts that political friendship is established in accordance with utility (*Eud. Eth.* 7.10.1242a6–9). I concede that Aristotle does make this assertion, but we must observe that he places qualifications on it. He states that political friendship was only most of all established in accordance with utility (*Eud. Eth.* 7.10.1242a6–7). He thus leaves open the possibility that people can form a political friendship for the sake of goodness. He also implies that people come together for the sake of living together (1242a8–9). But living together is a mark of good friendship (see *Eth.* 9.4.1166a6–7).

Price, too, recognizes that Aristotle allows for the possibility that a city can arise for the sake of living together when he states that political friendship is useful (Price, ch. 7, pp. 195–96).

Irwin notes a similar distinction between the desire to live together and the pursuit of self-interest. But he takes at face value Aristotle's statement at *Eud. Eth.* 7.10.1242a6–9 that political friendship is useful friendship (Irwin, "Good," pp. 87–88). He thus fails to take account of the qualifications that Aristotle places on his statement. Irwin also cites *Eth.* 8.9.1160a11–14, where Aristotle states that a political community comes to be and remains for the sake of our interest (Irwin, "Good," p. 88). But Aristotle there asserts explicitly that statesmen aim at our interest and say that our common interest is justice (*Eth.* 8.9.1160a12–14). He thus implies that statesmen concern themselves with the happiness of others (see *Eth.* 5.1.1129b14–19).

Irwin also argues that friendship for the sake of advantage cannot explain the intrinsic value of political actions. Friendship of this type can only explain how action might have instrumental value. He suggests that political friendship of this sort might be appropriate only in some circumstances (Irwin, "Good," p. 88). I agree that political friendship for the sake of utility is appropriate for some circumstances and that it has only instrumental value. But I would also point out that the important issue is not whether political activity has value for itself but whether it has value for others.

2. Cooper argues that neither a kingship nor an aristocracy can exist for the sake of the common advantage of its citizens. He argues that kingship would collapse into tyranny. He implies that a king cannot rule for the sake of other citizens because he is the sole citizen. He also asserts that aristocracy would not be distinct from oligarchy. Presumably, aristocrats cannot rule for the sake of other citizens because they, too, are the only citizens. He suggests accordingly that Aristotle's definition of a citizen as someone who holds a deliberative or judicial office is too narrow. Citing *Pol.* 3.6.1279a21, he recommends that we define a citizen more broadly as someone who is free (Cooper, "Animals," pp. 228–29).

But I do not think that we need to reject Aristotle's definition of a citizen. Though he mentions it, Cooper does not attach sufficient importance to the fact that a king almost always appoints subjects to hold lesser offices for him (*Pol.* 3.16.1287b8–15). A king would thus rule for the sake of those who hold these lesser offices. But even a king who does not make appointments would differ from a tyrant. Though he might not rule for other citizens, he would rule those whom he rules for their sake. A tyrant rules only for his own sake (see *Pol.* 3.15.1286b8–11). I would also argue that aristocrats hold their offices by turn so that they can rule for those not currently in office and that aristocrats hold offices of different kinds and can fulfill their different offices for one another (*Pol.* 7.9.1329a2–19; *Pol.* 7.14.1332b27–41). Aristocrats also rule for the sake of those who are citizens in a qualified sense. That is, for those who are too young or too old to hold office (*Pol.* 3.1.1275a7–18). Finally, Aristotle does assert that a city is a community of free men, but he does so merely to distinguish citizenship from slavery (*Pol.* 3.6.1279a17–21).

Kraut argues that correctly governed constitutions have rulers who are not egoistic. He asserts that these rulers seek to advance the good of other citizens and do not promote their own good (Kraut, *Aristotle,* ch. 2, pp. 97–98). He even observes explicitly that these rulers seek the good of other citizens for the sake of those citizens (p. 98 n. 25). And yet he does not appear to assert that healthy constitutions are altruistic.

3. Though he does not distinguish essential from accidental good will, Cooper also argues that an oligarchy does not have political friendship because oligarchs establish only a commercial relationship. Citing *Pol.* 3.9.1280b1–5, he points out that oligarchs do not concern themselves with the characters of each other (Cooper, "Animals," pp. 229–30). I

agree. Oligarchs do not act for the sake of the virtue or the happiness of one another.

However, Cooper goes on to argue that citizens who are political friends do have a commercial relationship based on their expectations of mutual benefit but that they also have some concern for the characters of each other. That is, they exhibit good will and mutual trust in some measure (Cooper, "Animals," pp. 232–36; see also Cooper, "Forms," pp. 645–48). Aristotle would argue that those who enter a political relationship for the sake of commercial benefit have only an egoistic political friendship and that they bear only accidental good will for one another. For people in a relationship of this sort act for the sake of one another only as a means to their own ends. They thus act essentially for the sake of benefits received (see *Eth.* 8.3.1156a10–19).

Irwin criticizes Cooper for advocating an advantage friendship that includes some concern for others for their sake. He argues that if we act out of friendship for the sake of another person, we cannot choose the activity characteristic of friendship for its own sake (Irwin, "Good," p. 88 n. 20). I agree with his argument. It clearly shows why we ought not to choose friendship and its activity for its own sake. But I suspect that Irwin intends it to show why we ought not to choose friendship and its activity for the sake of others (see Irwin, "Good," p. 88).

Fraisse argues that political friends do have a useful friendship. Referring to *Eth.* 8.15.1162b21–1163a1, he divides useful friendships into two kinds. The one kind he also calls useful friendship, the other kind he calls moral friendship. The useful kind requires written law and allows only precisely defined contracts, but the moral kind rests on unwritten law and permits implied promises. Only the moral kind is friendship fully achieved (Fraisse, pt. 2, pp. 214–17). But we can see that even useful friendship of the moral kind cannot be good friendship. Aristotle does argue that useful friendship need not have fixed terms and that it can rely on mutual trust (*Eth.* 8.13.1162b25–33). But he also implies that friendship of this kind remains egoistic. He argues that this friendship is full of complaints, for those who enter it only wish to do good by one another without receiving something in return, but they actually choose to do good with the expectation of gaining something advantageous (1162b33–1163a1).

Grant would apparently agree. He asserts that Aristotle writes of a vacillation between a disinterested wish and a self-interested choice (Grant, vol. 2, p. 277).

Fraisse also argues that friendship of the useful kind realizes a mean accidentally without intention and that the moral kind of friendship realizes a mean essentially and apparently by intention. He cites *Eth.* 8.8.1159b19–23 (Fraisse, pt. 2, pp. 214–17, 215 n. 55). Aristotle does argue that useful friends aim at a contrary because they seek what they lack (*Eth.* 8.8.1159b12–15). He also suggests that these friends may aim at a contrary only accidentally and essentially may seek what is intermediate (1159b19–23). The implication is that if they have an excess or a deficiency, they will attempt to attain a mean (see *Eth.* 2.9.1109a30–1109b13). But if they seek a mean, even useful friends of the moral kind still seek a mean for themselves and not for their friends.

Irwin recognizes that oligarchy and democracy are merely instrumental constitutions (Irwin, *Principles,* ch. 20, pp. 433–34). He also asserts that oligarchy is a partnership for producing wealth and democracy an association for attaining gratification (pp. 435–37). Nevertheless, he fails to connect these constitutions with friendships of the useful and pleasant sorts.

4. Stewart argues that friendship does not exist between a king and his subjects because his subjects never have a turn at ruling, and that friendship does not exist between aristocrats and those subjected to their rule because those whom aristocrats rule do not rule in turn either (Stewart, vol. 2, pp. 312–13). But he overlooks the fact that a king who holds all offices in his kingdom is extremely rare; a king most often appoints some subjects to hold lesser offices for him (see again *Pol.* 3.16.1287b8–15). And a king who makes appointments at least would find that the subjects appointed to lesser offices would be his friends. They would not take a turn at being king, but they would fulfill their lesser offices for him. Aristotle explicitly argues that aristocrats do rule by turns, for they rule when they are mature, but when they are immature, they are ruled (*Pol.* 7.9.1329a2–17; *Pol.* 7.14.1332b27–41). I would also note that those who do not take a turn at ruling in an aristocracy would appear to be only natural slaves (*Pol.* 7.8.1328a21–37).

Newman apparently argues that a king and his subjects can be friends because they exchange advantage and honor. He asserts that a king rules for the advantage of his subjects and that his subjects render him honor (Newman, vol. 2, pp. 392–93). We would add that an argument of this sort would apply even to a king who does not make appointments. For his subjects would still grant him the honor of his office (see *Pol.* 3.10.1281a31).

Though he neglects reciprocity, Price recognizes that unanimity requires mutual recognition (Price, ch. 7, pp. 198–200). Irwin, too, remarks that the citizens know each other (Irwin, "Good," p. 95).

5. Millgram argues that fellow citizens love one another because they procreate one another. They thus make one another other selves, for they educate each other in virtue. They also love one another only in weak form, for they are responsible for the virtues of each other in a small degree (Millgram, p. 371 n. 18). I would agree, but I would add that fellow citizens do not always procreate each other in a moral or intellectual sense. They also do favors for each other, for they not only make others other selves but also make other selves theirs.

Price, too, agrees that political friendship is less intimate than personal friendship and that citizenship makes lesser demands than comradeship. He also recognizes that a city promotes moral education (Price, ch. 7, pp. 198–200).

Irwin argues that Aristotle's discussion of good friendship and its motive explains why we enjoy political activity. He explains that good friendship promotes our own good because friendship of this sort includes an awareness of our friend and his life. That is, we find our own good in sharing rational communication with our friend (Irwin, "Good," pp. 89–90). But, again, do we engage in intellectual or other activity with our friend for its own sake? To do so would be to engage in a friendship with ourself, for we would be acting for our own benefit. Rather, we engage a friend in any activity for his benefit. At least, in a good friendship we act essentially for another.

Irwin also argues that we attain our own good when we regard another person as another self. To regard another as another self is to make his thoughts and desires count as our own. That is, we cooperate in deliberation, decision, and action. My thoughts apparently are to his thoughts and actions as they are to my own. Our thoughts and actions provide each other with reasons for future thoughts and actions (Irwin, *Principles,* ch. 18, p. 392; Irwin, "Good," p. 91). We thus realize ourself more fully than we otherwise might. With cooperation we gain many more opportunities for action through one another (*Principles,* ch. 18, pp. 393–94; "Good," pp. 91–92). But I would argue that even without cooperating we may yet regard another as another self. We need only act for his sake as we act for our own sake. Nor do we realize more opportunities for action with another self. We, rather, give more opportunities for action to another self, for we act essentially for his sake.

And yet Irwin avers that good friendship cannot be extended to the political arena. Citing *Eth.* 9.10.1171a19–20, he asserts that friendship of this kind holds only for a few select people and that it cannot be extended to many (Irwin, *Principles,* ch. 18, pp. 397–98; Irwin, "Good," p. 90). But in *Eth.* 9.10. Aristotle discusses only good friendship of the personal kind.

We clearly cannot have a relationship of this sort with many people because it requires intimacy. We can, however, have a good friendship of the political kind with many people. A friendship of this sort is much less intimate; it requires that we share only a common legal system with others.

What Irwin claims is that fellow citizens have a relationship of friendliness rather than one of friendship proper. He cites *Eth.* 4.6.1126b20–25. He argues that a friendly person does not act for the sake of pleasure or advantage. But if he finds that another has sufficient virtue to have similar aims, a virtuous person can extend his practical reason in the same way as a friend can (Irwin, *Principles,* ch. 18, pp. 398–99; Irwin, "Good," p. 93). One citizen can thus treat another citizen as another self, for he extends his own self-realization by sharing the aims of another (*Principles,* ch. 18, p. 399; "Good," pp. 94–95). I think that a person who could establish merely a friendly relationship with another self rather than a friendship would be an improbability. Aristotle explicitly asserts that friendliness occurs without any feeling of fondness (*Eth.* 4.6.1126b20–25). But someone who is another self is a lovable object (see *Eth.* 9.9.1170a5–10). And, once more, to extend our self-realization to include the actions of another is to make our relationship with another egoistic.

Irwin, however, does rightly state that fellow citizens do not share lives to the same extent that friends do. He states too that fellow citizens need not be virtuous and, hence, are not other selves in the same way virtuous people are (Irwin, *Principles,* ch. 18, p. 399; Irwin, "Good," p. 93). He is right again. But we ought not to forget that we do sometimes make friends with those who are only potentially other selves when we first encounter them. Parents do, for example. So do kings (see *Pol.* 3.15.1286b8–13).

Couloubaritsis agrees that friendliness differs from friendship in that it lacks any feeling of fondness (Couloubaritsis, "Philia," p. 40). He attempts to argue also that friendliness expresses nothing other than a rational ideality (pp. 39–40, 53–54). But any virtue must rest on a particular emotion appropriate to it (see *Eth.* 2.6.1106b16–24). Though he does not specify what emotion it concerns, Aristotle denies only that friendliness occurs with the emotion appropriate to friendship (again *Eth.* 4.6.1126b20–25).

Couloubaritsis also argues that, with the addition of a feeling of fondness, friendliness surpasses itself and becomes friendship (Couloubaritsis, "Philia," pp. 41–42). He even assumes that without friendliness there could be no friendship (pp. 54–55). But if they are to be friends, those who are friendly with one another need to do more than feel fondness for each other. They must also wish and do what is good for the sake of one another, and they must do so with reciprocity and recognition

(*Eth.* 8.2.1156a3–5). In other words, they must change the activities of their relationship. For friendly people exhibit a mean only with regard to social pleasures and pains (*Eth.* 4.6.1126b28–35). And without having exhibited friendliness, people may, of course, wish and do what is good for one another.

Couloubaritsis agrees with Irwin that friendship can occur only among very few people. And he, too, argues that, when he speaks of political friendship, Aristotle refers to political friendliness. Friendliness of this sort is unanimity because it rests on a reciprocity that conforms to rationality (Couloubaritsis, "Philia," pp. 57–58, see also pp. 39–40). But Aristotle argues only that friendship is a relationship that entails reciprocity (again *Eth.* 8.2.1156a3–5); he does not state that friendliness does (see *Eth.* 4.6; *Eth.* 2.7.1108a9–30). And because it entails reciprocity, friendship also conforms to principle, for its mean lies in its reciprocity.

6. Cooper argues—with scant textual evidence—that the common advantage is both a cooperative advantage and an individual advantage. He asserts that all citizens attain part of their own good by cooperatively seeking the good of other citizens. When he cooperates with ordinary citizens for their good, an aristocrat, for example, fulfills a conscious objective and hence attains his own good, for his conscious objectives include his civic function. He also asserts that each citizen separately seeks his individual good from the just actions of other citizens. For example, an aristocrat benefits from the intellectual and moral virtues that he receives through education and from the opportunities that he receives to exercise these virtues (Cooper, "Animals," pp. 237–38; see also Cooper, "Forms," pp. 622, 648). I would note, first of all, that Cooper describes a ruler who seeks both public and private advantage from his office. Aristotle describes a ruler of this sort as someone who is sick and hopes to regain his health by always holding office (*Pol.* 3.6.1279a8–16). I would also argue that if we act merely for the sake of fulfilling our civic function, we engage in a political friendship with ourself, for we act for the sake of the virtue and activity of friendship itself. We thus would act essentially for the sake of the virtue and activity of ourself and accidentally for the sake of the virtue and activity of others. Again, to engage in a political friendship for the sake of advantages received from others is to engage in an egoistic political friendship. To engage in a friendship of utility.

Cooper does cite *Pol.* 1.2.1253a7–18 and *His. Ani.* 1.1.487b33–488a14 to the effect that human beings all have some work that we engage in together and that this cooperative activity is a city (Cooper, "Animals," pp. 222–27). But what Aristotle says in the passage from the *Politics* is only that our language enables us to define what justice and injustice are as well as what is beneficial and harmful. He does not define these terms, as Cooper himself notes (Cooper, "Good," pp. 5–6). What Aristotle does argue in the *Politics* is that rulers in healthy constitutions act only for the sake of those whom they rule. And so we might expect him to define justice as a virtue exercised for the sake of others (see, of course, *Eth.* 5.1). In the *History of Animals* Aristotle asserts only that political animals have some single function that all share (*His. Ani.* 1.1.488a7–9). The function shared by humans would, of course, be that of holding office. But to rule we need not perform a cooperative activity. Even to rule by turns we need not cooperate; we need only act for the sake of the happiness of those ruled.

Price also argues that we cannot fully achieve our own happiness unless our fellow citizens do. He attempts to argue that we act for the happiness of other citizens for their sake. That we bear them good will, in other words (Price, ch. 7, pp. 196–97). He explains that our life includes cooperation with other citizens as a constituent. Our happiness, in fact, includes as its finest part our contribution toward the happiness of other citizens. And by our contribution we appropriate their happiness and value it for itself (pp. 203–4). Again, if we act for the sake of cooperation with others, we act only for the sake of political friendship itself. And thus we act essentially for the sake of ourself, for our happiness includes political friendship and its activity. And if we appropriate their happiness, we obviously act accidentally for the sake of others. But Price does agree with me that citizens do not promote virtue and happiness in other citizens so that they might in turn be treated justly. He argues that, if they did, they would not act with good will (Price, ch.7, pp. 196–97).

Irwin, too, argues that we value political activity as an end in itself, for we value political activity as an intrinsic good. A complete and happy life ought to include political activity, for a rational agent wants to participate in human associations, and the most comprehensive association is a city, which includes everything needed for complete goodness. We thus realize ourself more fully by extending our practical reason beyond our own life (Irwin, *Principles,* ch. 18, pp. 400–402). But, again, if we act for the sake of civic activity itself, we act for the sake of a friendship with ourself; we advance our own happiness, for we act for the sake of our own virtuous activity. And we also act for our own happiness when we realize ourself by extending our rationality beyond our life.

Irwin cites *Pol.* 1.2.1253a12–18, too, where Aristotle argues that language enables us to define what is just and what beneficial. He asks why could we not develop our rational capacity through communication with rivals and enemies. He answers that we can fully realize our rational capacity only through a cooperative community (Irwin, *Principles,* ch. 18, p. 401; Irwin, "Good," pp. 84–85, 89). But we can develop our rationality without working together on a cooperative project. We can help one another with our projects, or we can simply work alone. And we do realize our rational capacity with antagonists, perhaps even doing so for their sake.

Irwin continues that we ought to distinguish living together in a city from living together in smaller associations. Living together in a city requires sharing in deliberation and choice about what is just and beneficial; participation in city life is a cooperative activity of ruling (Irwin, *Principles,* ch. 18, p. 403; Irwin, "Good," pp. 86–87). But, again, citizens can participate in political power without engaging in a cooperative scheme—they may simply hold office by turns. Aristotle clearly advocates rule of this kind (*Pol.* 3.6.1279a8–16, e.g.).

Striker agrees with me. What Aristotle demands, she says, is not deliberating cooperatively but taking turns at government. Fairness requires that those clearly qualified be allowed to exercise their capacity to rule (Striker, p. 99). Unfortunately she also agrees with Irwin that our happiness includes participation in government as an indispensable part (pp. 99–100). She would thus imply that we hold office for our own sake and that political rule is essentially egoistic.

Sherman, too, argues that unanimity is cooperative activity of some kind. She explains that those who are unanimous exhibit reciprocal choice and that choice of this sort results in a project of shared happiness. Friends make mutual decisions together and other looser agreements (Sherman, ch. 4, pp. 132–35). But, again, we can share a conception of happiness without cooperating, and we can reciprocally choose things for one another without cooperating.

With their emphasis on cooperative activities, Cooper, Price, and Irwin appear to share the same supposition that fellow citizens can be other selves only if they engage in an activity that is numerically one. On their supposition fellow citizens would thus be different in the usual sense, for they are different individuals. But they would be the same in an unusual sense, for they engage in one and the same activity. They would share a numerical identity of form in their shared activity.

But I argue that fellow citizens need not share a numerically identical form to be other selves. They may share numerically distinct forms that are only formally identical. On my account fellow citizens remain individuals who differ numerically; yet they are also individuals who are formally the same, for they share the same conception of happiness. And they can

do so without engaging in the very same action. I do not deny that political friends can engage in a cooperative activity. What I do deny is that they
must. Aristotle himself does not specify that political friends must cooperate; he indicates only that they act for the sake of one another. That they
hold political offices by turns. Nor do I deny that we can fulfill these offices for our own sake (*Pol.* 3.6.1279a8–16, e.g.). But I would again argue
that we need not fulfill these offices only for our sake. We can also fulfill
them for the sake of other citizens. Indeed, Aristotle avers that we ought
to do so (1279a17–21).

7. Commenting on this argument, Newman does refer us to *Eth.* 9.9
and 9.7. But he cites these passages merely to show that life is good and
pleasant. He apparently does not see that in them Aristotle discusses good
life not mere life. He also fails to make a connection with friendship (Newman, vol. 3, pp. 187–88).

8. One might even gather up more material here for the focal analysis debate. Are the definitions of healthy constitutions implied by those of
corrupt constitutions? They are. Aristotle himself remarks that healthy constitutions are prior to unhealthy ones (*Pol.* 3.1.1275a38–1275b2). And he
uses comparisons with healthy constitutions to define corrupt ones (*Pol.*
3.7.1279b4–10; *Eth.*8.10.1160a36–1160b22).

Fortenbaugh agrees but does not cite the *Ethics* (Fortenbaugh, esp.
pp. 129–30).

9. That kingship is a transitional constitution, Irwin fails to notice.
He claims that Aristotle is inconsistent. He argues that a king cannot rule
over virtuous people, for the criterion for citizenship is to have sufficient virtue to attain the happiness that constitutes political rule. If he
does rule, a king denies others political activity and deprives them of its
intrinsic good (Irwin, "Good," pp. 95–97). But the criterion for citizenship is not whether we have enough virtue to make ourself happy by
ruling but whether we have virtue enough to make others happy, for
rulers ought to rule for the sake of those whom they rule (once more *Pol.*
3.9.1279a8–16). I agree that one virtuous person ought not to rule over
other virtuous people—unless he has more virtue than they all do taken
together (see *Pol.* 3.17.1288a6–29; *Pol.* 3.13.1284a3–1284b34). Thus,
kingship is appropriate when people have little or no virtue (*Pol.*
3.15.1286b8–13 again). And if he is good, a king soon relinquishes his rule
because he makes his people virtuous and happy (*Pol.* 3.16.1287a23–27,
1287b29–35). That is, he qualifies them for citizenship.

10. Wood and Wood argue that Aristotle offers an analogy between his conception of an aristocracy and his conception of a household. They argue that Aristotle's distinction between the ruler and the ruled in an aristocracy is similar to that between husband and wife or father and child in a household, and that his distinction between the parts and the conditions of an aristocracy is similar to that between master and slave in a household (Wood and Wood, ch. 5, pp. 232–33). But they also argue that the Aristotelian conception of aristocracy subordinates the analogy of husband and wife to that of master and slave (pp. 236–37). I agree that Aristotle does draw an analogy between an aristocracy and a marriage. He does so explicitly, in fact (see *Eth.* 8.10.1160b33–35; *Eth.* 8.11.1161a22–25). But the analogy to husband and wife is the essential one, for aristocrats rule for the sake of those whom they rule (see *Eth.* 8.10.1160b35–1161a3; *Eth.* 8.11.1161a22–25). Wood and Wood themselves note that they do (Wood and Wood, ch. 5, pp. 232–33). And Aristotle argues only that the conditions of an aristocracy are not free men but only natural slaves (see esp. *Pol.* 7.8–9). But, again, he doubts that men are sufficiently different to establish an aristocracy. Do not forget that he does not believe the caste system in India to be natural (see again *Pol.* 7.14.1332b16–27).

11. Wood and Wood contend that polity is oligarchized democracy. They argue that by mixing oligarchic and democratic measures the rulers of a polity attempt to secure the domination of the wealthy over the poor (Wood and Wood, ch. 5, pp. 243–45, 248–49). Polity, however, is essentially altruistic, and oligarchy and democracy are essentially egoistic. Rulers of a polity do use measures the same as those used in an oligarchy or a democracy; but these rulers use oligarchic or democratic measures for the sake of those whom they rule, not for their own sake. Aristotle, in fact, warns against deceiving the people (*Pol.* 4.12.1297a7–13).

Mulgan argues that those citizens with moderate wealth are not more given to similarity or to friendship and that these citizens are not more fit for ruling and being ruled (Mulgan, ch. 6, pp. 108–10). He apparently forgets that those with moderate wealth are more apt to obey a principle (but see pp. 107–8). They are accordingly more likely to be friends because they are likely to be good men and to be similar.

Cooper rightly recognizes that political friendship is best achieved only if the middle class has political power. He also asserts that each citizen has friendship of this kind with all other citizens. But unfortunately he again argues that political friendship is only advantage friendship. He also asserts that each citizen feels this friendship for other citizens en masse (Cooper, "Animals," pp. 233–34 n. 16).

CHAPTER VI. POLITICAL JUSTICE

1. By referring to some other grounds of sovereignty, Aristotle might seem to refer to tyranny, oligarchy, and democracy. Most commentators believe that he does (e.g., see Stewart, vol. 1, pp. 390–91; or Burnet, p. 207). But Aristotle clearly cannot refer to corrupt constitutions, for rulers of corrupt constitutions do not promote the happiness of their citizens. He appears more likely to refer to some ground such as the possession of armor, which is necessary for the exercise of military virtue (see *Pol.* 3.7.1279a40–1279b4).

2. Irwin maintains that whole justice concerns the collective good of a city and that partial justice concerns the separate good of citizens. Whole justice apparently does not benefit any person in particular, but partial justice does. For whole injustice does not inflict harm on any particular person, but partial injustice does (Irwin, *Principles,* ch. 20, pp. 426–27). Irwin might better argue that whole justice does benefit particular persons, for it benefits those who cooperate for a collective good, and that partial justice does benefit a collective good, for it benefits those who engage in a cooperation. But I would argue that justice takes as its end the happiness of other citizens and that their activities need not be cooperative activities. They may also be separate activities, for happiness can be cooperative or separate. I would also argue that both whole and partial justice benefit particular citizens, for whole justice finds its end in the happiness of individuals, and partial justice distributes and secures external goods necessary for their happiness.

Irwin also argues that general justice promotes our common interest in cooperative activities and that special justice protects our self-interest in these activities. We are not entirely altruistic; we do not wish to sacrifice our self-interest for the common interest (Irwin, *Principles,* ch. 20, pp. 430–31). I would agree that we are not entirely altruistic; we perform not only altruistic actions but also egoistic ones. But I would argue that both whole justice and particular justice promote both altruistic and egoistic actions. For whole justice concerns happiness, which includes altruistic and egoistic activities, and partial justice concerns external means to happiness.

Hardie would agree with me. He offers examples to show that whole justice concerns more than public activities, and partial justice more than private activities (Hardie, ch. 10, pp. 186–87). Stewart also agrees, but he discusses conduct alone rather than conduct and resources (Stewart, vol. 1, pp. 406–8).

3. Citing Trendelenberg, Stewart agrees about this relation between distributive and corrective justice (Stewart, vol. 1, pp. 414–15).

4. We thus agree with Newman when he says that men in a community are just with one another before they become friends. He argues that justice is a condition of friendship in any community. For men in a community must render honor and advantages to one another in accordance with their worth if they are to have friendship with one another (Newman, vol. 2, pp. 392–93).

Cooper would appear to agree, too. He asserts that people who do not care for one another can follow strict rules of justice but that people who are friends look after one another without resorting to strict rules of justice (Cooper, "Forms," pp. 646–47).

Fraisse maintains that friendship renders justice useless. Justice proceeds by constraint, for it requires both the recognition of merit and the sanction of law. But friendship neglects merit and finds its value in freedom, for it treats men as men (Fraisse, pt. 2, pp. 210–12). I would argue that friendship cannot neglect merit; it treats others not as mere men but as other selves. And it arises for the sake of the virtue and activity of another self. We might also note that justice of the best sort is without constraint. Being a virtuous activity, it proceeds from choice.

Barker puts the matter best, stating simply that friendship follows on the heels of justice (Barker, ch. 5, pp. 235–37).

Irwin, however, implies that political friendship is prior to justice. He argues that friendship provides an extension of altruistic concerns and that an extended concern of this sort provides a basis for justice. Consequently, we value just activities for their own sake and for the sake of other citizens (Irwin, *Principles*, ch. 18, pp. 397, 406). But surely we must have extended altruism before we have extended altruism that is reciprocated and recognized. For friendship is good will that is reciprocated and recognized (see *Eth.* 8.2.1156a3–5). We need not have extended altruism, however. Ordinary altruism will also do. And justice becomes egoistic if we perform just activities for their own sake and for the sake of our happiness, even if we view our happiness as extended.

Stewart also argues that friendship is prior to justice. He maintains that only in a community in which they feel confidence in one another can men effect private and public advantage for one another through contract and the division of labor. Otherwise, they secure their advantages by plunder and murder (Stewart, vol. 2, pp. 262–64). But justice and its laws can exist where friendship does not. Again, friends exhibit the marks of friendship, but not all who exhibit the marks of friendship are friends (*Eth.* 8.3.1156b29–32).

5. Kraut especially emphasizes the fact that distributive justice requires reciprocity. He bases his argument on the general proposition that justice requires equality (Kraut, *Aristotle*, ch. 2, p. 98). He explains that we must give up political power to others who are as worthy of office as we are. Even though we forfeit opportunities to act virtuously, we must still grant opportunities to our peers to exercise their political virtue. Otherwise, we deprive them of their happiness (pp. 98–101). Yet he concludes only that a just relationship is not egoistic, for we do not maximize our happiness when we give up political power (pp. 101–2). He thus stops short of calling justice altruistic. He appears to view sharing power with others as merely a self-sacrificing activity (see Kraut, *Aristotle*, ch. 2, p. 102; also Kraut, "Comments," pp. 22–23).

6. Cooper appears to argue that each community has friendship and justice specific to it, and he points out that unjust action destroys families less easily than it does a city (Cooper, "Animals," pp. 236–37; also Cooper, "Forms," pp. 646–47). I would add only that injustice is less destructive in a family than in a city because family members have a relationship more intensive and extensive than fellow citizens. They would thus be better able to tolerate some injustice.

CHAPTER VII. CONCLUSION

1. Kraut appears to agree, but he puts the point merely in terms of sharing pain. He maintains that an egoist would wish to share his pain with others because he prefers to reduce his own suffering, even though he increases theirs. He implies that an altruist would not wish to share his pain because he does not prefer to increase the suffering of others, even though he thus fails to lessen his own (Kraut, *Aristotle*, ch. 2, pp. 113–15).

2. Kraut rightly declares that the pie to be divided increases when one virtuous activity causes another. Unfortunately he assumes that the virtuous activity causing the other is an act of self-love (Kraut, *Aristotle*, ch. 2, pp. 124–25). He thus implies that the common good increases accidentally. Aristotle would argue that one virtuous action causes another essentially when we perform an action out of love for another. We would thus increase the common good purposefully.

Kraut also points out that the happiness of one person does not detract from that of another, for happiness does not consist in having a greater quantity of a good than another has. Happiness consists in acting virtuously (Kraut, *Aristotle,* ch. 2, p. 119).

APPENDIX A

1. The references are to Lawrence Blum, *Friendship, Altruism, and Morality* (New York: Routledge and Kegan Paul, 1980).

Other philosophers have also written about the issues raised by Blum, of course. For example, one might consider Barbara Herman, "Integrity and Impartiality," *The Monist,* vol. 66 (1983), pp. 233–50; or Barbara Herman, "Rules, Motives, and Helping Others," *Philosophical Studies,* vol. 45 (1984), pp. 369–77. And also Michael Stocker, "Duty and Friendship," *Women and Moral Theory,* Eva Feder Kittay and Diana T. Meyers, eds., (Totowa: Rowman and Littlefield, Publishers, 1987), pp. 56–68; or Michael Stocker, "Friendship and Duty," *Identity, Character, and Morality,* Owen Flanagan and Amélie Oksenberg Rorty, eds., (Cambridge: MIT Press, 1990), pp. 219–33. Another source worthy of consideration is "Symposium on Impartiality and Ethical Theory," *Ethics,* vol. 101 (1991), no. 4.

APPENDIX B

1. John Rawls, *A Theory of Justice* (Cambridge: Harvard University Press, 1971).

2. Cooper, of course, presents an interpretation of this kind (see ch. 5 nn. 3, 6; see also ch. 3 nn. 3, 6 and ch. 4 nn. 13, 14). And he cheerfully acknowledges Rawls's influence on his interpretation (Cooper, "Forms," p. 645 n. 23).

3. Irwin advocates an interpretation of this sort (see ch. 5 nn. 5, 6; see also ch. 2 n. 4, ch. 3 nn. 6, 10 and ch. 4 n. 8). Price, too, advances this interpretation (see ch. 5 n. 6; see also ch. 3 nn. 3, 6, 10 and ch. 4, nn. 13, 14).

SELECT BIBLIOGRAPHY

PRIMARY SOURCES

Aristoteles. *Analytica Priora et Posteriora*. Edited by W. D. Ross. Oxford: Clarendon Press, 1964.

———. *Ethica Nicomachea*. Edited by I. Bywater. Oxford: Clarendon Press, 1894.

———. *Politica*. Edited by W. D. Ross. Oxford: Clarendon Press, 1957.

Barnes, Jonathan, ed. *The Complete Works of Aristotle*. 2 vols. Princeton: Princeton University Press, 1984.

McKeon, Richard, ed. *The Basic Works of Aristotle*. New York: Random House, 1941.

SECONDARY SOURCES

Adkins, A. W. H. " 'Friendship' and 'Self-Sufficiency' in Homer and Aristotle." *Classical Quarterly,* vol. 13 (1963), pp. 30–45.

Alpern, Kenneth D. "Aristotle on the Friendships of Utility and Pleasure." *Journal of the History of Philosophy,* vol. 21 (1983), pp. 303–15.

Annas, Julia. "Comments on J. Cooper." In *Aristoteles' "Politik,"* edited by Günther Patzig, pp. 242–48. Göttingen: Vandenhoeck und Ruprecht, 1990.

————. "Plato and Aristotle on Friendship and Altruism." *Mind,* vol. 86 (1977), pp. 532–54.

————. "Self-Love in Aristotle." *Southern Journal of Philosophy,* vol. 27 (1988), sup., pp. 1–18.

Barker, Ernest. *The Political Thought of Plato and Aristotle.* New York: Dover Publications, 1959.

Burnet, John. *The Ethics of Aristotle.* London: Methuen and Co., 1900.

Cooper, John M. "Aristotle on the Forms of Friendship." *The Review of Metaphysics,* vol. 30 (1977), pp. 617–48.

————. "Friendship and the Good in Aristotle." *The Philosophical Review,* vol. 86 (1977), pp. 290–315.

————. "Political Animals and Civic Friendship." In *Aristoteles' "Politik,"* edited by Günther Patzig, pp. 220–41. Göttingen: Vandenhoeck und Ruprecht, 1990.

Couloubaritsis, L. "La philia à l'origine d'une mise en question du bonheur aristotélicien comme seule fin ultime de l'Ethique." *Annales de l'Institut de Philosophie,* vol. 2 (1970), pp. 25–78.

————. "Le rôle du *pathos* dans l'amitié aristotélicienne." *Diotima,* vol. 8 (1980), pp. 175–82.

Fortenbaugh, W. W. "Aristotle on Prior and Posterior, Correct and Mistaken, Constitutions." *Transactions of the American Philological Association,* vol. 106 (1976), pp. 125–37.

————. "Aristotle's Analysis of Friendship." *Phronesis,* vol. 20 (1975), pp. 51–62.

Fraisse, Jean-Claude. *Philia.* Paris: Librairie Philosophique J. Vrin, 1984.

Gauthier, René Antoine, and Jolif, Jean Yves, trans. and comms. *L'éthique à Nicomaque.* 2nd ed. 2 vols. Paris: Béatrice-Nauwelaerts, 1970.

Grant, Alexander. *The Ethics of Aristotle.* 4th ed. 2 vols. London: Longmans, Green, and Co., 1885.

Hardie, W. F. R. *Aristotle's Ethical Theory.* 2nd ed. Oxford: Clarendon Press, 1980.

Irwin, Terence. *Aristotle's First Principles.* Oxford: Clarendon Press, 1989.

————. "The Good of Political Activity." In *Aristoteles' "Politik,"* edited by Günther Patzig, pp. 73–98. Göttingen: Vandenhoeck und Ruprecht, 1990.

————, trans. *Nicomachean Ethics.* Indianapolis: Hackett Publishing Company, 1985.

Kahn, Charles H. "Aristotle and Altruism." *Mind,* vol. 90 (1981), pp. 20–40.

Kraut, Richard. *Aristotle on the Human Good.* Princeton: Princeton University Press, 1989.

————. "Comments on Julian Annas' 'Self-Love in Aristotle.'" *Southern Journal of Philosophy,* vol. 27 (1988), sup., pp. 19–22.

Millgram, Elijah. "Aristotle on Making Other Selves." *Canadian Journal of Philosophy,* vol. 17 (1987), pp. 361–76.

Monan, J. Donald. *Moral Knowledge and its Methodology in Aristotle.* Oxford: Clarendon Press, 1968.

Moravcsik, J. M. E. "The Perils of Friendship and Conceptions of Self." In *Human Agency,* edited by Jonathan Dancy, J. M. E. Moravcsik, and C. C. W. Taylor, pp. 133–51, 293–94. Stanford: Stanford University Press, 1988.

Morrall, John B. *Aristotle.* London: George Allen and Unwin, 1977.

Mulgan, R. G. *Aristotle's Political Theory.* Oxford: Clarendon Press, 1977.

Newman, W. L. *The Politics of Aristotle.* 4 vols. Oxford: Clarendon Press, 1897–1902.

Owens, Joseph. "An Ambiguity in Aristotle, EE VII 2 1236a23–4." *Apeiron,* vol. 22 (1989), pp. 127–37.

Price, A. W. *Love and Friendship in Plato and Aristotle.* Oxford: Clarendon Press, 1989.

Robin, Léon. *Aristote.* Paris: Presses Universitaires de France, 1944.

Ross, David. Introduction to *The Nichomachean Ethics,* translated by David Ross and revised by J. L. Ackrill and J. O. Urmson, pp. v–xxiv. New York: Oxford University Press, 1980.

Ross, W. D. *Aristotle.* London: Methuen and Co., 1923.

———, trans. and ed. *Ethica Nicomachea.* Vol. 9 of *The Works of Aristotle,* edited by W. D. Ross. 12 vols. London: Oxford University Press, 1944.

Sherman, Nancy. *The Fabric of Character.* Oxford: Clarendon Press, 1989.

Stewart, J. A. *Notes on the Nicomachean Ethics.* 2 vols. Oxford: Clarendon Press, 1892.

Stocker, Michael. "Values and Purposes." *Journal of Philosophy,* vol. 78 (1981), pp. 747–65.

Striker, Gisela. "Comments on T. Irwin." In *Aristoteles' "Politik,"* edited by Günther Patzig, pp. 99–100. Göttingen: Vandenhoeck und Ruprecht, 1990.

Urmson, J. D. *Aristotle's Ethics.* Oxford: Basil Blackwell, 1988.

Walker, A. D. M. "Aristotle's Account of Friendship in the *Nicomachean Ethics.*" *Phronesis,* vol. 24 (1979), pp. 180–96.

Wood, Ellen Meiksins, and Wood, Neal. *Class Ideology and Ancient Political Theory.* New York: Oxford University Press, 1978.

SUBJECT INDEX

Numbers and letters set in bold refer to chapters or appendices; numbers set in roman refer to pages.

Altruistic, definition, **2**, 30
Apperception, pleasant, **1**, 3, 3–4, 4; **4**, 64–68, 71–72; **5**, 84; **6**, 104; **7**, 116
    See also Friendship, personal or political: motivation; Justice: motivation

Beneficence, **4**, 68–69
    See also Good will; Love
Blum, Lawrence, and personal friendship
    definition, **A**, 123–26
    marks, **A**, 124, 125
    altruistic and egoistic, **A**, 125–26
    motivation, **A**, 126
    and other selves, **A**, 126, 127
    partial and impartial, **A**, 127, 131–32, 133–36, 136–37
    personal and impersonal, **A**, 127, 131–32, 132–33
    and happiness, **A**, 127
    rationality, **A**, 127–29, 129–30, 131
    emotion, **A**, 127–29, 130–31
    and Aristotle, **A**, 123, 127, 130, 132, 132–33, 136, 137

and morality, **A**, 131–32, 133–37
and justice, **A**, 136–37

Citizens
    See City; entries for Constitutions; Friendship, political
City, **1**, 6, 9, 9–10, 11–12, 12–13; **3**, 40–41; **5**, 76–77, 78, 86, 87, 93, 94–96; **6**, 110; **7**, 114, 119, 120–22
    See also entries for Constitutions; Friendship, political
Comradeship, **1**, 6–7, 9; **5**, 81; **6**, 110
Constitutions
    healthy and corrupt, **1**, 3, 4; **5**, 78–83, 84–87; **7**, 114, 116–17
    essential and accidental, **5**, 78–83, 84–87
    altruistic and egoistic, **5**, 78–83, 84–87; **7**, 114
    good, useful, and pleasant, **5**, 80–83
    See also Friendship, political
Constitutions, division, **5**, 79–80, 87–89; **7**, 114
Constitutions, kinds

kingship, **5**, 78, 78–79, 79,
    79–80, 80–81, 84–85, 87–88,
    89–92; **7**, 114, 120
aristocracy, **5**, 78, 78–79, 79, 81,
    84–85, 87–88, 92–94; **6**, 102;
    7, 114, 120
polity, **5**, 79, 80, 81, 88, 94–96;
    7, 114, 120, 120–22
tyranny, **5**, 79, 81–82, 83; **7**, 114,
    120–21
oligarchy, **5**, 79–80, 82; **6**, 102; **7**,
    114, 120–22
democracy, **5**, 80, 82; **6**, 102; **7**,
    114, 120–22
Courage, **2**, 24–26; **3**, 48; **4**, 55–56,
    72–73; **5**, 88, 93, 94; **6**,
    99–100; **7**, 120
Craftsman
    and beneficence, **4**, 68–69
    Egoistic, definition
        See Altruistic
Emotion
    in political friendship, **1**, 4; **6**, 98,
        107–9
    in justice, **1**, 4; **6**, 98, 107–9
    in moral virtue, **2**, 26
    control of, **2**, 21; **4**, 57–58; **7**,
        118–19, 120
    in personal friendship, **3**, 42–44,
        46–47
    See also Beneficence; Good will;
        Love; Self-Love
Emotion, acquisitive, **6**, 109
Extremes, The
    in personal friendship, **3**, 46
    in moral virtue, **2**, 25–26, 26

Faction, **1**, 6; **5**, 75–76, 77–78, 78; **7**,
    120–22
Friends
    See various entries for Friendship
"Friendship," range, **1**, 4–5, 6
Friendship, activeness, **7**, 117–18,
    118–19, 120

Friendship, advantages, **7**, 116–22
Friendship, conventional, **1**, 6–7, 9–13
Friendship, development, **1**, 6–13
Friendship, division, **1**, 4–13, 14; **7**,
    113–114, 115, 116
    See also Friendship, unity and
        diversity
Friendship, feasibility
    personal friendship, **1**, 2; **4**, 73
    political friendship, **1**, 2, 4; **5**,
        89–96; **7**, 120
Friendship, extensity and intensity, **5**,
    84; **6**, 109–10
    See also Happiness, personal and
        political
Friendship, kinds
    See Friendship, personal; Friend-
        ship, political; other entries un-
        der Friendship
Friendship, marks
    of personal friendship, **4**, 53–62;
        6, 109, 110–11
    of political friendship, **5**, 76–78, 96
    and justice, **1**, 4; **6**, 97–98,
        98–101, 101–4
Friendship, natural, **1**, 6–7, 7–9
Friendship, object
    See Friendship, personal or politi-
        cal: motivation; Other selves
Friendship, personal
    definition
    of activity, **1**, 1, 2–3, 5; **3**, 35–37;
        7, 114–16
    of virtue, **1**, 5; **3**, 42–47
    motivation, **1**, 1–2, 3, 5–6; **4**,
        60–62, 62–68; **7**, 114–16
    essential and accidental, **1**, 2–3;
        3, 37–39, 40–41, 50–51
    altruistic and egoistic, **1**, 1, 1–2,
        2, 3; **3**, 38–39, 49–51; **7**,
        113–14, 117–18
    good, useful, and pleasant, **1**,
        2–3; **3**, 36, 37–38, 40–41,
        41, 47–48; **4**, 69–71; **7**,
        113–14, 116

origin, **4**, 53–62
affinity with justice, **6**, 109–10
See also other entries under
    Friendship; Good will; Love;
    Other selves
Friendship, political
definition
    of activity, **1**, 2, 3, 6–7; **5**, 75–38;
    7, 114–16
    of virtue, **5**, 83
motivation, **1**, 2; **5**, 83–84; **7**,
    114–16
essential and accidental, **5**, 78–80
altruistic and egoistic, **1**, 2, 3;
    5, 75–83, 84–87; **7**, 114,
    117–18, 120
good, useful, and pleasant, **5**,
    80–83, 87–89
affinity with justice, **1**, 2, 4, 6; **5**,
    77, 77–78, 78, 80–82, 86–87,
    91–92, 93; **6**, 97–98, 105–7,
    108–9
See also other entries for Friend-
    ship; entries for Constitutions;
    Unanimity; Other selves; Good
    will; Love
Friendship, pluralistic
personal friendship, **1**, 2, 3; **4**,
    71–73
political friendship, **1**, 2, 3–4; **5**,
    84–89; **7**, 120–22
Friendship, stability
personal friendship, **3**, 41, 47–48;
    7, 116
political friendship, **5**, 83; **7**,
    116–17
Friendship, sublimity, **1**, 13
Friendship, unity and diversity,
    1, 6, 13, 14; **2**, 29–30; **7**,
    113–14, 115
See also Friendship, division
Friendship, with self, **3**, 50–51; **4**,
    53–62, 62–68; **6**, 110–11; **7**,
    118–19, 119–20
See also Self-Love

God
and self-identity, **4**, 58–59
Good will
in personal friendship, **3**, 36–37,
    37–40; **6**, 107–8
in political friendship, **6**, 107–8
in justice, **6**, 107–9, 109
Good wishes, **3**, 36
See also Good will
Goods, external
and personal friendship, **1**, 5–6
and happiness, **2**, 19–20
and self-love, **3**, 49, 50; **7**, 119–20
and political friendship, **7**, 119–20
and polity, **5**, 95–96; **7**, 120
and justice, **6**, 101–4
See also Emotion, acquisitive;
    Greed
Greed, **3**, 49; **5**, 77–78; **6**, 98–99

Habit
of moral virtue, **2**, 26–27
of personal friendship, **3**, 42–44,
    47–48
of political friendship, **5**, 83
of justice, **6**, 98
See Also Friendship, stability
Happiness
definition, **2**, 17–20
primary and secondary, **1**, 3, 3–4,
    4; **2**, 27–28; **4**, 60, 71–73; **5**,
    84–85, 87–89; **7**, 114, 116, 120
personal and political, **1**, 4;
    2, 29–30; **5**, 84; **6**, 104, 110;
    7, 116
and personal friendship, **1**, 2, 3; **2**,
    29–30; **3**, 48–50
and political friendship, **1**, 2, 3–4,
    4; **2**, 29–30; **5**, 83–84; **7**,
    118–19
and justice, **1**, 4; **6**, 98–104, 104
See also Friendship, personal and
    political; Justice; Virtue; Goods,
    external; Other selves

Household, **5**, 82–83, 85–86; **6**, 111
  See also entries under Kindship,
    kinds
  Human being, **2**, 30
  Humboldt, Wilhelm von, **B**, 144

Justice, personal
  affinity with friendship, **3**, 49–50;
    6, 109–10; **7**, 118–19
  and marks of friendship, **6**, 109
Justice, political
  definition
  general, **6**, 98–99
  lawfulness, **1**, 4; **6**, 99–101
  fairness, **6**, 101–4
  distributive, **2**, 24–25; **6**, 102–3
  corrective, **6**, 103–4
  motivation, **1**, 4; **6**, 104
  whole and partial, **6**, 101–2
  essential and accidental, **6**, 100
  altruistic and egoistic, **6**, 98–101,
    100, 102–3
  good, useful, and pleasant, **6**,
    102–3
  affinity with political friendship, **1**,
    2, 4, 6, 13; **6**, 97–98, 105–7,
    107–9
Justice, object
  See Justice, political: motivation
Justice, with self, **6**, 110–11

Kinship, **1**, 6–7, 11, 12
Kinship, kinds
  marriage, **1**, 9–10, 11; **5**, 81, 82,
    85–86
  family, **1**, 9–10, 11, 12–13; **5**, 90
  parenthood and childhood, **1**, 6,
    7–8, 9, 9–10; **3**, 47; **5**, 80–81,
    83, 85–86; **6**, 110
  brotherhood, **1**, 8–9, 9; **5**, 81;
    6, 110
  grandparenthood and grandchild-
    hood, **1**, 10

cousinship, **1**, 11
  See also Household; Village

Love
  of husband and wife, **1**, 9–10
  of parents and children, **1**, 7–8
  of brothers, **1**, 8–9
  of villagers, **1**, 9
  of citizens, **1**, 9
  of personal friends, **3**, 36, 42–44,
    45, 46–47; **6**, 107–8
  of political friends, **6**, 108–9, 109
  of just persons, **6**, 108–9, 109
  See also Beneficence; Good will;
    Self-Love
Love, erotic, **3**, 39–40; **4**, 71–72;
  6, 108

Mean, The:
  in personal friendship, **3**, 45–46;
    6, 106–7
  in political friendship, **5**, 83; **6**,
    106–7
  in justice, **6**, 105–7
  in moral virtue, **2**, 25–26
Methodology, **2**, 31–33
Monistic, definition
  See Pluralistic, definition

Other selves
  definition, **2**, 28–29
  and happiness, **1**, 2, 3; **2**, 28–29
  and development of friendship,
    1, 6–13
  family, **1**, 9–10
  parents and children, **1**, 7–8, 9,
    9–10, 11
  brothers, **1**, 8–9, 9, 11
  grandparents and grandchildren,
    1, 10
  cousins, **1**, 11
  comrades, **1**, 9

villagers, **1**, 9, 10–11
villagerlike people, **1**, 10–11
citizens, **1**, 9, 12–13
personal friends, **1**, 3; **4**, 61–62,
   66, 68–69; **6**, 110–11; **7**, 116
political friends, **1**, 4; **5**, 83–84,
   85; **7**, 116
just persons, **6**, 104, 111
See also Human being

Passion
   See Emotion
Principle
   and Aristotle, **1**, 2–4, 4–5; **2**,
     28–30
   and polity, **5**, 95–96
   See also Happiness
Pluralistic, definition, **2**, 30–31

Rawls, John, and political friendship
   original position, **B**, 139–41
   altruistic and egoistic, **B**, 140–41,
     141–43, 143–47, 147–49,
     149–51
   common institutions, **B**, 141–42,
     143–47
   thin and full theory of the good,
     B, 142–43
   social union, **B**, 144–45
   Aristotelian principle, **B**,
     145–46
   moral virtue, **B**, 147–49
   moral development, **B**, 149–51
   and Aristotle, **B**, 139, 140–41,
     146–47, 150–51
   and interpretation of Aristotle, **B**,
     139, 151–53
Reciprocity and recognition
   in personal friendship, **3**, 36–37
   in political friendship, **5**, 83
   in justice, **6**, 105

Rulers
   See Constitutions.

Self-Love, **3**, 49–50; **7**, 118–19,
   119–20
   See also Friendship, with self
Sidgwick, Henry, **A**, 136
Slavery, **5**, 81–82, 83, 85, 93–94,
   95–96; **6**, 111

Temperance, **2**, 24–26; **3**, 49–50;
   4, 55–56, 72–73; **5**, 93; **6**,
   99–100; **7**, 118–19; 120

Unanimity
   definition, **1**, 3, 6; **5**, 75–78
   essential and accidental, **5**, 78–79
   altruistic and egoistic, **5**, 78–79;
     7, 114
   affinity with justice, **5**, 77,
     77–78, 78
   See also Friendship, political; en-
     tries under Constitutions

Village, **1**, 9, 9–10, 10–11, 12–13
Villagelike relationships, **1**, 6–7,
   11–12; **6**, 109–10
Virtue, definition
   intellectual, **2**, 20–24
   moral, **2**, 24–26
   See also Habit

Wisdom
   theoretical, **2**, 20–22; **4**, 59–60,
     69–71, 72; **5**, 87–88, 93; **7**,
     114, 120
   practical, **2**, 22–24; **3**, 49–50; **4**,
     55–56, 57–58, 63–64; **5**,
     92–93; **7**, 119

AUTHOR INDEX

Numbers or letters set in bold refer to chapters and appendices; numbers set in roman refer to notes.

Adkins, A. W. H.
    definition of friendship, **1**, 3, 6;
        3, 4
    altruistic and egoistic friendship,
        1, 3, 6; **3**, 4
    good, useful, and pleasant friend-
        ship, **1**, 3; **3**, 4
    good will, **3**, 6
Alpern, Kenneth D.
    good will, **3**, 5
Annas, Julia
    essential and accidental friendship,
        3, 2
    altruistic and egoistic friendship,
        1, 5; **3**, 10
    good, useful, and pleasant friend-
        ship, **3**, 2
    motivation for friendship, **1**, 5;
        3, 10
    origin of friendship, **4**, 1, 6
    marks of friendship, **1**, 18; **4**, 2;
        5, 1
    practical intellect, **4**, 3
    political friendship, **5**, 1
    "altruistic" and "egoistic", **2**, 5

Barker, Ernest
    development of friendship, **1**, 19

other selves, **1**, 19
altruistic and egoistic friendship,
    4, 14
motivation for friendship, **4**, 14
unanimity, **5**, 1
marks of friendship, **5**, 1
affinity between friendship and
    justice, **6**, 4
Blum, Lawrence
    See subject index
Burnet, John
    altruistic and egoistic friendship,
        1, 4; **4**, 8
    motivation for friendship, **1**, 4;
        4, 8, 9
    reciprocal love, **3**, 8
    theoretical intellect, **4**, 3
    marks of friendship, **4**, 5
    grounds of sovereignty, **6**, 1

Cooper, John M.
    definition of friendship, **1**, 2, 6; **3**, 3
    essential and accidental friendship,
        3, 2, 3; **5**, 3, 6
    altruistic and egoistic friendship,
        1, 2, 6, 7; **3**, 3; **5**, 2, 3, 6
    good, useful, and pleasant friend-
        ship, **1**, 2; **3**, 2, 3; **4**, 13, 14, 15

good will, **3**, 6
motivation for friendship, **1**, 7; **4**,
    7, 8, 10, 13, 14
marks of friendship, **1**, 18
feasibility of friendship, **1**, 10; **4**, 15
other selves, **4**, 7; **5**, 6
contemplation of actions, **4**, 12
kingship, **5**, 2
aristocracy, **5**, 2
polity, **5**, 11
oligarchy, **5**, 3
citizenship, **5**, 2
political friendship, **1**, 7; **5**, 3, 6
cooperation, **5**, 6
affinity between friendship and
    justice, **6**, 4, 6
and interpretation of Aristotle, **B**, 2
and Rawls, **B**, 2
designation of "friendship", **1**, 14
αἰσθάνεσθαι, **4**, 13
διά, **3**, 3
Couloubaritsis, L.
marks of friendship, **1**, 18
good will, **3**, 6
virtue of friendship, **3**, 9
motivation for friendship, **4**, 13
political friendship, **5**, 5
friendliness, **5**, 5
feasibility of friendship, **5**, 5

Dahl, Norman O.
practical intuition, **2**, 2

Engberg-Pederson, Troels
practical intuition, **2**, 2

Fortenbaugh, W. W.
focal analysis, **3**, 7; **5**, 8
Fraisse, Jean-Claude
and other selves, **1**, 17
focal analysis, **3**, 7
marks of friendship, **4**, 2; **5**, 1
origin of friendship, **4**, 6

motivation for friendship, **4**, 8
unanimity, **5**, 1
political friendship, **5**, 3
good, useful, and pleasant friend-
    ship, **5**, 3
affinity between friendship and
    justice, **6**, 4

Gauthier, René
focal analysis, **3**, 7
reciprocal love, **3**, 8
marks of friendship, **4**, 2; **5**, 1
theoretical intellect, **4**, 3
motivation for friendship, **4**, 13
unanimity, **5**, 1
Grant, Alexander
altruistic and egoistic friendship,
    1, 4
virtue of friendship, **3**, 9
motivation for friendship, **1**, 4;
    4, 8
good wishes, **4**, 4
marks of friendship, **4**, 5
good, useful, and pleasant friend-
    ship, **5**, 3

Hardie, W. F. R.
altruistic and egoistic friendship,
    1, 5; **3**, 10
motivation for friendship, **1**, 5; **4**,
    7, 8
other selves, **4**, 7
dominant and inclusive happiness,
    2, 3
whole and partial justice, **6**, 2
Hirsch, E. D.
weighing evidence, **2**, 6

Irwin, Terence
altruistic and egoistic friendship,
    1, 5, 7; **3**, 10; **4**, 8; **5**, 6, 9
good wishes, **3**, 1; **4**, 4
good will, **3**, 6

motivation for friendship, **1**, 5, 7;
4, 8, 13; **5**, 5
marks of friendship, **1**, 18; **4**, 8
practical intellect, **4**, 3
other selves, **1**, 17, 19; **2**, 4;
5, 5, 6
cooperation, **2**, 4; **4**, 8; **5**, 5, 6
political friendship, **1**, 7; **5**, 1, 3,
4, 5, 6
good, useful, and pleasant friendship, **5**, 1, 3, 5
kingship, **5**, 9
oligarchy, **5**, 3
democracy, **5**, 3
feasibility of friendship, **5**, 5
friendliness, **5**, 5
extensity and intensity of friendship, **5**, 5
whole and partial justice, **6**, 2
affinity between friendship and
justice, **6**, 4
and interpretation of Aristotle,
B, 3
and Aristotle's principle, **1**, 11
"altruistic" and "egoistic", **2**, 5
διά, **3**, 3

Kahn, Charles H.
altruistic and egoistic friendship,
1, 5; **3**, 10; **4**, 8, 14
motivation for friendship, **1**, 5; **4**,
8, 14
other selves, **1**, 17; **2**, 4
"altruistic" and "egoistic", **2**, 5
Kraut, Richard
essential and accidental friendship,
3, 10
altruistic and egoistic friendship,
3, 10; **4**, 8; **5**, 2
good, useful, and pleasant friendship, **4**, 15
motivation for friendship, **4**, 8
origin of friendship, **4**, 6
other selves, **4**, 11

feasibility of friendship, **4**, 15
distributive justice, **6**, 5
activeness of friendship, **7**, 1, 2

Millgram, Elijah
other selves, **1**, 17; **4**, 11; **5**, 5
practical intellect, **4**, 3
motivation for friendship, **4**, 8, 13
altruistic and egoistic friendship,
4, 8
beneficence, **4**, 11
extensity and intensity of friendship, **5**, 5
Monan, J. Donald
reflective method, **2**, 6
Moravcsik, J. M. E.
altruistic and egoistic friendship,
3, 10
other selves, **4**, 11
Morrall, John B.
unanimity, **5**, 1
good, useful, and pleasant friendship, **5**, 1
Mulgan, R. G.
polity, **5**, 11

Newman, W. L.
natural and conventional friendship, **1**, 16
marks of friendship, **1**, 18
kingship, **5**, 4
and altruistic and egoistic friendship, **5**, 7
affinity between friendship and
justice, **1**, 8; **6**, 4

Owens, Joseph
focal analysis, **3**, 7

Price, A. W.
altruistic and egoistic friendship,
1, 7; **3**, 3, 10; **4**, 8, 14; **5**, 6

good, useful, and pleasant friendship, **3**, 3
good will, **3**, 5, 6
focal analysis, **3**, 7
practical intellect, **4**, 3
motivation for friendship, **1**, 7; **4**,
13, 14
beneficence, **4**, 11
other selves, **1**, 17; **4**, 11; **5**, 6
cooperation, **4**, 13, 14; **5**, 6
unanimity, **5**, 1, 4
good, useful, and pleasant friendship, **5**, 1
extensity and intensity of friendship, **5**, 5
political friendship, **1**, 7; **5**, 6
and interpretation of Aristotle,
B, 3
and Aristotle's principle, **1**, 11
διά, **3**, 3

Rawls, John
See subject index
Robin, Léon
altruistic and egoistic friendship,
1, 4; **4**, 8
motivation for friendship, **1**, 4; **4**, 8
Ross, W. D.
faulty editing of the *Ethics*, **1**, 1
altruistic and egoistic friendship,
4, 8
motivation for friendship, **4**, 8, 9
marks of friendship, **4**, 2

Sherman, Nancy
altruistic and egoistic friendship,
4, 8
motivation for friendship, **4**, 8
cooperation, **4**, 8; **5**, 6
other selves, **4**, 11

Stewart, J. A.
other selves, **1**, 17
reciprocal love, **3**, 8
marks of friendship, **4**, 2, 5
practical intellect, **4**, 3
good wishes, **4**, 4
origin of friendship, **4**, 6
motivation for friendship, **4**, 8
contemplation of actions, **4**, 12
kingship, **5**, 4
aristocracy, **5**, 4
grounds of sovereignty, **6**, 1
distributive and corrective justice,
6, 3
affinity between friendship and
justice, **1**, 9; **6**, 4
designation of "friendship",
1, 14
Stocker, Michael
virtue of friendship, **3**, 9
altruistic and egoistic friendship,
3, 10
Striker, Gisela
cooperation, **5**, 6
and altruistic and egoistic friendship, **5**, 6

Urmson, J. O.
faulty editing of the *Ethics*, **1**, 1
altruistic and egoistic friendship,
3, 10
designation of "friendship",
1, 14

Walker, A. D. M.
good will, **3**, 5
focal analysis, **3**, 7
Wood, Ellen Meiksins and Neal
aristocracy, **5**, 10
polity, **5**, 11